PROFESSOR HOFFMANN'S
MODERN MAGIC

PROFESSOR HOFFMANN'S
MODERN MAGIC

EDITED BY
RICHARD ROBINSON

quick fox

New York   London   Tokyo

International Standard Book Number: 0-8256-3073-8
Library of Congress Catalog Card Number: 77-78530

In Great Britain: Book Sales Ltd., 78 Newman Street, London W1, England.
In Canada: Gage Trade Publishing, P.O. Box 5000, 164 Commander Blvd.,
Agincourt, Ontario M1S 3C7.

Book and cover design by Iris Weinstein.
Cover illustration by Ruth Marten.
Photographs by Mark Stein.
Photographs posed by Richard Robinson and Cyrinda Foxe.
Back cover photo by Bob Gruen.

TABLE OF CONTENTS

PREFACE: THE MYSTERY OF PROFESSOR HOFFMANN'S MODERN MAGIC

In 1874, a young London lawyer named Angelo John Lewis wrote to publisher Edmund Routledge offering to contribute articles on conjuring tricks for the new series of Routledge's *Every Boy's Magazine.* Routledge met with Lewis, and, impressed by his knowledge of conjuring, asked him to write enough so that once the material had run through the magazine it could be published as a book. *Modern Magic* appeared in 1876 and was an immediate success: the first edition of 2,000 copies sold out in seven weeks. Lewis got £100 for writing the book, a small fee considering the illustrations cost £320.

"Messrs. Routledge suggested bringing out the book under my own name, but to this I objected," Lewis wrote in *The Magician Annual 1908–9.* "I was then practising in a modest way at the Chancery Bar, and I did not think that being known to dabble in magic would increase my professional prestige."

So Angelo Lewis became Professor Hoffmann. "'Professor' being at that date the brevet rank of every respectable wizard." (Besides, Routledge insisted on it.) And "'Hoffman,' as a name of uncertain nationality."

As Professor Hoffmann, Lewis wrote a number of landmark conjuring texts: he followed *Modern Magic* with *More Magic, Later Magic,* and *Latest Magic;* translated the works of the French magician Robert-Houdin; wrote several other books and magazine articles on particular aspects of the conjuring art; and with one volume, *Conjurer Dick,* even tried his hand at fiction with a magic theme.

Modern Magic "marked the border line between old and new conjuring," says Raymond Toole Stott in his *A Bibliography of English Conjuring 1581–1876.* Stott quotes conjuring-book collector Harold A. Smith as saying, *"Modern Magic* fell like a bombshell among the conjurers of the time, and had an almost incalculable effect in revolutionising and revivifying the art of conjuring. . . ."

Harry Houdini, himself an avid magic book collector and historian, noted that *Modern Magic* "at the time of its publication was by far the greatest book of its kind in this or any other language." David Devant and Howard Thurston, two of the great illusionists of the early twentieth century, credited it as their initial introduction to the art of magic.

How did an amateur magician whose performances, as he admitted, were "confined to the Theatre Royal, Back Drawingroom," produce a work of such monumental impact?

There is no obvious answer. Certainly, Lewis had a talent for describing the modus operandi, as he liked to call it: he wrote about magic the way Arthur Conan Doyle wrote about murder. He savored the mystery produced by good magic, and when he explained how it was done, he tempered his prose with a legal eye that scrutinized each detail in logical sequence.

Lewis's lively style and precise explanations contributed not only to the popularity of *Modern Magic* and its sequels but also to the creation of a persona for Professor Hoffmann. In later years, Lewis furthered the illusion that there was a Professor Hoffmann by giving the Professor the first name of Louis and putting his own photograph as the frontispiece of later editions. Lewis looked the part: by then he was a portly old gentleman with a white moustache and chin beard who stared at the camera through small round spectacles. (A few years before his death on

December 23, 1920, Lewis apparently realized how completely he was identified with Professor Hoffmann, for in his last works he added *Angelo Lewis, M.A.,* in brackets under the name Professor Hoffmann on the title pages.)

Modern Magic was not by any means the first book of tricks. The literature of conjuring began almost 300 years before its publication. So while the Hoffmann persona and excellent style made it superior literature to most earlier works, these elements added to the book's commercial success rather than its revolutionary impact on magic. Perhaps the real key to Lewis's book is found in the word *Modern* of the title, for the book heralded a distinct change in the process of performing magic—a change that had philosophical as well as practical ramifications.

Lewis was born in London on July 23, 1839. His public school French teacher taught him his first conjuring tricks as a reward for his aptitude in French. His interest in conjuring continued through his childhood, but only after he graduated Oxford and studied the law did he delve into the why's and wherefore's of the art.

It was an interesting time in the history of magic. The conjurers of the late 1700s and early 1800s took after the medieval notion of Merlin. They often wore pointed caps and long robes covered with cabalistic signs, and performed on elaborately outfitted stages filled with odd-looking apparatus. These conjurers frequently relied on assistants hidden beneath heavily draped tables to accomplish their effects. Just after he left Oxford, Lewis saw one of the greatest of these early wizards, Professor Anderson, the celebrated "Wizard of the North," in one of his final performances at the Crystal Palace. "I cannot say that I was much impressed by it," Lewis wrote years later.

By 1868 or '69, Lewis acquired copies of three conjuring books by French magicians that changed his thinking about how the show business of magic could work its effect on an audience. One of the books was Jean Eugène Robert-Houdin's *Secrets de la Prestidigitation et de la Magie.* Houdin had opened a theater in 1845 where he presented his *Soirées Fantastiques.* He performed in evening dress on a simple, open stage, eschewing the traditional cluttered stage and long robes of his predecessors.

Lewis was inspired by Houdin's writings, which characterized the conjurer as "an actor playing the part of a magician." Lewis combined this axiom with Houdin's advice that "the ordinary dress of a gentleman is the only costume appropriate to a high-class conjurer." The result was the prototype for the modern magician.

Without question, Lewis borrowed heavily from Houdin to write *Modern Magic.* Many of the basic sleights with coins, cards, and other small objects are lifted from Houdin. But Lewis went much further than Houdin in exposing the modus operandi of contemporary tricks. He included many commercial tricks sold only by manufacturers of magical apparatus, and gave much more attention to the details of presentation crucial to the successful execution of any magic trick. Lewis sought out two professional magicians, Robert Hellis and a Monsieur Charlier, to assist him in this task.

I titled this edition of Lewis's work *Professor Hoffmann's Modern Magic* because it is a compilation of material from *Modern Magic* and its immediate sequel, *More Magic.* The two volumes offered 1030 octavo pages from which I chose the best magic. My guide-lines were the same as Lewis's—to produce an introduction to *modern* magic. As I began the process of reducing the two books to a manageable size, I was forced to eliminate a great deal of information of historical interest, but the result is of real value to any aspiring conjurer. In fact, knowledgeable magicians will discover several effects and methods in this volume that are, as magicians phrase it, "in the miracle class." In preparing this edition I also 'up-dated' Lewis's chronological references from 1876 to 1977 so that the contributions of more contemporary magicians and advances in the apparatus of conjuring are included when pertinent.

It is a pleasure to have instigated the return of Professor Hoffmann after all these years. Like every successful illusionist, I must acknowledge invaluable assistance behind the scenes. So, after rolling up my sleeves, and showing my hands convincingly empty, allow me to pluck red roses from thin air and distribute them with my thanks to my parents, Cedric and Regina Robinson, who bought me my first Mysto Magic Set long ago; to Jeffrey Weiss who listened when I told him about the magic book I wanted to do; to Cyrinda Foxe for her help in making the magic so it could be photographed; and to Lisa Robinson who loves me even though she hates card tricks.

Richard Robinson
New York City
13 January 1977

INTRODUCTION TO THE FIRST EDITION

Considering the great antiquity and the unfading popularity of the magic art, it seems at first sight a matter of wonder that its literature should be so extremely scanty. In England, in particular, is this the case. Until within the last few years it would have been difficult to name a single book worth reading upon this subject, the whole literature of the art consisting of single chapters in books written for the amusement of youth (which were chiefly remarkable for the unanimity with which each copied, without acknowledgment, from its predecessors), and handbooks sold at the entertainments of various public performers, who took care not to reveal therein any trick which they deemed worthy of performance by themselves. Upon a little consideration, however, the scarcity of treatises on "White Magic" is easily accounted for. The more important secrets of the art have been known but to few, and those few have jealously guarded them, knowing that the more closely they concealed the clue to their mysteries, the more would those mysteries be valued. Indeed, the more noted conjurers of fifty years ago strove to keep the secret of their best tricks not only from the outside world, but from their *confrères*. At the present day the secrets of the art are not so well kept; and there is hardly a trick performed upon the stage which the amateur may not, at a sufficient expenditure, procure at the conjuring *depôts*. There being, therefore, no longer the same strict secrecy, the literature of magic has improved a little, though it still leaves much to be desired.

There is a vast difference between telling how a trick is done and teaching how to do it. The existing treatises, with few exceptions, do the former only. The intention of the present work is to do the latter also; to teach sleight-of-hand generally, as well as particular tricks; and to conduct the neophyte from the very A B C of the magic art gradually up to those marvels which are exhibited on the public stage.

The student may rest assured that, if he will diligently follow the instructions here given, he will be able, in due time, not merely to astonish his friends *extempore* with a borrowed coin or pack of cards, but to roll two rabbits into one, compel chosen cards to rise spontaneously from the pack, produce lighted lanterns from empty hats, and bowls of goldfish from empty pocket-handkerchiefs; in a word, to execute all those wonders which he has hitherto deemed the exclusive property of the public performer.

There are, of course, different degrees of natural aptitude. It is not everyone that can be a Robert-Houdin or a Buatier, but, given the usual number of fingers and thumbs, fair intelligence, and a sufficiency of perseverance, anyone who will may become at least a tolerable conjurer. Be it remembered that we especially stipulate for *perseverance*. A wizard is not to be made in a day, and he who would attain excellence must be content to proceed as he would with music, drawing, or any other accomplishment—viz., begin at the beginning, and practice diligently until he attains the coveted dexterity. The student need not, however, wait the termination of the somewhat formidable course of study we have indicated before he begins to astonish his friends; on the contrary, there are numerous tricks requiring very little manual dexterity, which are yet, if neatly performed, brilliant in effect. These simpler tricks, for which we shall give full instructions, will supply the beginner, even at the outset, with a fair programme, which he may from time to time enlarge as he feels able to undertake more elaborate illusions.

The first rule to be borne in mind by the aspirant is this: *Never tell your audience beforehand what you are going to do*. If you do so, you at once give their vigilance the direction which it is most necessary to avoid, and increase tenfold the chances of detection. We will give an illustration. There is a very good trick in which the performer, after borrowing a handkerchief, gives it to someone to hold. When it is returned, it proves to be torn into small pieces. It is again handed to the holder, who is instructed, in order to restore it, to rub it in a particular manner; but when again unfolded, it is found in a long strip. These effects are produced by successive adroit substitutions, and the whole magic of the trick consists in the concealment of the particular moment at which each substitution is effected. Now, if you were to announce to the audience beforehand that you were about to cause the handkerchief to appear in several pieces, or in a long strip, they would at once conjecture that the trick depended on an exchange, and, their whole vigilance being directed to discover the moment of that exchange, you would find it all but impossible to perform the trick without detection. If, on the other hand, you merely roll up the handkerchief and ask someone to hold it, the audience, not knowing what you are about to do, have no reason to suspect that you have handed that person a substitute; and when the transformation is exhibited, the opportunity of detection will have already passed away.

It follows, as a practical consequence of this first rule, that *you should never perform the same trick twice on the same evening.* The best trick loses half its effect on repetition, but besides this, the audience knows precisely what is coming, and have all their faculties directed to find out at what point you cheated their eyes on the first occasion. It is sometimes hard to resist an encore, but a little tact will get you out of the difficulty, especially if you have studied, as every conjurer should do, the variation and combination of tricks. There are a score of different ways of vanishing a given article, and as many of reproducing it; and either one of the first may be used in conjunction with either of the second. Thus, by varying either the beginning or the end, you make the trick to some extent a new one. The power of doing this readily is very useful, and among other advantages will enable you to meet an encore by performing some other trick having some element of similarity to that which you have just completed, but terminating in a different and therefore unexpected manner.

The student must cultivate from the outset the art of "talking," and especially the power of using the eyes and tongue independently of the movement of the hands. To do this, it will be necessary to prepare beforehand not only what you intend to *do,* but what you intend to *say,* and to rehearse frequently and carefully even the simplest trick before attempting it in public. It is surprising how many little difficulties are discovered on first attempting to carry into effect even the clearest written directions; and nothing but practice will overcome these difficulties. The novice may be encouraged by assuming, as he safely may, that the most finished of popular performers was once as awkward as himself, and were he to attempt any unfamiliar feat, would probably be as awkward still.

THE MAGIC WAND

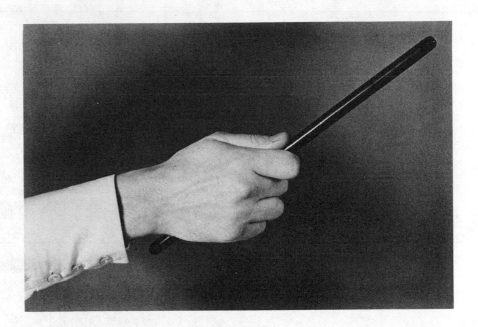

From the time of the Pharaoh downward, the wand has been and will always remain the chosen emblem and instrument of the magician's power. The wand is a light rod twelve to fifteen inches in length, and about three-quarters of an inch in diameter. It may be of any material, and decorated in any manner the fancy of the owner may dictate.

To the uninitiated its use may appear a mere affectation, but such is by no means the case. Apart from the prestige derived from the traditional properties of the wand, and its use by the wizards of all ages, it affords a plausible pretext for many necessary movements, which would otherwise appear awkward and unnatural, and would thereby arouse the vigilance of the audience at possibly the most critical period of the trick. Thus, if when performing you desire to hold anything concealed in your hand, by holding the wand in the same hand you are able to keep it closed without exciting suspicion. If it is necessary, as frequently happens, to turn your back upon the audience for an instant, the momentary turn to the table, in order to take up or lay down the wand, affords the required opportunity. We most strongly advise the would-be magician to cultivate from the outset the habitual use of the wand. Even where its employment is not absolutely necessary for the purpose of the trick, its use is in strict accordance with the character the conjurer professes to fill, and the dainty touch of the wand, for the supposed purpose of operating a magical transformation, assists materially in leading the audience to believe that such transformation did actually take place at that particular moment, instead of having been (as is really the case) secretly effected at an earlier period.

THE MAGICIAN'S TABLE

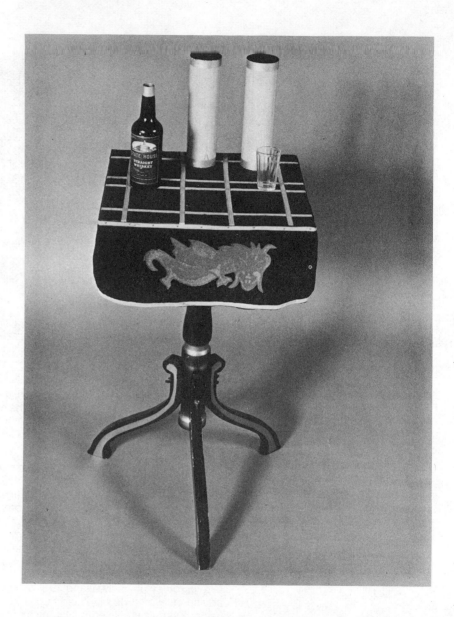

There are plenty of good minor tricks that may be performed anywhere, and with little or no previous preparation, but as soon as the student has outgrown these humbler feats, and aspires to amuse friends or the public with a prearranged séance, the first necessity will be a proper table.

Until the early 1800s, conjurers used a table with a long hanging cover, within which an assistant was concealed. These conjurers, having occasion to cause the disappearance of any object, placed it on one of these cumbrous tables, and concealed it beneath a gorgeously japanned tin cone, under cover of which it fell through a trap into the hands of the hidden assistant. When Robert-Houdin opened his *Théâtre Robert-Houdin* in Paris in 1845, he made the first great step in the direction of simplification with a center table of carved wood, gilt, and of light and elegant appearance, clearly excluding the supposition of any concealed assistant. Another conjurer of his time, Wiljalba Frikell, went further and may be regarded as the founder of the non-apparatus school of conjurers, the principal characteristics of his entertainment being the absence of visible accessories. Since the late 1800s many high-class performers have given what is known as a "carpet-bag show," from the fact that a moderate-sized suitcase suffices to contain all the apparatus necessary for their performance.

Today conjurers vary in their use of specially constructed and decorated magic tables: many conjurers use tables and other apparatus which represent to the eye of the spectator merely the appliances of everyday life, and are not obviously designed for conjuring purposes. But although the contemporary conjurer has dispensed with special tables, he has not dispensed with the aid of a *servante* attached to a "normal-looking" table.

The table necessary for a magic exhibition differs from an ordinary table in two points only: its height, which should be six or eight inches greater than that of an ordinary table, and the addition of a hidden shelf or ledge at the back or a hole in the table's top. The precise height of the table is best determined by the stature of the performer. The *servante,* or hidden shelf, should be just so high from the ground as to be level with the knuckles of the performer as the arm hangs by the side; and the top of the table should be about six inches higher than this. It will be found that this height will enable the performer secretly to take up or lay down any article thereon without stooping or bending the arm; either movement would suggest to the spectators that the conjurer's hand was occupied in some manner behind the table. One of the first tasks of the novice should be to acquire the power of readily picking up or laying down any article on the *servante,* without making any corresponding movement of the body, and especially without looking down at the hands. If the performer is uncertain as to the precise whereabouts of a given article, it must be located with a quick glance while approaching the table, and not after walking behind it. From this moment the conjurer must not again look down. If the audience suspects that there is a secret receptacle behind the table, half the magic of the tricks will be destroyed. Many manufactured magician's tables have a hole cut in the table top with a short cloth bag attached beneath the hole. This type of *servante* is called a *well,* and allows for secretly obtaining or disposing of articles in the act of picking up or placing an object on the table.

An oblong box, twelve or fourteen inches in length by three in depth, well padded with cotton and placed on the *servante,* will be found very useful in getting rid of small articles such as coins or oranges. Such articles may be dropped into the box without causing any sound, and therefore without attracting attention.

Without a table made for the purpose, the amateur may with little difficulty adapt an ordinary table for use. A common kitchen table having a drawer on one side, and raised on four blocks of wood to the requisite height, will answer the purpose. The table must be covered with a cloth, and should have the drawer pulled out about six inches (the drawer side being, of course, away from the audience) to form the *servante.* A card table can be used, the *servante* taking the form of a net bag stretched upon a coathanger-wire framework, and attached to the table by means of a couple of minute screw-eyes. A *servante* can also be attached to the back of a solid-backed chair.

The conjurer, however, may be called upon to give a sample of the art when neither a regular or extemporized table is available; and even when sufficiently provided in this respect, there will frequently be an occasion to produce or get rid of a given article without retiring behind a table to do so. The wizards of two centuries ago met this necessity by wearing openly in front of them a sort of bag or apron. French conjurers called it a *gibecière,* from its supposed resemblance to a game-bag. This was used not only to carry the cups and balls and other minor paraphernalia of the art, but for the purpose of procuring, exchanging, or getting rid of any small article at the pleasure of the performer. In fact, this bag acted as the *servante,* which was not then known. During the past century conjurers have relied on external *servantes* or specially prepared places of concealment in their clothing or pockets to take the place of the *gibecière.* Recently, Doug Henning has re-introduced the use of the shoulder bag as a portable bag of tricks and *servante* for close-up conjuring.

THE MAGICIAN'S DRESS

Centuries ago the orthodox dress of the conjurer was a long and flowing robe, embroidered more or less with hieroglyphic characters, and giving ample space for the concealment of any reasonable-sized article—say from a flower vase downward. From the mid-1800s, the costume *de rigueur* of the magician has been ordinary "evening dress." Compared with the flowing robe, the effect of the feats performed is greatly heightened by the close fit and comparative scantiness of such a costume, which appears to allow no space for secret pockets or other places of concealment. In reality, however, the magician in "evening dress" is provided with two special pockets, known as *profondes*, placed in the tails of his dress-coat. Each is from four to six inches in depth and seven in width, and the opening, which is across the inside. of the coat-tail, slanting slightly downward from the center to the side, is, like the *servante*, so placed as to be just level with the knuckles of the performer, as the hand hangs by the side. He can thus, by the mere action of dropping either hand to his side, let fall any article instantly into the *profonde* on that side, or take anything from thence in like manner. The action is so natural that it may be used under the very eyes of the audience, at very small risk of their observing it; and if the performer at the same moment slightly turns his other side to the spectator, he may be perfectly secure from detection.

The amateur conjurer, dressed in a business-suit or wearing a sports-jacket, is at a slight disadvantage to the professional with his specially tailored clothes, but the amateur will find that the naturalness of "street clothes" will disarm the audience, while still providing numerous places to conceal objects. With practice small objects can be *sleeved:* hidden up the sleeve after a vanish or before a production. A number of mechanical devices are available to pull objects up the sleeve to perform a vanish. Articles for production can be secreted inside the coat near the bottom, often held by spring clips pinned to the coat lining, and secured by the hand in the same manner as an object is obtained from a *profonde:* as the arm hangs naturally by the side and the body turns slightly away from the audience on the side where the load is hanging. Many professors have also a spacious pocket, opening perpendicularly, inside the breast of the coat, under each arm, for the purpose of what is called "loading," i.e., bringing a rabbit, dove, or other article into a hat, bunch of silks, etc. Other pockets may be added, as the fancy or invention of the performer may dictate; but the above are those generally used.

CARD TRICKS:

General Principles of Sleight-of-Hand with Cards

Among the various branches of the conjurer's art, none will better repay the labor of the student, whether artist or amateur, than the magic of cards. It has the especial advantage of being, in a great measure, independent of time and place. The materials for half its mysteries are procurable at five minutes' notice in every home circle; and, even in the case of those tricks for which specially prepared cards are requisite, the necessary appliances cost little, and are easily portable—two virtues not too common in magical apparatus.

Further, the majority of card tricks are dependent mainly on personal address and dexterity, and as such will always be highly esteemed by connoisseurs in the art. Before very large audiences, indeed, the spectators being at a distance from the performer, much of the effect of a card trick is lost; but at close-up, tricks with cards can be the basis for brilliant and puzzling performances.

Cards to Use

Those adept in sleight-of-hand should accustom themselves to the use of every description of cards. Where, however, the choice is open to them, they should use in the actual performance of tricks bridge-size cards. Many conjurers prefer red- or blue-backed "Aviator" design playing cards made by the United States Playing Card Company of Cincinnati, Ohio, probably because of their ready availability and because of the many specially printed gimmick cards and decks made in the "Aviator" design as "Fox Lake" playing cards by Haines House of Cards of Norwood, Ohio.

The Pass

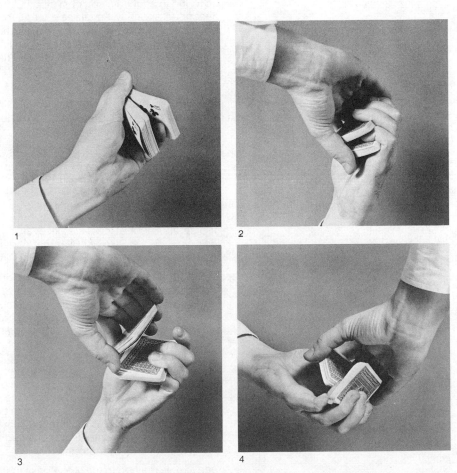

The oldest and most essential sleight to the skilled conjurer with cards is the "pass." While it is no longer the very backbone of card-conjuring, it will prove invaluable to those who take the time to master it. The effect of this sleight is to reverse the respective positions of the top and bottom halves of the pack, i.e., to make those cards which at first formed the lower half of the pack come uppermost, when those cards which at first formed the upper half will of course be undermost. It is used by card-sharpers, immediately after the cards have been cut, to replace them in the position they occupied before the cut.

There are various methods of producing this effect, some requiring the use of both hands, some of one hand only; some requiring a good amount of practice, some only nerve. We shall describe first the most difficult and effective, and second the easiest.

In the first method, hold the pack in the left hand, lengthways, with the face downward, as if about to deal. In this position the thumb will naturally be on the left side of the pack, and the four fingers on the other. Insert the top joint of the little finger immediately above those cards which are to be brought to the top of the pack (and which are now undermost), and let the remaining three fingers close naturally on the remaining cards, which are now uppermost. In this position you will find that the uppermost part of the pack is held between the little finger, which is underneath, and the remaining fingers, which are upon it.

Now advance the right hand, and cover the pack with it. Grasp the lower portion of the pack lengthways between the second finger at the upper and the thumb at the lower end, the left thumb lying, slightly bent, across the pack. Press the inner edge of the lower packet into the fork of the left thumb. Next draw away the upper packet, by slightly extending the fingers of the left hand, at the same time lifting up the *outer* edge of the lower packet, till the edges of the two packets just clear each other, when by the mere act of closing the left hand they will be brought together as at first, save that they will have changed places.

Do this at first very slowly, aiming only at neatness and noiselessness of execution. At the outset the task will be found somewhat difficult, but gradually the hands will be found to acquire a sort of sympathetic action; the different movements we have described above will melt, as it were, into one, and the two packets will change places with such lightness and rapidity that they will seem to actually pass through each other. A slight momentary depression and elevation of the hands (apparently a mere careless gesture) in the act of making the pass will completely cover the transposition of the cards, which in the hands of an adept is invisible, even to the most watchful spectator.

The above is the most orthodox and the most perfect method of making the pass, and if the student be proficient in this, he need be troubled very little about other methods.

In this, as in all other branches of prestidigitation, you will find it of the greatest possible advantage to practice before a mirror. By this means, better than any other, you will be enabled to judge how far your movements succeed in deceiving the eyes of a spectator. One caution may here be given with advantage: as a student of legerdemain, you must learn to perform all necessary movements *without looking at your hands,* unless for some special reason you desire the spectators to look at them also. In every case, wherever you desire your audience to look, your own eyes must take that particular direction; and wherever you desire your audience not to look, you yourself must carefully abstain from looking.

Let us suppose, for instance, that a person has drawn a card, and has replaced it in the middle of the pack. You desire to bring it to the top, for which purpose it is necessary to introduce the little finger above the card in question, and to make the pass, as above described. When the card is replaced in the pack, the eyes of the drawer are naturally directed toward it; and if you, the performer, were yourself to look downward at the cards, it would multiply tenfold the chances of detection. You should pause for a moment, and, looking full at the person who drew the card, ask, "You are certain that you will know that card again?" or make any similar observation. As you speak, a natural impulse will draw the eyes of the audience to your own face, and you may then make the pass without the slight necessary movement attracting the least attention. It is hard to believe, until tested by actual experience, what apparently obvious movements may be executed under the very noses of an audience, if only their attention is diverted at the right moment by a dexterous use of the eye and voice of the operator.

One simple method to make the pass that suffices to bring the selected card to the top of the pack can be accomplished as follows: A card is selected and drawn from the pack. Square the pack, holding it backs-up in your left palm. Cut the pack in two and take the top half with your right hand. Ask the drawer to return the selected card to the pack and to place it face down on top of the lower half held in your left hand. Upon the selected card being put on the top of the bottom half, use your right hand to return the top half of the pack onto the bottom half. As this is done, insert the little finger of your left hand on top of the selected card so that a "break" is held in the pack. Then cut the pack twice in the following manner: Square the pack with your right hand and take about a third of the pack from the top, placing it on the table or on the drawer's outstretched palm. Next, take another section of the pack and place it on top of the first section. This second section is cut at the break held by the little finger. In this way the final section of the pack, when taken from the left hand and placed on top of the other two cuts, will have the selected card uppermost so that it arrives at the top of the pack. Performed rapidly in an off-hand manner, it will appear that you have cut the pack in three and mixed the sections to further bury the selected card.

The Force

"Forcing a card" is compelling a person to draw such a card as you desire, though he is apparently allowed absolute freedom of choice. Your first step is to get sight of the bottom card, or if you want to force a predetermined card, to get that card to the bottom. Having done this, take the pack in the left hand, and insert the little finger halfway down, in readiness to make the pass. Make the pass by the first method, but before uniting the two halves of the pack in their new position, again slip the little finger of the left hand between them. (The two halves will now be united at the end that is toward the spectators, but will be divided by the little finger at the end nearest to yourself as in the simple pass already described; in this instance, however, the original bottom card, which is the one you desire to force, will now be at the bottom of the top heap, resting on the little finger.)

Using both hands, with the thumbs above and the fingers below the pack, spread out the cards fanwise from left to right, at the same time offering them to the person who is to draw, and requesting him to select a card. Keep the little finger of the left hand still on the face of the card to be chosen, or you may now use, if more convenient, the same finger of the right hand, both being underneath the cards. As the person advances his hand to draw, move the cards onward with the thumb, so that the particular card shall reach his fingers just at the moment when he closes them in order to draw; and, if you have followed these directions properly, it is ten to one that he will draw the card you wish.

It may possibly be imagined that forcing is a very difficult matter, and requires an extraordinary degree of dexterity; but this is by no means the case. The principal thing against which a beginner must guard is a tendency to offer the particular card a little *too soon*. When the cards are first presented to the drawer, the pack should be barely spread at all, and the card in question should be ten or fifteen cards off. The momentary hesitation of the drawer in making his choice will give time, by moving the cards quicker or slower, as may be necessary, to bring that card opposite his fingers at the right moment. Should you, however, miscalculate your time, and the card pass the drawer's fingers before the choice is made, you need not be embarrassed. Still keeping the little finger on the card, you should sharply close the cards, and making some remark as to the drawer being "difficult to please," or the like, again spread them as before, and offer them for the choice.

A moderate degree of practice will make the student so proficient that even a person acquainted with the secret of forcing will have to be very wide awake in order not to take the desired card. You will, however, sometimes find a person, suspecting your design and wishing to embarrass you, suddenly jerk his hand away from the card he was apparently about to take, and draw another from a different part of the pack. In the great majority of tricks this is of little consequence, inasmuch as there are numerous ways (which will be hereafter explained) of ascertaining what the drawn card was; but there are some illusions that depend upon the drawer taking a card similar in suit and number to one already prepared elsewhere for the purpose of the trick. In this case it is, of course, absolutely necessary that the card drawn should be the right one; and as even the most accomplished performer cannot always be certain of forcing a single card, another expedient must be used in order to ensure success.

The Forcing Pack

To make absolutely certain that the required card will be selected, a "forcing pack" is used. This is a pack in which all the cards are alike. Thus, if the jack of hearts is the card to be drawn, the whole pack will consist of jacks of hearts, and the drawer may therefore do his or her utmost to exercise a free choice, but the card drawn will certainly be the jack of hearts, and no other. Where more than one card is to be drawn, as, for instance, in the well-known trick of the "rising cards," the pack may consist, instead of similar cards throughout, of groups of two or more particular cards. Thus, one third may be jack of hearts, one third ace of diamonds, and the remaining third seven of clubs—the cards of each kind being together. These are known as a "two-way" and a "three-way" pack, respectively. With the aid of such a pack, it will require very little skill to ensure one of each sort being drawn.

More complicated, specially assembled packs are available from magic suppliers. As with the one-, two-, and three-way packs they will not stand examination, but some of them are so cleverly devised that they may be fanned face-up to display different faces, while the conjurer has full control over the card actually drawn. Among the most popular "gimmicked packs" are the Svengali Deck, the Psychomatic Deck, and the Nu-Idea Pop-Eyed Eye Popper Deck. The drawbacks of "forcing" packs are that they can only be used for one trick, that they are obviously the conjurer's pack of cards, and that if they should stray into the hands of the audience they will immediately yield their secret. The serious conjurer would do well to avoid their use.

The False Shuffle

False shuffles are of two kinds, according to the object to which they are made. Those of the first kind are designed simply to keep in view a particular card or cards, the remainder of the pack being really shuffled. Those of the second are designed to keep the pack in a prearranged order, and are shuffles in appearance only, all the cards being brought back to the same relative positions they occupied before the shuffle.

The Over-Hand Shuffle

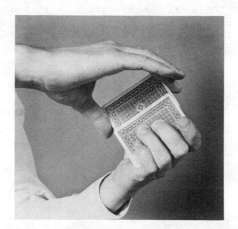

Bring the card in question, as before directed, to the top of the pack. Take the pack in the left hand, holding it upright on its side, the edges of the cards resting on the palm, the four fingers being at the back or top, and the thumb on the face of the pack. Now, with the thumb and middle finger of the right hand lift out edgeways that portion of the cards which now forms the middle of the pack, and drop them by packets of five or six at a time upon *the face* of the cards remaining in the left hand, moving aside the left thumb to allow their passage. The pressure of the fingers will always keep the top card in its place, however many of the remaining cards you lift out with the right hand; and as you only shuffle on to the face of the pack, however often you repeat the process this card will still remain at the top.

False-Pack Shuffle

To retain the whole pack in a prearranged order, make the pass so as to bring the lower half of the pack uppermost. Take the pack in the right hand, keeping the two portions of the pack separated by the little finger of that hand. Hold the cards face-downward a few inches from the table, and let fall, by five or six at a time, those cards which now form the lower half of the pack. You should so arrange that these cards form four little heaps, falling across the table so they are from left to right the third pile, first pile, fourth pile, and second pile. The bottom cards fall as the first pile, the next lowest as the second pile, the next (comprising all that remain of the lower packet) as the third pile, and the remaining cards (being the whole of the upper part) as the fourth pile. Now (with the left hand) quickly place packet one on packet four, and (with the right hand) packet two on packet one, and finally (with the left hand) packet three on the top of all, when the cards will occupy precisely the same relative positions as at first. The use of the two hands alternately, coupled with the rapidity of the performer, gives to these motions an appearance of carelessness which effectually baffles the spectators, and prevents their suspecting that the heaps are rearranged in any determinate order.

Card Palming

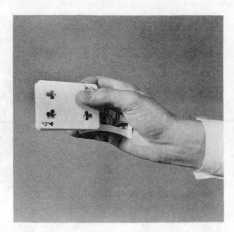 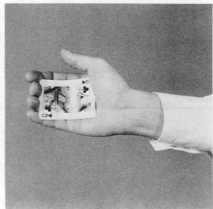

Bring the card you desire to palm to the top of the pack. Hold the pack face-downward in the left hand, covering it lengthways with the right. With the left thumb push the top card till it projects about an inch beyond the edge of the pack. With the third finger of the left hand, which is now immediately below the card, press it upward into the right hand, which should half-close over it. You must not mind about bending the card, which will lie curled up against the inside of the hand. You may either let the hand drop negligently to your side, or, still better, take the pack between the fingers and thumb of the same hand and offer it to be shuffled. This will give you the opportunity, often very valuable, of seeing what the card in question is. When it becomes necessary to return the card to the pack, the mere motion of taking the pack in the right hand, whether from the left hand or from the table, will effect that object in the most natural manner. If the card retains a curve from its bent position in the hand, you may readily straighten it up by ruffling the cards.

To "ruffle" the cards, hold the pack tightly by its lower end between the fingers and thumb of the left hand, the thumb being above and the fingers below the cards. Cover the pack lengthways with the right hand, and clip the cards between the fingers and thumb as if you were about to make the pass. Keep the thumb unmoved, but draw the fingers smartly upward, so as to bend the cards slightly. The springing of the cards, as they escape one by one from the pressure of the fingers and again straighten themselves, causes a peculiar sharp sound.

The ruffle is a mere flourish, but it is by no means without its value. We have indicated one of its uses, vis., to straighten a card that has been palmed. Apart from this, there are many tricks in which it is desirable to mislead the spectator as to the particular movement by which, or the point of time at which, a particular effect was produced. This may be effected by a judicious use of the ruffle. Suppose, for instance, that the trick consists in magically bringing a given card to a particular position in the pack, and that the performer has already, without the knowledge of the audience, placed the card in the required position. If, before showing that it is so placed, the conjurer ostentatiously ruffles the cards, nine out of ten of the audience will be persuaded that this noisy movement is in some way the cause of the transposition, and will be proportionately the less likely to discover the true explanation of the feat.

Changing a Card

Some of the most brilliant effects in card-conjuring are produced by the aid of this sleight, by means of which a card, fairly exhibited, is forthwith apparently transformed into a different one.

Hold the card to be changed face downward between the thumb and first and second fingers of the right hand, the thumb being above and the two fingers below the card. Hold the pack in the left hand, as if about to deal the cards, the card for which that first mentioned is to be changed being on the top. Bring the hands rapidly together, pushing the top card with the left thumb about an inch beyond the rest of the pack, and at the same moment place the card held in the right hand with a sliding motion upon the top of the pack. Both this card and the original top card (which is now second) will now be between the two fingers and thumb of the right hand. Press lightly on the top card with the left thumb to keep it back, and quickly draw away the right hand, pressing gently upwards with the two fingers on the face of the second card, which you will thereby draw away in place of the top card.

If neatly done, the keenest eyesight cannot detect the substitution of the second card. Your only difficulty will be to find a colorable pretext for placing the card you hold on the top of the pack. This achieved, the rest is easy. The nature of the trick you are performing will frequently suggest a plausible excuse. A very successful plan is to boldly request the company to observe that you do *not* do that which you at the same moment actually do: "You will observe, ladies and gentlemen, that I do not, even for one moment, replace the card in the pack, but simply . . ." etc., etc. At the words "replace the card in the pack," the hands are brought together, and the change is made. The action, suiting the words, is taken by the audience as an indicative gesture only, and thus the change is effected under their very eyes without exciting the least suspicion. In this mode of making the change, you should aim at being easy and natural, rather than very rapid. The main movement (that which brings the hands together) is undisguised, but attributed to a fictitious motive; and the subsidiary movement of the fingers, which actually effects the change, is so slight as to be practically imperceptible.

The Double-Lift

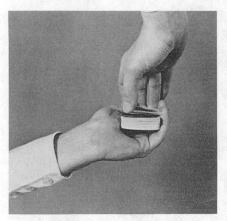 

It is sometimes necessary to demonstrate that the top card of the pack is *not* the selected card, when in reality it is just that. This is accomplished by lifting the two top cards off the deck as one and displaying the face of the second card as the face of the top card. The pack is held in the left hand. The ball of the thumb ruffles the corner of the pack, allowing the two top cards to snap off the ball and then pushing the edge of the thumb between the ball and the side of the nail into the break between these two cards and the rest of the pack. The right hand now approaches the pack. The right thumb takes the back edge closest to the performer, the right middle finger contacts the two top cards at the opposite end just to the right of where the left thumb holds the break, and the right index finger touches the back of the top card in the exact center. The two top cards are lifted away as one, by the thumb and right middle finger. As the two cards are lifted, the right thumb and middle finger squeeze the cards slightly, the right index finger pushing forward to exaggerate this bowing effect. The result is that the two cards appear to be only one. The bowing of the cards keeps the top and bottom edges at a slight angle away from the view of the audience so the double thickness cannot be seen. The cards are then returned to the top of the pack, from which point the conjurer may remove the top card only to show that it has changed from an indifferent card to the selected card.

Sighting the Chosen Card

The power of doing this is a *sine quâ non* for the conjurer. As already mentioned, even the most expert operator cannot be absolutely *certain* of "forcing" the card that he desires, and a novice is very likely indeed to find a wrong card occasionally drawn. It is therefore necessary to be provided with a remedy for such a contretemps. One mode of meeting the difficulty is to allow the card to be returned to the pack, make the pass to bring it to the top, and palm it, immediately giving the pack to be shuffled, and in so doing to get sight of the card, which remains in your own hand, and can in due time be reproduced in any way you please. For the present purpose, we assume that you do not desire to retain possession of the card, but merely wish to know its suit and value.

Ask the drawer to return the chosen card to the pack, which you offer for that purpose in the left hand, spreading the pack fanwise, in order that the card may be inserted where the drawer pleases. As the drawer replaces the card, slip the little finger of the left hand *below* it, and close the fan. You now have the pack held in the palm of the left hand, but divided just below the chosen card by the little finger, the three remaining fingers being on the top. Offer the cards to be shuffled, or make any gesture you like with the pack, at the same moment slightly straightening the fingers. The effect of this movement will be to lift the upper packet, and thus open the back bookwise, the opening being toward yourself, and the lowest card of the top heap, which is the card you desire to ascertain, being for the moment in full view.

The Glide

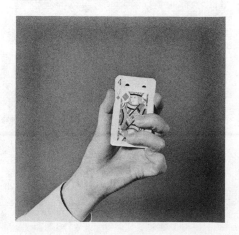

The performer shows the bottom card and then, dropping the pack into a horizontal position, face downward, draws out, with the thumb and second finger of the other hand, apparently that card, but really the next above it. This is effected as follows: Hold the pack upright in the left hand between the first finger and thumb, the back of the cards toward the palm, and the thumb and finger about the middle of each side of the pack. Let the third finger rest on the face of the cards. You will find that in this position, by moving the third finger, you can draw back the bottom card about an inch below the remaining cards, and thereby leave exposed a corresponding portion of the next card. This is the whole mechanism of the operation. You must, of course, take care, after showing the bottom card, to turn the pack downward before you slide back that card in order to draw the next card in its place.

Conjuring with Cards

We have endeavored to be as explicit as possible in the foregoing description of the different sleight-of-hand processes, so that the reader may, by following our instructions closely, be able to teach himself, unassisted, to perform the various movements described. We have done our best to make our descriptions intelligible, and trust that we have fairly succeeded. We should, however, strongly advise any student who desires to make rapid progress to take, if possible, a few preliminary lessons under the personal guidance of a competent performer, professional or amateur. It is an old saying that an ounce of example is worth a pound of precept, and a reader who has once or twice seen the processes we have described practically illustrated by skillful hands will not only avoid the difficulties sure to be at first found in even the clearest written instructions, but will escape the formation of bad habits, which it may take much time and trouble to eradicate. Should the novice seek such assistance, it must not be expected that any one performer uses indifferently all the processes we have described. Every Professor has favorite methods of procedure, and, generally speaking, pours scorn and contumely upon all others; or, in the words of Byron (a little altered):

Compounds for *sleights* he has a mind to,
By damning those he's not inclined to.

The student who commences his labors without such assistance must make his own selection. The various sleights above described will cost the student some time and perseverance before they are fairly mastered, and until they are so it is hopeless to attempt any of the more brilliant feats. For your amusement in the meantime, we subjoin a few tricks for which sleight-of-hand is not necessary, but which, if performed with neatness and tact, will cause considerable astonishment to the uninitiated.

EASY CARD TRICKS

There is a large class of tricks that may be described as consisting of two elements: the discovery of a chosen card by the performer; and the revelation of that knowledge in a more or less striking manner. We propose to give, in the first place, a few methods of discovering a given card, and then a similar variety of methods of concluding the trick. It must be remembered that for our present purpose we exclude all tricks for which any special dexterity is requisite. There will be little that is absolutely novel in this chapter, but it will be up to the student to supply the want of freshness in the materials with the ingenuity of his combinations.

How to Discover a Given Card

1. Hold the pack face-downward in the left hand, having previously noticed the bottom card. Secretly draw down this card about three-quarters of an inch, and hold the part so drawn down between the thumb and fourth finger of the right hand, the palm of the right hand being above the cards.

Now, with the tip of the first or second finger of the right hand, draw down the cards one by one about half an inch (beginning with the top card, and so on), inviting your audience to stop you at any card they may choose. When they do so, draw down all the cards, as far as you have gone, completely away from the remaining cards; but with them draw down at the same time the bottom card. This card, coalescing with the upper portion, will be, to the eyes of the spectators, that at which you were directed to stop. Holding the cards with their backs toward you, request the spectators to observe what the card is. The pack may now be shuffled to any extent, but, being acquainted with the card, you can find or name it at pleasure.

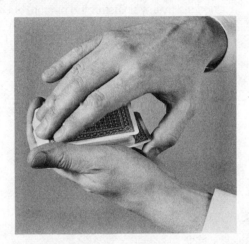

The above may be employed as a means of "forcing," when it is essential to force a given card and you are not sufficiently proficient to feel certain of effecting that object by the regular method. Thus, if the card you desire to force is the seven of diamonds, place that card at the bottom of the pack, and proceed as above directed. When the audience desire you to stop, draw off the upper packet, and with it the seven of diamonds, which will thereby become the bottom card of that packet. Request them to note the card, and at once hand the pack to be shuffled. This is a very simple and easy mode of forcing.

2. Deal the cards into three packs, face upward, and request a spectator to note a card and remember in which heap it is. When you have dealt twenty-one cards, put the rest aside, these not being employed in the trick. Ask in which heap the chosen card is, and place that heap between the other two; deal again as before. Again ask the question, place the heap indicated in the middle, and deal again a third time.

Note particularly the fourth or middle card of each heap, as one or other of those three cards will be the card thought of. Ask, for the last time, in which heap the chosen card now is, when you may be certain that it was the card which you noted as being the middle card of that heap.

This same effect will be produced with any number of cards, so long as such number is odd, and a multiple of three. The process and result will be the same, save that if fifteen cards are used, each heap will consist of five cards, and the *third* card of each will be the middle one; if twenty-seven cards, each heap will consist of nine cards, and the *fifth* will be the selected one, and so on.

3. Take any number of the cards, and deal them face upward upon the table, noting in your own mind the *first* card dealt. Ask any number of persons each to note a card, and to remember at what number it falls. When you have dealt all the cards you first took in your hand, take them up again, without disturbing their order, and turn them face downward. In order to show that the trick is not performed by any arithmetical calculation (you should lay great stress upon this, the fact being precisely the reverse), invite the company to take any number they choose of the remaining cards (such number being unknown to you), and place them either above or below the cards you have dealt. Allow the cards to be cut (not shuffled) as many times as the audience please. You now, for the first time, ask each person the number of the chosen card, and, on being informed, again deal the cards, turning them face upward. When the original *first* card appears, count on (silently) from this as number one to the number mentioned, at which number the noted card will again appear. Should the whole of the cards be dealt out without reaching the required number, turn the cards over again, and continue from the top of the pack until that number is reached.

4. A card having been selected, offer the pack fanwise, that the drawer may replace it. As this is done, let the forefinger of the right hand, which is naturally under the cards, come up and meet it, and with the fingernail press crossways upon the edge of the card. This will make a minute notch or indentation, too slight to be noticed by any uninstructed person, but readily perceptible, either by hand or eye, to the initiated. Similarly, a selected card can be made identifiable by bending one of the corners or bowing the card sharply prior to returning it to the deck.

Revealing the Chosen Card

Having indicated how a card may be discovered, we proceed to describe various modes of disclosing the card thus ascertained.

1. Get the card to the top of the pack. Give the pack to some person to hold. The cards should face upward, so that the chosen card will be undermost, with the thumb of the holder above and the fingers below the pack. The fingers should extend under the pack for about an inch, but the thumb above not more than half an inch. Request the person to nip the cards tightly, and as he does so give them a smart downward rap with your forefinger, which will knock all the cards out of his hand except the lowest card, which will be retained by the greater friction of the fingers, and will remain staring him in the face. This is a very old and simple finish, but it appears marvelous to those who witness it for the first time.

You may, if you prefer, hold the cards yourself as above directed, and allow another person to strike them downward.

2. Get the chosen card to the top, and hold the pack in the right hand, lengthways and face downward, about two feet above the floor or table. Push the top card a little off the pack sideways, so as to make it project throughout its whole length about an inch beyond the rest of the cards. Now let fall the pack, when the resistance of the air will cause the top card to turn over in its fall, and to appear face upward, all the other cards remaining face downward.

3. Place the card in question and seven other indifferent cards in two rows, face downward, on the table. Keep in your own mind which is the chosen card, but do not let the audience see the face of any of the cards. Ask the drawer if he is sure that he will know his card again. He will, of course, answer yes. Now ask either the same or another person to touch four of the eight cards upon the table. Necessarily, the four touched will either include or not include the chosen card. In either case, take up (whether touched or not) the four that do *not* include the chosen card, remarking, "I will return these to the pack." Invite the same person to touch two out of the four that remain. Again take up the two (whether touched or not touched) that do not include the chosen card, saying, "I return these also to the pack." You have now only two cards left on the table, one of which is the chosen card.

Invite one of the spectators to touch one of these cards. As before, whichever the person touches, pick up and return to the pack the non-chosen card, remarking, "We have now only one card left. You have all seen that I dealt out eight cards on the table, and that I have withdrawn seven, you yourselves choosing which I should withdraw. Now, sir, be kind enough to name the card you drew." The card having been named, you turn over the card left on the table, and show that it is the right one.

This trick is based upon a kind of *double entendre*, which, though apparently obvious, is rarely seen through by the audience if performed in a quick and lively manner. The secret lies in the performer interpreting the touching of the cards in two different senses, as may best suit his purpose.

If the chosen card is *not* among the cards touched, he interprets the touching as meaning that the cards touched are rejected, and to be returned to the pack. If the card is among those touched, he interprets the touching in the opposite sense— namely, that the cards touched are to be retained, and the others rejected. If he is lucky in the cards touched, he may be able to interpret the touching in the same sense throughtout the trick, in which case there will be no clue whatever to the secret; but even in the opposite case, where compelled to put aside first the cards touched and then the cards not touched, the difference generally passes unnoticed by the spectators, or, if noticed, is put down as a slip on the part of the performer, rather than as being, as it really is, the key to the trick.

Where the performer is proficient in sleight-of-hand, the above may be worked up into a really brilliant trick. Any indifferent card being drawn and returned is brought to the top by the pass, palmed, and the back shuffled. Eight cards are laid out, and the drawn card revealed as above.

Having described these few commencements and terminations, we will next proceed to the discussion of some complete card tricks.

The One that Got Away

A card vanishes from the pack and is found in a person's pocket.

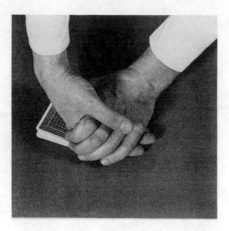

Slightly moisten the back of your left hand. Offer the pack to be shuffled. Place it face downward on the table, and request one of the company (Mr. A) to look at the top card. Request him to place the back of his left hand upon the cards, and press heavily upon it with his right. In order that he may better comprehend your meaning, place your own hands as described and request him to imitate you. When you remove your left hand, the back being moistened, the card will stick to it. Put your hands carelessly behind you, and with the right hand remove the card. All will crowd round to see the trick. Pretend to be very particular that Mr. A places his hand on the card in precisely the right position. This will not only give you time but will draw all eyes to his hands. Meanwhile, watch your opportunity and slip the card into the coat pocket of one or other of the spectators (Mr. B). Now announce that you are about to order the top card, which all have seen, and which Mr. A is holding down so exceedingly tight, to fly away from the pack and into the pocket of Mr. B., making the choice apparently haphazard. On examination your commands will be found to have been fulfilled. It has a good effect, when practicable, to slip the card into the pocket of the same person who is pressing on the back. (Magician's wax, available at magic shops, is an excellent alternative to wetting the back of the hand.)

The Traveling Kings

The four kings are placed in different parts of the pack and with one cut they are found all together.

Take the four kings (or any other four cards at pleasure), and exhibit them fanwise, but secretly place behind the second one two other court cards of any description, which, being thus hidden behind the king, will not be visible.

The audience being satisfied that the four cards are really the four kings and none other, fold them together, and place them at the top of the pack. Draw attention to the fact that you are about to distribute these four kings in different parts of the pack. Take up the top card, which, being really a king, you may exhibit without apparent intention, and place it at the bottom. Take the next card, which the spectators suppose to be also a king, and place it about halfway down the pack, and the next, in like manner, a little higher. Take the fourth card, which, being actually a king, you may show carelessly, and replace it on the top of the pack. You have now really three kings at the top and one at the bottom, though the audience imagine that they have seen them distributed in different parts of the pack, and are proportionately surprised, when the cards are cut, to find that all the kings are again together.

It is best to use jacks or queens for the two extra cards, as being less distinguishable from the kings, should a spectator catch a glimpse of their faces.

The Secret Card Code

This is an old trick, but a very good one, that lets you name all the cards in the pack in succession.

To perform it, you must arrange the cards beforehand, according to a given formula, which forms a sort of *memoria technica*. There are several used, but all are similar in effect. The following is one of the simplest:

> Eight kings threatened to save
> Ninety-five ladies for one sick knave.

These words suggest, as you will readily see, eight, king, three, ten, two, seven, nine, five, queen, four, ace, six, knave (or jack). You must also have a determinate order for the suits, which should be red and black alternately, say, diamonds, clubs, hearts, spades, which can be recalled as *DiCHeS*.

Sort the pack for convenience into the four suits, and then arrange the cards as follows: Take in your left hand, *face upward*, the eight of diamonds, on this place the king of clubs, on this the three of hearts, then the ten of spades, then the two of diamonds, and so on, till all the cards are exhausted. This arrangement must be made privately beforehand, and you either must make this the first of your series of tricks, or (which is better, as it negatives the idea of arrangement) have two packs of the same pattern, and secretly exchange the prepared pack, at a suitable opportunity, for that which you have already been performing. Spread the cards (which may previously be cut any number of times), and offer them to a person to draw one. While he is looking at the card, glance quickly at the card next above that which he has drawn, which we will suppose is the five of diamonds. You will remember that in your *memoria technica* "five" is followed by "ladies" (queen). You know then that the next card, the one drawn, was a queen; you know also that clubs follow diamonds; ergo, the card drawn is the queen of clubs. Name it, and request the drawer to replace it.

Ask someone again to cut the cards, and repeat the trick in the same form with another person, but this time pass all the cards that were above the card drawn, below the remainder of the pack. This is equivalent to cutting the pack at that particular card. After naming the card drawn, ask if the company would like to know any more. Name the cards next following the card already drawn, taking them one by one from the pack and laying them face upward on the table, to show that you have named them correctly. After a little practice, it will cost you but a slight effort of memory to name in succession all the cards in the pack.

Another trick performed by the aid of this prepared pack is to have the pack cut and to tell the audience whether the number cut is odd or even.

Notice whether the bottom card for the time being is red or black. Place the pack on the table, and invite any person to cut, announcing that you will tell by the weight of the cards cut whether the number is odd or even. Take the cut cards (i.e., the cards which before the cut were at the top of the pack), and poising them carefully in your hand, as though testing their weight, glance slyly at the bottom card. If it is of the same color as the bottom card of the other or lowest portion, the cards cut are an even number; if of a different color, they are odd.

Mental Coincidence

One person thinks of a card and that card appears at such a number in the pack as another person names.

Allow the pack to be shuffled and cut as freely as the company please. When they are fully satisfied that the cards are well mixed, offer the pack to any of the spectators, and request that person to look over the cards, and think of any one, and to remember the number at which it stands in the pack, reckoning from the bottom card upward.

Then remark: "Ladies and gentlemen, you will take particular notice that I have not asked a single question, and yet I already know the card; and if anyone will kindly indicate the place in the pack at which you desire it to appear, I will at once cause it to take that position. I must only ask that, by arrangement between yourselves, you will make the number at which the card is to appear higher than that which it originally held."

We will suppose that the audience decide that the card shall appear at number twenty-two. Carelessly remark, "It is not even necessary for me to see the cards." So saying, hold the pack under the table or behind your back, and rapidly count off twenty-two cards from the bottom of the pack, and place them on the top. (When the number named is more than half the total number of the pack, i.e. more than twenty-six, it is quicker, and has precisely the same effect, to count off the difference between that and the total number from the top, and place them at the bottom. Thus, if the number called be twelve, you would count off twelve from the bottom, and place them on top; but if the number called were thirty, you would achieve the same object by counting twenty-two from the top, and passing them to the bottom.)

You then continue: "Having already placed the card thought of in the desired position, I may now, without suspicion, ask for the original number of the card, as I shall commence my counting with that number." We will suppose you are told the card was originally number ten. You begin to count from the top of the pack, calling the first card ten, the next eleven, and so on. When you come to twenty-two, the number appointed, you say, "If I have kept my promise, this should be the card you thought of. To avoid the suspicion of confederacy, will you please say, before I turn it over, what your card was." The card being named, you turn it up, and show that it is the right one.

In all tricks which depend on the naming of a card drawn or thought of, it adds greatly to the effect to have the card named before you turn it up.

This trick, unlike most, will bear repetition; but it is well on a second performance to vary it a little. Thus you may on the second occasion say, when the card has been thought of, "I will choose for myself this time; your card will appear at number forty-five." It is desirable to name a number very near the total number of the pack, as the difference between that and the total number being very small, it is easy to see at a glance the number of cards representing such difference, and pass them to the bottom of the pack. If you are able to make the pass, you will, of course, avail yourself of it to transfer the requisite number of cards to the top or bottom of the pack.

Let Me Guess

The conjurer guesses correctly four cards thought of by four different persons.

Offer the pack to be shuffled. Place it on the table, and taking off the four top cards with the right hand, offer them to any person, and ask him to notice one of them, shuffle them, and return them to you. When they are returned, place them, face downward, in your left hand. Take the next four cards, and offer them to another person in like manner. Proceed in like manner with a third and fourth group of four. When all the sixteen cards are returned, deal them out in four heaps, face upward. Ask each person in which heap his card now is. That of the first person will be the uppermost of his heap, that of the second person second in his heap, and so on. It will sometimes occur that two of the cards chosen are in the same heap, but the rule will still apply. Should there be three persons only to choose, you should give them three cards each, and deal in three heaps.

Tricks with Special Cards

We have already explained the nature and use of the "forcing" pack of cards. It may be well, before we go further, to give a short account of one or two other species of prepared cards.

The Key Card

The "key" card is the technical name for a card that is different in some fashion from the rest of the pack. Key cards can be slightly longer, wider, or shorter than the rest of the pack. Whether longer, wider, or shorter by about the thickness of a dime, the performer is able to cut the pack at that particular card whenever he chooses to do so. A short card is easily made: simply trim one of the short ends of a card (some conjurers trim straight across the short end, others trim the two diagonal corners, still others trim the center of the short end, leaving the corners intact). Place the short card in the deck and shuffle. A ruffle of the pack will make it obvious which card is short, for at that point in the ruffle the fingers will feel the indentation. With the aid of such a card, and a tolerable proficiency in "forcing" and "making the pass," many excellent tricks can be performed.

A useful variation of the key card is the tapered or "shaved" pack, in which any card may in turn become the key card. In a tapered pack, all cards are a shade narrower at one end than the other. If the whole pack is at the outset placed with all the cards alike (i.e., their ends tapering in the same direction), by reversing any card and returning it to the pack, its wide end will be made to correspond with the narrow ends of the remaining cards, thereby making it for the time being a key card.

By offering the pack for a person to draw a card, and turning the pack round before the card is replaced, the position of that card will thus be reversed, and you will be able to find it again in an instant, however thoroughly the cards may be shuffled. By prearranging the pack beforehand, with the narrow ends of all the red cards in one direction, and those of the black cards in the other direction, you may, by grasping the pack between the finger and thumb at each end, and, drawing the hands apart, separate the black cards from the red at a single stroke, or, by preparing the pack accordingly, you may divide the court cards from the plain cards in like manner. Tapered packs are available at magic shops for little more than the cost of a normal pack.

Many other recreations may be performed with a pack of this kind, which will be noticed in due course. The key card and the tapered pack have each their special advantages and disadvantages. The key card, such as the short card, is the more reliable, as it can always be distinguished with certainty from the rest of the pack; but after having made use of it for one trick, it is clear that you cannot immediately venture upon another with the same card. It is further comparatively useless unless you are proficient in "forcing."

The tapered pack may be used without any knowledge of forcing, and has the advantage that any card may in turn become the key card, but it is treacherous. The necessary turning of the pack is likely to attract observation, and any little mistake, such as allowing the card to be replaced in its original direction, or a few of the cards getting turned round in shuffling, will cause a breakdown. Notwithstanding these disadvantages, both the key card and the tapered pack will be found very useful to the amateur; but it should be borne in mind that both these appliances are in reality only makeshifts or substitutes for sleight-of-hand. Professionals of the highest class discard them altogether, and rely wholly on the more subtle magic of their own fingers.

The Selected Card Revealed

Request some person to draw a card, spreading the deck before him for that purpose. If you use a key-card pack you must force the key card; if you are using a tapered pack any card may be drawn, the pack being reversed before the card is replaced. The card being returned, the pack may be shuffled to any extent, but you will always be able to cut by feel at the chosen card.

You may vary the trick by taking the cards upright between the second finger and thumb of the right hand, and requesting someone to say, "One, two, three!" At the word *three* drop all the cards save the card chosen, which its projecting edges will enable you to retain when you relax the pressure upon the other cards of the tapered pack. The same effect may be accomplished with the key card by cutting it to the top of the deck and pinching it between thumb and fingers as you drop the rest of the pack.

Another mode of finishing the trick is to request anyone present to put the pack (previously well shuffled) in his pocket, at which point you proceed, with his permission, to pick his pocket of the chosen card.

The trick can also be finished by flinging the pack in the air, and catching the chosen card. For this purpose, after forcing the key card, and after giving the pack to be shuffled, you cut the pack at the key card as before, but without showing it, and place the original lower half of the pack on the top. The chosen card will now be at the top. Take the pack upon the right hand, and quickly transfer it to the left, at the same time palming (with the right hand) the top card. Spread the cards a little, and fling them into the air, clutching at them with the right hand as they descend, and at the same moment bring the chosen card to the tips of the fingers. The effect to the spectators will be as if you actually caught it among the falling cards.

The Magic Touch

The conjurer demonstrates an ability to distinguish the court cards from the rest of the pack—by touch.

This trick is performed by means of a preliminary preparation of the court cards, to be made as follows: Take each court card separately, edge upward, and draw a tolerably sharp knife, the blade held sloping backwards at an angle of about forty-five degrees, once or twice along the edge from left to right. This will be found to turn the edge of the card, so to speak, and to leave on each side a minute ridge, not noticeable by the eye, but immediately perceptible, if sought for, to the touch. Prepare the opposite edge of the card in the same way, and again mix the court cards with the pack, which is now ready for use.

Offer the prepared pack to be shuffled. When the pack is returned to you, you may either hold it above your head, and, showing the cards in succession, call "court card" or "plain card," as the case may be, or you may offer to deal the cards into two heaps, consisting of court cards in one heap and plain cards in the other, every now and then offering the cards to be again shuffled. You can, of course, perform the trick blindfolded with equal facility.

You should endeavor to conceal, as much as possible, the fact that you distinguish the court cards by the sense of touch, and rather seek to make your audience believe that the trick is performed by means of some mathematical principle, or by any other means remote from the true explanation. This advice, indeed, applies more or less to all tricks. Thus, while your knowledge of a forced card depends, of course, on sleight-of-hand, you should by no means let this be suspected, but rather claim credit for some clairvoyant faculty, and vice versa, when you perform a trick depending on a mathematical combination, endeavor to lead your audience to believe that it is performed by means of some impossible piece of sleight-of-hand. Further, endeavor to vary your modus operandi. If you have just performed a trick depending purely on sleight-of-hand, do not let the next be of the same character, but rather one based on a mathematical principle, or on the use of special apparatus.

Sightless Vision

The conjurer names any number of cards in succession without seeing them.

This trick, in its original form, is well known; but we describe it for the sake of completeness, and for the better comprehension of the improved method.

Take your pack, and secretly notice the bottom card. Then announce that you will name all the cards of the pack in succession without seeing them. Holding the pack behind you for an instant, turn the top card face-outward on the top of the pack; then holding the pack with the bottom card toward the audience, name that card. From the position in which you hold the pack, the top card, which you have turned, is toward you, and in full view.

Again placing your hands behind you, transfer the last named to the bottom, and turn the next, and so on in like manner. Even in an audience of half-a-dozen only, it is very likely that there will be someone acquainted with this form of the trick who will proclaim aloud his knowledge of "how it is done." We will suppose that you have performed the trick with this result. Passing your hands again behind you, but this time merely passing the top card to the bottom, without turning any other card, you reply that you doubt his pretended knowledge, and name the card as before. He will naturally justify his assertion by explaining the mode of performing the trick.

You reply, "According to your theory, there should be an exposed card at each end of the pack. Observe that there is nothing of the kind in this case" (here you show the opposite side of the pack), "but, to give still more conclusive proof, I will for the future keep the whole of the pack behind me, and name each card *before* I bring it forward. Perhaps, to preclude any idea of arrangement of the cards, someone will kindly shuffle them."

When the cards are returned, give them a slight additional shuffle yourself, remarking, "They are pretty well shuffled now, I think," and continue the trick by the *second method*: Glance, as before, at the bottom card. Place the cards behind you, and name the card you have just seen. Passing the right hand behind you, palm the top card, and then taking hold of the bottom card (the one you have just named) face-outward, with the first two fingers and thumb of the same hand, bring it forward and throw it on the table. Pause for a moment before you throw it down, as if asking the company to verify the correctness of your assertion, and glance secretly at the card which is curled up in your palm. Again place your hands behind you, call the name of the card you last palmed, and palm another.

You can, of course, continue the trick as long as you please, each time naming the card you palmed at the last call. You should take care to have a tolerably wide space between yourself and your audience, in which case, with very little management on your part, there is little fear of their discovering the secret of the palmed card.

You should not be in too great a hurry to name the card you have just seen, or the audience may suspect that you gained your knowledge in the act of bringing forward the card you last named. To negate this idea, you should take care first to bring forward again the right hand, manifestly empty, and do your best to simulate thought and mental exertion before naming the next card.

The Three-Card Monte

This well-known trick has long been banished from the repertoire of the conjurer, and is now used by itinerant card-sharpers. We insert the explanation of it in this place as exemplifying one form of sleight-of-hand, and also as a useful warning to the unwary.

The effect of the trick is as follows: Three cards are used, one of them being a court card, the two others "plain" or low cards. We will suppose, for the sake of illustration, that the cards used are the king of hearts, the seven of spades, and the nine of diamonds. The performer takes one of the low cards, say the nine of diamonds, in his left hand, face downward, between the tips of the second finger and thumb. The other two cards are held in the right hand in like manner one above the other, about an inch apart, but the uppermost card, which we will suppose to be the seven, is held between the thumb and the tip of the first finger, while the undermost (the king) is supported between the thumb and the second finger. The hold on the cards can be facilitated by giving each card a lengthwise bend.

The performer now throws the three cards in succession face downward upon a table or on the ground before him (in the latter case kneeling to his work), shuffles them about with more or less rapidity, and then invites the spectators to guess (or, in the card-sharping form of the trick, to bet) which is the court card.

This would seem to be a perfectly easy matter. The spectators have observed where the king originally fell; and the subsequent shifting of the cards has not made it much more difficult to keep note of its position; but if the trick has been skillfully performed they will be much more often wrong than right.

The main secret lies in the position of the cards in the right hand, coupled with a dexterity acquired by much practice. The performer professedly throws down the *undermost* of the two cards in the right hand first, and this card has been seen to be the king. As a matter of fact, however, he can at pleasure let the uppermost card fall first, the first finger, which supported it, taking the place of the middle finger at the top of the second card. The change is so subtle that even the keenest eye cannot detect whether it has or has not been made, and this makes practically two chances to one against the person guessing.

After this has gone on for a little time, and a sufficient ring of spectators has been got together, the operator makes use of some plausible pretext to look aside from the cards for a moment. While he does so one of the confederates, with a wink at the bystanders, slyly bends up one corner of the court card, ostensibly as a means of recognition.

The performer takes up the cards without apparently noticing the trick that has been played upon him, but secretly (that corner of the card being concealed by the third and fourth fingers of the right hand) straightens the bent corner, and at the same moment bends in like manner the corresponding corner of the other card in the same hand. He then throws down the cards as before. The bent corner is plainly visible, and the spectators, who do not suspect the change that has just been made, are fully persuaded that the card so bent, and no other, is the court card. Speculating, as they imagine, on a certainty, they are easily induced to bet that they will discover the court card, and they naturally name the one with the bent corner. When the card is turned, they find, to their disgust, that they have been duped, and that the dishonest advantage which they imagined they had obtained over the dealer was in reality a device for their confusion.

A Throw of the Dice

The effect of this surprising trick is as follows: You invite a person to draw a card, allowing the utmost freedom of selection. You allow the drawer to replace the card in any part of the pack he pleases, and you thoroughly shuffle the cards, finally inviting the drawer to "cut." Then dealing out six rows of six cards each, face downward on the table, you offer the drawer a dice-cup and a pair of dice, and after he has thrown any number of times to satisfy himself that the dice are fair and unprepared, you invite him to throw each singly, the first to ascertain the row in which his card is, and the second to discover at what number it stands in the row. He throws, say, "six" first, and "three" afterward, and on examination the card he drew proves to be the third card of the sixth row.

The whole mystery consists in the use of a forcing pack, all the cards of which are alike. The dice are perfectly fair, but as each card of each row is the same, it is a matter of perfect indifference what numbers are thrown. It is advisable to gather up all the other cards, and to request the person to name his card, before allowing the one designated by the dice to be turned up. This will draw the attention of the company to the card on the table, and will give you the opportunity to re-exchange the cards you have used for an ordinary pack (from which, by the way, the card answering to the forced card should have been withdrawn). This pack you may carelessly leave on the table; so that in the event of suspicion attaching to the cards, it will be at once negated by an examination of the pack.

The trick may be made an illustration of second sight, by pretending to mesmerize some person in the company, and ordering him to write down beforehand, while under the supposed mesmeric influence, the row and number at which the drawn card shall be found. The mode of conducting the trick is the same, but the dice are not used.

CARD TRICKS REQUIRING SPECIAL APPARATUS

We propose to describe such card tricks as require the aid of some mechanical appliance or apparatus, but are still appropriate for performance at close quarters.

We may here anticipate a not unlikely question on the part of the student, viz., "How can I best obtain the necessary apparatus?" In some instances, an amateur with a mechanical turn may be able to manufacture his own appliances; and where this is the case, we would by no means discourage it, as doing so will thereby double one's amusement from the study of the magic art. But where the student has not the ability or inclination to do this, we strongly advise not to attempt to have apparatus made to order by persons unaccustomed to this class of work, but to go direct to one or other of the regular magic shops. Magical apparatus requires so much precision in its details, and so much attention to apparent trifles, that the first attempt of any workman, however skillful, is almost sure to be a failure; and by the time the defects are rectified, the purchaser will find that more has been paid for a clumsy makeshift than would have been charged for a thoroughly good article from the right quarter. Experience will quickly prove that inferior apparatus is dear at any price.

The novice must be warned against imagining that once in the region of apparatus the necessity of personal address and dexterity will be diminished. On the contrary, there is hardly a trick among those we are about to describe which does not demand more or less practical knowledge of sleight-of-hand. We shall assume, in the following pages, that the reader has carefully followed and studied the directions already given, in which case there will be little difficulty in this portion of the work.

The Rising Cards

This is one of the best of card tricks. The performer advances, pack in hand, to the company. Three persons are invited each to draw a card. The cards having been drawn, they are replaced in different parts of the pack, which is thoroughly shuffled. The performer then places the pack in a metal or wood box or case with a cut-out design front and no top, just large enough to hold the pack in an upright position. This case, called a *houlette* by conjurers, is generally supported on a shaft or metal tube, twelve to fifteen inches high, which itself sits on a metal base. The performer then asks each person in succession to call for his card, which is forthwith seen to rise slowly from the pack, without any visible assistance, the performer standing quite apart.

The ingenuity of different professors has added little embellishments of a humorous character. For instance, the performer may remark, addressing one of the persons who drew, "I will not even ask the name of your card. You have only to say, 'I command the card I drew to appear,' and you will be obeyed." He does so, but no effect is produced; the cards remain obstinately motionless. The command is repeated, but with the same result. The performer feigns embarrassment, and says, "I must really apologize for the disobedience of the cards. I cannot tell how it is; they never behaved in this way before. I am afraid I must ask you to name the card, after all, when I will try my own authority." The card proves to have been a queen, say the queen of spades. "Oh," the performer says, "that quite explains it. Queens are not accustomed to be ordered about. If we try again in becoming language, I dare say we shall be more successful. Let us try the experiment. Say, 'Will your majesty oblige the company by appearing?'" Thus propitiated, the card rises instantly.

Sometimes a card, after coming up half-way, begins to retire again, but at the command of the performer starts afresh, and rises completely out of the pack.

These apparently surprising effects are produced by very simple means. In the first place, the cards that rise from the pack are not those actually drawn, but duplicates of them, arranged beforehand. The performer ensures the corresponding cards being drawn by using a forcing pack, made up of repetitions of the three cards in question, which we will suppose to be the queen of spades, the ten of hearts, and the seven of diamonds, with some other single card at the bottom.

The case or *houlette* in the original form of the trick has two compartments—the one to the front being large enough to hold a complete pack, but the back one adapted to contain six or eight cards only. In this back compartment are placed six cards, three of them being those which are intended to rise, and the other three indifferent cards. A black silk thread is fastened to the upper edge of the partition between the two compartments, and is thence brought under the foremost card (which is, say, the queen of spades), over the next (an indifferent card), under the third (the ten of hearts), over the fourth (an indifferent card), under the fifth (the seven of diamonds), over the sixth (an indifferent card), finally passing out through a minute hole at the bottom of the back compartment. If the thread is pulled, the three cards named will rise in succession, beginning with the hindmost—viz., the seven of diamonds. The three indifferent cards are put in as partitions, or fulcrums, for the thread to run over. if these partitions were omitted, the three chosen cards would rise all together.

The thread may be drawn in various ways. Sometimes this is done by the performer himself, standing behind or beside the table. Another plan is to have the thread drawn by means of a clockwork motor. The arrangement that we ourselves prefer, where practicable, is to have the thread drawn by an assistant, who may either be placed behind a sceen, or may even stand in full view of the audience, so long as he or she is at some little distance from the table. The black thread is quite invisible, if only you have a tolerably dark background and no overhead lighting. The only portion of the thread you need feel any anxiety about is that immediately connected with the cards. To conceal this it is well, if you use a magic table, to have a small hole bored in the top, through which the thread may pass. The card-stand being placed immediately in front of the hole, the thread will pass perpendicularly downward for the first portion of its length, and will thus be concealed behind the stand. In default of a hole, a ring of bent wire attached to the table will answer the same purpose. The great advantage of having the thread pulled by a living person instead of a mechanical power or small electric motor is that you can take your own time in the performance of the trick; whereas if you use a motor or clockwork, there is always a danger of a card beginning to rise before you have called for it, or possibly not rising at all.

In the latest and best form of the trick, the second compartment in the case is dispensed with. In this case three cards are forced and returned as already mentioned; but the performer, on reaching the table, exchanges the forcing pack for another already prepared, and placed on the *servante* if a conjuring table, or, if not, concealed behind some object on the table. This pack is prepared as follows:

The last six cards are arranged with the thread traveling in and out between them (a short slit in the top of the indifferent cards through which the thread rides will keep the thread in place), just as the six cards in the back compartment in the older form of the trick. A knot is made in the thread, which is hitched into a notch an eighth of an inch deep, made in the lower edge of the *sixth* card. The knot prevents the thread from slipping, but does not interfere with its being instantaneously detached when, the trick being over, you hand the whole apparatus, cards and all, to be examined.

To our own taste the trick is best performed without any special card-case whatever, the pack being placed in an ordinary glass tumbler with straight sides, first handed round to the audience for inspection. It is here absolutely self-evident that the glass can give no assistance; and as the audience know nothing of the exchange of the packs, the immediate rising of the cards at the word of command appears little short of miraculous.

The Magic Card

This little trick is hardly of sufficient importance to be performed by itself; but as an incident introduced in the course of some more pretentious illusion, it produces a very good effect. A great deal of the sparkle of a conjuring entertainment depends upon the performer's readiness in what may be called "by-play," consisting of a number of minor tricks not supposed to form part of the settled program, but merely introduced incidentally, and used, as it were, as a garnish to the more important feats.

When a coin, an egg, or other small article is required for the purpose of a trick, the performer may fetch it openly from behind the scenes, or have it handed to him by his assistant; but this is a commonplace proceeding. The higher class of performers prefer in such cases to produce the article from the pocket of one of the audience; and in like manner, when the article has served its purpose, to make it vanish by some magical process, rather than by the prosaic methods of everyday life. These little incidents serve to keep the audience surprised, and they further assist materially in keeping up the *continuity* of an entertainment. In a thoroughly good performance the audience should have no time to think, but should be led direct from one surprise to the contemplation of another.

The trick we are about to describe is of the class above alluded to. In the course of one or other of your card tricks, you make occasion to ask some person to go and place a given card on the table, or to examine a card already placed there. He does so, and is about to return to his seat; but you stop him. "No, that won't do. I want everybody to see what the card is. Will you be good enough to stand it up on end, with its face to the audience, so that everybody can see it?" He looks foolish, and finally says that he can't do it. "Not do it?" you reply. "Why, it's the simplest thing in the world. Allow *me*!" And taking the card from him, you place it upright on the table, and leave it standing without any visible support. Taking it up again, you hand it round, to show that there is no preparation about it, and on receiving it back, again stand it upright, but with the other end upward; or, if challenged, allow the audience themselves to choose a card, which you cause to stand alone with equal facility.

The secret lies in the use of a very small and simple piece of apparatus, being, in fact, merely a strip of sheet metal, 1½ inches long, and ⅝ inch wide, bent at a shade less than a right angle—say eighty-five degrees; its shorter arm being one-third its length. On the outer surface of the long arm is spread a thin layer of magician's wax (or double-sided adhesive tape), and to the inner surface of the shorter arm is soldered a small piece of lead, about ⅛ inch thick (a fishing weight will do).

When you desire to perform the trick, have this little appliance concealed in your right hand, the longer arm between the first and second fingers, and the shorter arm pointing toward the little finger. Picking up the card with the left hand, you transfer it to the right, taking hold of it in such manner that the fingers shall be behind and the thumb in front of the card. As you place the card on the table (which, by the way, must be covered with a cloth), you press against it the waxed side of the metal which will slightly adhere to it, and thus form a prop or foot, the little lump of lead acting as a counterpoise to the weight of the card. Pick it up with the same hand, and as you transfer it to the other, you will find no difficulty in removing and secreting between the fingers the little prop.

The Card-Box

This simple apparatus is capable of vanishing and producing cards.

On the left is a metal flap that hides the card when placed in the box.

The card-box in its simplest form is a small flat box in wood, metal, or plastic. Its outside measurement is four inches by three, and not quite an inch deep. Inside, it is just large enough to admit an ordinary-sized playing card. The upper and lower portions of the box, which are connected by hinges, are exactly alike in depth so that the box, which, when open, lies flat like a book, may be closed either way up; and either portion will, according to its placement, become box or lid in turn.

Thus, by using a card which, unknown to the audience, has two faces—e.g., is an ace of hearts on one side and an ace of spades on the other—and placing such a card in one side of the open box, you have only to close the box with that side uppermost, or to turn over the box as you place it on the table, to transform the card just shown into a different one. There is nothing in the appearance of the box itself to indicate that it has been turned, so to speak, wrong side up, and very little practice will enable you to turn it over as you place it on the table without attracting observation.

There is a further appliance in connection with the box in question, which, however, may be used with or without it, as may best suit the trick in hand. This is a loose flap of the same material of which the interior of the box is made, of the thickness of cardboard, and of such a size as to fit closely, though not tightly, in either half of the box.

When the box is closed in such manner that the part in which this flap is uppermost, the flap falls into the lower portion, thus forming a false bottom on whichever side happens to be undermost. If a card (say the ace of hearts) be secretly placed in either side of the box, and this flap placed on it, the box will appear empty. If now another card (say the jack of spades) be openly placed in either side, and the box closed in such manner that the portion containing the false bottom is undermost, no change will take place; but if, either in closing the box or subsequently, it is so placed that the side containing the false bottom becomes uppermost, the false bottom will at once drop into the opposite division, and on re-opening the box the ace of hearts will be revealed, and the jack of spades will in its turn be concealed. The effect on the spectators is as if the jack of spades had changed into the ace of hearts.

Card-boxes are frequently worked in pairs, as follows: The boxes are prepared by placing a different card secretly in each, say an ace of hearts in one and a jack of spades in the other. The performer brings them forward to the company, each hanging wide open, and held by one corner only, with the first and second finger inside, and the thumb outside the box, taking care, however, to hold each by the side containing the false bottom, which is thus kept in position by the pressure of the fingers. So held, the boxes appear absolutely empty.

Having drawn attention to the entire absence of any preparation, the performer lays them open upon the table, and, taking up a pack of cards, requests two of the company each to draw one. They, of course, imagine that they are making a free choice, but in reality the conjurer forces (either by sleight-of-hand or by means of a forcing pack) the ace of hearts and the jack of spades. Again bringing forward the two boxes, he requests each person to place the chosen card in one of them, taking care so to arrange that the person who has drawn the ace of hearts shall place it in the box already containing the concealed jack of spades, and vice versa. Closing each box with the portion containing the false bottom uppermost, he now announces that at his command the cards will change places, which, on re-opening the boxes, they appear to have done. By again turning over the boxes, they may be made to return to their original quarters.

Numerous other good tricks may be performed with the aid of these boxes, which should form part of the collection of every conjurer. By placing a given card beforehand beneath the false bottom, and forcing a like card, you may allow the card drawn to be torn into twenty pieces, and yet, by placing the fragments in the box, or firing them at it from a pistol, restore the card instantly, as at first. In like manner, you may cause a given card to be found in the apparently empty box, or may cause a card openly placed therein to vanish altogether. The changing-box is also sometimes employed by those not proficient in sleight-of-hand as a substitute for forcing, in the following manner: The performer requests some person to draw a card, and, without looking at it, to place it face downward in the box for supposed safekeeping. The box is presently opened by the same or some other person, who is requested to note what the card is. He does so, believing the card to be that which was drawn, and which he had just before seen placed in the box; whereas the card he now examines is, in reality, one concealed beforehand in the box by the performer to suit his purpose, the card actually drawn being now hidden by the false bottom.

Cards Up the Sleeve

The performer having illustrated by some minor trick how completely the cards obey his commands, offers to give further proof of their perfect training by ordering a few of them to pass up his sleeve and inside his jacket pocket.

This is at first usually regarded as a mere conjurer's joke, an undertaking to be "got out of" in some more or less ingenious manner; but the performer proceeds, apparently, to fulfill it in a literal sense. He invites someone to draw a card, to replace it, and to shuffle freely; after which, holding the pack at arm's length in the left hand, he says, "I shall now order the cards to pass one by one up my sleeve and inside my jacket pocket, here," indicating with the right hand a spot about the region of the heart. "Attention, please, that you may hear them pass! First card, pass!"

A slight snap or "click" is heard to proceed from the pack, and the performer, inserting his right hand in the opening of his jacket, takes out a card, which he exhibits and throws on the table. "One card has passed, you see. Now, madam, at what number would you like the card you drew just now to pass? You will remember that the cards have been well shuffled since you replaced it, so that neither you nor I know in what part of the pack it may be, but that will make no difference. Whenever you would like that particular card to pass up the sleeve it will do so. What do you say? At what number shall it go—second, third, fourth? Whatever number you like."

The lady says, we will suppose, "Sixth."

"Sixth, very good. One card has already passed, so the next will be number two. Second card, pass! Third card, pass! Fourth card, pass! Fifth card, pass!" At each command the little "click" is heard, and the performer draws a card out of his jacket pocket, shows it, and throws it on the table.

"Sixth card, pass!" Again he withdraws a card, but this time holds it face downward. "May I ask you to name the card you selected?"

The answer is, say, "The queen of spades."

"Then, madam, as you wished your card to pass sixth, this should be the queen of spades." He turns up the card and shows that it is so.

But the trick is not yet finished. "Some of you, ladies and gentlemen," the performer continues, "have probably formed in your own minds a theory as to how this is done. I find most people imagine that I have a second pack here inside my jacket, and that the cards which I produce are merely duplicates. Fortunately, that is easily disproved; for, if you watch the cards in my hand, you will see that they become gradually fewer and fewer, till at last only one card will be left; and if you pay attention, you will see that card fly up the sleeve after the rest. In order, however, to save time, I shall now say 'pass' a little louder, when two or three cards will pass at a time. I begin. 'Pass!' Three cards have passed, you see.'' (He produces three cards from his pocket accordingly.) ''Pass! Here are two more. Pass! Three more. Pass! Three more. You can see for yourselves that the cards in the hand are rapidly diminishing.'' (He spreads them fanwise.) ''We have now only about half the pack left. Once again, pass! Three cards have passed. Again, pass! Two cards.

''Let us see how many we have still left. One, two, three, *four* cards only. Note what they are, please: the king of diamonds, ten of hearts, jack and seven of spades. Shall they pass one at a time, or altogether?'' (The answer is, invariably, ''Altogether.'') ''Very good. All four cards, pass!'' The cards vanish from the left hand, which is seen empty, and a moment later the four cards are produced from the performer's inside jacket pocket, identified, and thrown on the table.

The whole secret of this trick, one of the most brilliant in the whole range of sleight-of-hand conjuring, lies in dexterous card-palming supplemented by unflinching audacity on the part of the performer. If the neophyte has not full confidence in himself, he had better leave the trick alone, for he will infallibly spoil it. But, given the necessary dexterity, and the address to use it to advantage, I know no feat that produces a more perfect illusion.

It is worked as follows. The chosen card, on being replaced, is brought to the top by the pass, palmed off, and the pack shuffled without it. The performer receives back the pack in his left hand, replaces the drawn card on the top, and forthwith again palms off some nine or ten of the uppermost cards, the card previously palmed being naturally uppermost of these. When he says, ''I shall now order these cards to pass one by one up my sleeve, and inside my jacket pocket,'' he thrusts the right hand into the pocket, as if merely to indicate the quarter referred to, but in removing the hand he leaves the palmed cards behind.

He now says, ''First card, pass,'' and as he does so, draws back the corner of the uppermost cards with the third finger of the left hand, producing the little ''click'' described. Showing, with a careless gesture, that the right hand is empty, he inserts it into the opening of the pocket, and withdraws the *undermost* of the packet of cards just before placed therein. He shows this card, and throws it on the table, then asks at what number the chosen card shall pass. This decided, and being, as we have supposed, sixth, he again, four times in succession, says, ''Pass,'' each time withdrawing the undermost card of the packet; but when he says ''pass'' for the fifth (in all, the sixth) time, he brings out the *uppermost* card of the packet, which, it will be remembered, is the one that was chosen.

The card being shown and identified, the audience naturally imagine that the trick is over, and their vigilance is for the time being suspended. Taking advantage of this momentary lull of attention, the performer coolly palms off another eight or ten cards from the top of the pack. These he retains in the hand, taking care to keep the palm turned to the body, and continues the trick as above described. When he again says ''pass'' he places the hand in the vest, as if merely to take out a card as before, but in so doing introduces the palmed cards. He brings out two or three of these, leaving the rest behind, then produces them, two or three at a time, till the supply in the vest is exhausted. When it becomes necessary to replenish it, he calls attention, as above described, to the diminished number of the cards in the left hand, spreading them fanwise for that purpose. As he closes the fan, he inserts the little finger above the last four cards, and palms off all above these. The cards thus palmed are produced in due course, and when they are exhausted, he again calls attention to the cards in the left hand, now reduced to four only. He spreads them fanwise, shows what cards they are, then closes the fan. Remarking, ''Now watch these cards closely, and you will see them go up the sleeve,'' he makes a quick upward movement of both hands, at the same moment palming the four cards in the right, and smartly ''snapping'' the second finger and thumb of the left. This is taken by the audience to be the same little ''click'' that they heard in the case of the previous ''passes.'' The right hand, with the cards palmed, is slowly lowered, its outstretched forefinger pointing to the empty palm of the left; and then, when all have sufficiently realized the fact of the disappearance of the cards from the left hand, the right is thrust into the vest, and immediately produces thence the four cards, which are seen to be the same as were a moment previously in the left hand.

The Diminishing Cards

The illusion above described forms a natural introduction to the feat of the diminishing cards, the performer offering to explain, as to the feat just exhibited, "how it's done." His explanation is that the cards have a good deal of rubber in their composition, and that by means of judicious compression, they can be reduced in size until they are no larger than a postage stamp, in which condition their flying up the sleeve becomes a comparatively easy matter. This explanation being received with some amount of incredulity, he proceeds to justify it by making a few of the cards visibly smaller, till ultimately they vanish altogether.

The diminishing cards pictured use metal clips to hold the various sizes in place before being brought into view.

One master of this illusion was Robert-Houdin, who produced it entirely by his address in showing an increased or diminished amount of the surface of the cards. Placing an ace at bottom, for a reason that will presently appear, and spreading the cards fanwise, he showed first that they were ordinary size. Closing the fan, he made believe to "stretch" the cards by pulling them strongly in the direction of their longer diameter; then again spread them fanwise, but allowing them to project a little farther from the hand, and boldly asserting that they had grown larger, which, from the larger amount of surface exhibited, really appeared to be the case. This was repeated, the cards being made to project yet a little more from the hand. The fan again being closed, the performer, giving the cards a squeeze, and again spreading them as at first, showed that they had returned to their original dimensions.

Once more the fan was closed, and pressure again applied. The cards were again spread, but this time only a very little way, and covered in great part by the fingers, in which condition they appeared to have diminished to much less than their normal dimensions. An ace was put at the bottom, as the size of the pattern on the face of the cards would otherwise tend to destroy the illusion.

The trick, as above described, is really illusive in competent hands, but its effect is uncertain. Many persons are completely taken in by it, and are even prepared to make affidavit that the cards really grow larger and smaller; but others, of a more hard-headed and unimaginative turn, decline to listen to the voice of the charmer, and jump at once to the true explanation.

To remove all possible question as to the fact of the diminution, a graduated series of packs is now used for the purpose of this trick. The series usually sold consists of, in the first place, the ordinary-sized pack, which we will call No. 1; secondly, of about a dozen cards (No. 2) of exactly half the size, secured together by a rivet at one corner. The first card of this pack is a full-sized card folded in half. On the back of each card of this pack is pasted a still smaller card, and the set is completed by a quite miniature pack (No. 3) of cards not exceeding an inch in length, fastened together in like manner by a rivet, or in some cases with a simple loop of thread. The pattern of the cards, back and front, should correspond in design throughout the series.

Pack No. 2, with the full-sized card extended, and with two or three loose cards of the same size lying on its face, is secretly substituted at the right moment for the ordinary pack previously in use. The loose full-sized cards are handed to the audience, or carelessly shown and thrown on the table, to prove, ostensibly, that all are ordinary cards; and the performer then, under pretense of squeezing the pack, folds down the one full-sized card, and spreads the pack (No. 2), as far as the rivet will permit. Another squeeze, under cover of which the pack is turned round, showing the still smaller cards on the reverse side. Another squeeze, and pack No.

2 is palmed off altogether, pack No. 3 being shown in its place. No. 2 is dropped into a pocket, or on the *servante*, and the performer, holding pack No. 3 between the second finger and thumb of the left hand, takes it (apparently) in the right, and by means of the "French drop" (explained in the section on coin tricks) vanishes it altogether.

The "make-believe" method of Robert-Houdin may in this case be employed with perfect safety for the first stage of the diminution; because the cards being at the next stage unmistakably reduced in size, any doubt in the minds of the spectators as to the reality of the change in the first instance is thereby set at rest.

The Velvet Cloth

This is a piece of black velvet, fifteen to eighteen inches square. The performer, having forced three cards, places them in a pistol and fires at the cloth, which is held up, by way of target, by his assistant. At the moment of firing, the three cards suddenly appear against the cloth, as if actually fixed there by the shot.

The secret lies in the fact that the cloth is in reality *two* pieces of velvet; one half of each being sewn together back to back. The portion sewn together constitutes a "flap," covering at pleasure either the one or the other half of the remaining portion. When first shown it is held by the assistant with the flap lifted, and the cards, which are lightly tacked or otherwise attached to the cloth, concealed behind it. When the pistol is fired, the assistant takes half a step backward, and at the same time quickly lowers and raises the cloth some six inches, as if startled by the report. Under cover of these two movements the flap is dropped, and the state of things is then changed, the three cards having apparently attached themselves to the velvet.

The edge of the flap should be weighted with a light iron rod, that it may fall the quicker.

The velvet cloth may be used for the reproduction of watches, bracelets, keys, and other borrowed articles, as well as of cards.

COIN TRICKS:

Principles of Sleight-of-Hand with Coins

Before attempting tricks with coins, it will be necessary for the student to practice certain sleights and passes which more especially belong to this particular branch of the magic art, though the sleight-of-hand used in coin tricks is more or less applicable to most other small objects.

The principles we have given for card tricks will not here be of any direct assistance to the student; but the readiness of hand and eye which will have been acquired, if the student has diligently put in practice the instructions already given, will be of great value as a preliminary training, and it may safely be predicated that any person who is a first-rate performer with cards will find little difficulty in any other branch of the art.

The first faculty the novice must seek to acquire is that of "palming"—i.e., secretly holding an object in the open hand by the contraction of the palm. To acquire this power, take a silver dollar, half-dollar, or quarter (these being the most convenient in point of size), and lay it on the palm of the open hand. Now close the hand very slightly, and if you have placed the coin on the right spot (which a few trials will quickly indicate), the contraction of the palm around its edges will hold it securely, and you may move the hand and arm in any direction without fear of dropping it.

You should next accustom yourself to use the hand and fingers easily and naturally, while still holding the coin as described. A very little practice will enable you to do this. You must bear in mind while practicing always to keep the inside of the palm either downward or toward your own body, as any reverse movement would expose the concealed coin. When you are able to hold the coin comfortably in the right hand, practice in like manner with the left, after which you may substitute for the coin an egg, small rubber ball, or other articles of frequent use in conjuring.

Being thoroughly master of this first lesson, you may proceed to the study of the various "passes." All of the passes have the same object—the apparent transfer of an article from one hand to the other, though such article really remains in the hand it has apparently just quitted. As the same movement frequently repeated would cause suspicion, and possibly detection, it is desirable to acquire different ways of effecting this object.

The Classic Palm

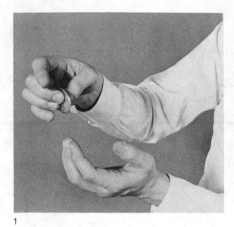 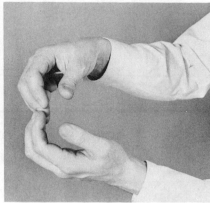 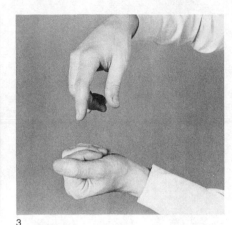

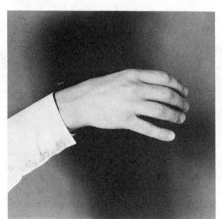 

1. Coin in right hand, approaches left.
2. Coin into classic palm in right hand, appears to be dropped into left hand.
3. Left hand closes as if holding coin.
4. Back of right hand with coin concealed in it.
5. Position of coin in right palm.

Take the coin in the right hand, between the second and third fingers and the thumb, letting it, however, really be supported by the fingers, and only steadied by the thumb. Now move the thumb out of the way, and close the second and third fingers, with the coin balanced on them, into the palm. If the coin was placed right in the first instance, you will find that this motion puts it precisely in the position above described as the proper one for palming; and on again extending the fingers, the coin is left palmed.

When you can do this easily with the hand at rest, you must practice doing the same thing with the right hand in motion toward the left, which should meet it open, but should close the moment that the fingers of the right hand touch its palm, as though upon the coin, which you have by this movement feigned to transfer to it. The left hand must thenceforward remain closed, as if holding the coin, and the right hand hang loosely open, as if empty.

In the case of an article of larger size than a coin you need not take the article with the fingers, but may let it simply lie on the palm of the right hand, slightly closing that hand as you move it toward the left. The greater extent of surface in this case will give you plenty of hold, without the necessity of pressing the article into the palm. Remember that, in any case, the two hands must work in harmony, as in the genuine act of passing an article from one hand to the other. The left hand must therefore rise to meet the right, but should not begin its journey until the right hand begins its own. Nothing looks more awkward or unnatural than to see the left hand extended with open palm, before the right hand has begun to move toward it.

After the pass is made, a judicious use of the wand will materially assist in concealing the fact that the object still remains in the right hand. For this purpose the performer should, before commencing the pass, carelessly place the wand under either arm, as though merely to leave his hands free. Immediately after the pass is made the right hand should with a sort of back-handed movement, which under the circumstance is perfectly natural, grasp the wand, draw it from under the arm, and thenceforth retain it till an opportunity occurs of disposing of the coin as may be necessary. The position of the fingers in the act of holding the wand is such as to effectively mask the concealed coin, while the hand appears perfectly easy and natural. The same expedient may be employed with equal advantage in the remaining passes. A pencil, pen, cigar, closed fan, or other object may be substituted for the wand.

The Finger Palm

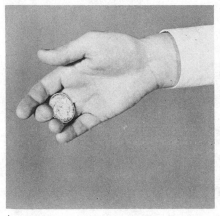 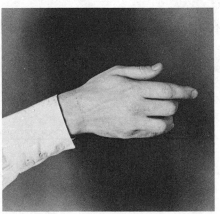

1

2

The coin rests in the right hand, in the area described by the first and third joints of the middle and third fingers. It will be noticed that a slight contraction of these two fingers will retain the coin between the first and third joints even though the hand is tipped over, palm down.

Repeat the actions of the classic palm, bringing the hands together, and pretend to tip the coin from the right hand into the left hand, closing the left hand over the imaginary coin, and letting the right hand hang loosely at your side. This variation of the classic palm requires precise timing for the illusion to be effective. It is, however, more practical than the classic palm when larger coins or other sizable objects are employed.

The Thumb Clip

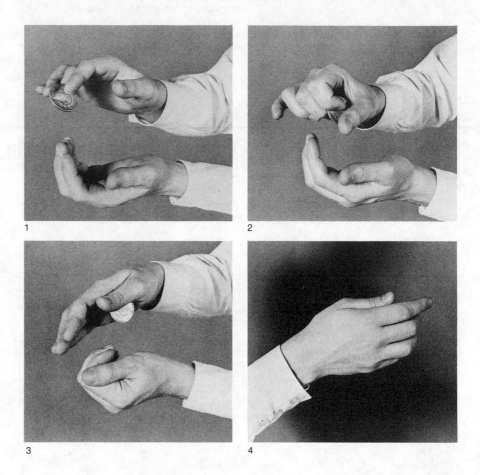

This is somewhat easier than the above passes, and may sometimes be usefully substituted for them. Take the coin edgeways between the index and middle fingertips of the right hand, the sides of those fingertips pressing against the sides of the coin, and the thumb steadying it on the index finger side.

Carry the right hand toward the left, and at the same time bend the index and middle fingers in toward the palm, which brings the coin into the crotch of the thumb and index finger. Clip the edge of the coin with the base of the thumb at this point, releasing the hold of the fingers. The coin is now securely clipped in the crotch of the thumb, hidden from view if the back of the hand is kept toward the audience.

As in the last case, the left hand must be closed the moment the right hand touches it. This is an especially quick mode of palming a coin, and if properly executed the illusion is perfect.

The French Drop

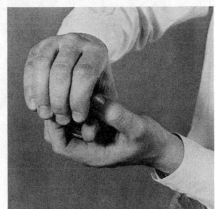

This is an easy and yet most effective pass. Hold the left hand palm upward, with the coin held parallel to the palm by the ball of the thumb and tip of the middle finger pressing against the edge of the coin. Now move the right hand toward the left, passing the thumb of the right hand under, and the fingers over the coin, closing them just as they pass it. The effect is the same to the eye of the spectator as if you seized the coin with thumb and fingers, but, in reality, at the moment when the coin is covered by the fingers of the right hand, you let it drop quietly into the palm of the left.

Carry the right hand upward and forward after it leaves the left hand, following it with your eyes, and thereby drawing away the attention of the audience from the other hand. Do not be in too great a hurry to drop the left hand, but turn the palm slightly toward you, with the fingers a little bent, and, after a moment's pause, let it fall gently to your side. The hollow made by the bent fingers will be sufficient to hold the coin.

This pass is available even for dimes or pennies which, because of their small size, cannot readily be palmed by the classic palm. It is also very useful for conjuring with balls.

The Jerk-Back Palm

Taking the coin—which must be one of large size, say a silver dollar or half-dollar—between the middle finger and thumb of the right hand, and holding the open left hand some four or five inches below it, the performer throws the coin with some force into the palm of the left hand. It should fall *flat* on the palm, with an audible smack. At the same moment, the left hand makes a quick upward movement to the extent of perhaps an inch, thereby jerking the coin back into the palm of the right hand, which closes just enough to retain it. The left hand is completely closed, and held up as though containing the coin, while the right picks up the wand or any other object.

This is a somewhat difficult sleight, one that will require a good deal of practice. At the outset the neophyte may be disposed to declare its acquirement altogether beyond him, but after some few dozens (or hundreds, as the case may be) of attempts will find that unexpected success, as if by accident, in jerking the coin back to the desired position in the palm of the right hand, and retaining it therein. From this point to the complete mastery of the sleight, progress will be rapid.

The Chink Pass

This pass is performed with two coins. The performer takes one of them in the right hand and, apparently transferring it to the left, palms it in the classic palm. Then, taking up the second coin between the fingers and thumb of the right hand, he apparently places that also in the left; but at the moment when the right hand is inverted over the left, lets the first coin drop from the palm, striking the second in its passage, and palms this latter in its place. The movement sounds complicated in description, but is not difficult in practice. The "chink" of the one coin against the other removes all doubt in the spectator's mind as to both coins having been really placed in the left hand.

This ingenious little sleight is, I believe, the invention of Professor Field.

Making the Pass

It must not be imagined that all of the passes above given are in turn used by every performer. Almost every conjurer has a favorite pass or passes, either selected from those above described, or invented by himself. Any mode by which a coin can be held in the hand without indicating its presence may be worked up into a pass. Thus, some performers will hold a coin by its edges between two of the fingers, or between the thumb and the side of the hand. Others, again, hold the coin flat against the first or second joint of the second or third finger, retaining it by slightly bending the finger. The novice should experiment till he ascertains which method best suits the conformation of his own hand. We have specified the hand to and from which each pass is generally used; but if the student desires to attain special excellence, practice is necessary to perfect the use of each from left to right, as well as from right to left.

In performing before a company of spectators, and standing with the left side toward them, it is well to use a pass that apparently transfers the coin from the right hand to the left, and vice versa. The coin is thus left in the hand farthest away from the spectators, and the performer has the benefit of the cover of the body in dropping it into his pocket or otherwise disposing of it.

When learning, you will here, as in card conjuring, find great advantage in practicing before a mirror, before which you should, in the first place, actually *do* that which you afterward pretend to do, and carefully notice the positions and motions of your hands in the first case, which you should then do your best to simulate, that there may be as little difference as possible between the pretense and the reality. You should further accustom yourself *always to follow with your eyes the hand in which the object is supposed to be*, this being the most certain means of leading the eyes and the minds of your audience in the same direction. When you are able to perform the passes neatly with a single half-dollar, you should then practice with coins of smaller size, with two coins at once, and afterward with three or four.

A word of caution may here be desirable. These passes must by no means be regarded as being themselves tricks, but only as processes to be used in the performance of tricks. If the operator, after pretending to pass the coin, say, from the right hand to the left, and showing that it had vanished from the left hand, were to allow the audience to discover that it had all along remained in the right hand, they might admire the dexterity with which in this instance their eyes had been deceived, but they would henceforth guess half the secret of any trick in which palming was employed. If it is necessary immediately to reproduce the coin, the performer should do so by appearing to find it in the hair of a spectator, or in any other place that may suit his purpose, remembering always to indicate beforehand that it has passed to such a place, thereby diverting the general attention from himself. As the coin is already in his hand, he has only to drop it to his fingertips as the hand reaches the place he has named, in order, to all appearance, to take it from there.

Having given this advice as to the hand in which the coin actually is, we must add a few words more as to the hand in which it is *not*.

Whenever you have (apparently) placed any article either in the closed hand or in some piece of apparatus from which it is afterward to disappear, you should not, as a rule, show that the article has departed from the spot where you have apparently placed it, without interposing some magical process, however slight, which may colorably account for its disappearance. A mere nothing will suffice—a touch of the wand, the pronouncing of a magic formula, the pressure of a finger; but in some form or other the ceremony should never be omitted.

To take a very simple example, we will suppose that by means of one of the passes above you have apparently placed in the left hand a coin, which really remains in the palm of the right hand. If you at once open the left hand, and show that the coin is not there, the spectators will naturally jump to the correct explanation—that you did not, in reality, put the coin there at all.

If, however, you delay opening the left hand for a minute or two, so as to let the audience get accustomed to the idea that the coin is therein, and then, before opening it, touch the hand mysteriously with your wand, or even simply, as you slowly open the left hand, rub the ball of the wrist with the second and third fingers of the hand which holds the coin, you not only give that hand an occupation apparently inconsistent with the fact of anything remaining concealed in it, but you suggest to the audience that the gesture in question is the cause of the disappearance of the coin. It is surprising what an effect even such a trifle as this has in misleading the judgment of a spectator. He knows perfectly well, in the abstract, that touching the closed hand with the wand, or rubbing it with a finger of the opposite hand, is not an adequate cause for the disappearance of a coin; but the fact being indisputable that the coin *has* disappeared, the mind unconsciously accepts the explanation which is thus indirectly offered. The advice here given becomes less important where, before the hand is opened, you are able to get rid of the object from that in which it originally appeared. Here the spectator is precluded from imagining that you retained it in the hand in which it was first seen, as that hand also is shown to be empty, and the absolute disappearance of the coin being a self-evident fact, you may leave the spectator to account for it in his own manner.

Coin Switching

The various passes may be employed not only to cause the disappearance of an article, as above described, but to secretly exchange it for a substitute of similar appearance. These exchanges are of continual use in conjuring; indeed, we may almost say that a good portion of its marvels depend on them. Such an exchange having been made, the substitute is left in sight of the audience, while the performer, having thus secretly gained possession of the original, disposes of it as may be necessary for the purpose of the trick.

Change 1: You desire, we will suppose, to exchange a half-dollar, marked by the audience, for another. You have the latter, which we will call the "substitute," already palmed in your left hand, of course taking care to keep the palm turned away from the audience. Taking the marked half-dollar in the right hand, you palm it in that hand in the classic palm position, but instead of closing the left hand as the fingers of the right touch it, keep the hand loosely open, and show lying on its palm the substitute, which the audience take to be the original just placed there by your right hand.

Change 2: This is the same as Change 1, except that you use the thumb clip with the right hand instead of the classic palm.

Change 3: Here also you use the thumb clip, but you have the substitute palmed in the right hand instead of the left. Taking up the marked coin with the same hand, you perform the thumb clip, at the same instant dropping the substitute from its palm into the left hand. This is a very neat and effective change. Some performers are expert enough to make this change by means of the classic palm instead of the thumb clip, the genuine coin taking the place of the substitute in the palm; but this demands dexterity of a more than average order.

Change 4: For this change you must have the substitute palmed in the right hand, and take the marked coin between the thumb and second finger of the left. Then using the French drop, appear to take it in the right hand, and at the proper moment exhibit the substitute, which you have already in that hand.

There are many other changes; indeed, they are almost too numerous to describe. If you are able to palm and to make the various passes neatly, you will readily invent methods of exchanging for yourself; in the meantime, you will find that the above will answer every necessary purpose, so far as coin tricks are concerned.

EASY COIN TRICKS

There is an immense variety of tricks with coins, some with apparatus, some without; some demanding a thorough mastery of sleight-of-hand; some so simple as to be within the compass of the beginner. The only classification we shall attempt will be to divide them into those that do and those that do not require special apparatus.

The Spinning Coin Mystery

You borrow a quarter and spin it, or invite some other person to spin it, on the table (which must be without a cloth). You allow it to spin itself out, and immediately announce, without seeing it, whether it has fallen head or tail upward. This may be repeated any number of times with the same result, though you may be blindfolded, and placed at the farther end of the room.

The secret lies in the use of a quarter of your own, on one face of which (say on the "tail" side) you have cut at the extreme edge a little notch, thereby causing a minute point or tooth of metal to project from that side of the coin. If a coin so prepared be spun on the table, and should chance to go down with the notched side upward, it will run down like an ordinary coin, with a long continuous "whirr," the sound growing fainter and fainter till it finally ceases; but if it should run down with the notched side downward, the friction of the point against the table will reduce this final whirr to half its ordinary length, and the coin will finally go down with a sort of "flop." The difference of sound is not sufficiently marked to attract the notice of the spectators, but is perfectly distinguishable by an attentive ear. If, therefore, you have notched the coin on the "tail" side and it runs down slowly, you will cry "tail"; if quickly, "head."

If you professedly use a borrowed coin, you must adroitly change it for your own, under pretense of showing how to spin it, or the like.

You should not allow your audience to imagine that you are guided by the sound of the coin, as, if once they have the clue, they will easily learn to distinguish the two sounds. They are not, however, likely to discover the secret of the notch, and if anyone professes to have found out the trick, you may, by again substituting an unprepared coin, safely challenge him to perform it.

The Coin Disappears

A coin is folded in a square of paper; when the paper is torn open, the coin has vanished.

The paper should be square, moderately stiff, and about four times the diameter of the coin each way. Place the coin in the center, and fold down each side fairly over it, showing at each stage that the coin is still there. Two sides having been folded, take the paper and coin upright in the right hand. Fold over the upper end, at the same time allowing the coin to slide down into the lower. Fold this latter over with the coin in it, and give all to someone to hold. The paper still contains the coin, but instead of being, as the spectators suppose, in the middle, it is really in the outer fold, whence you can let it slide out into your hand at pleasure.

The Coin in the Handkerchief

This is similar to the previous trick, only this time the coin disappears through a handkerchief.

Hold the coin in the left hand, the thumb and first finger on either side of the coin. Throw a handkerchief over it, then apparently take hold of the coin within the handkerchief with the thumb and first and second fingers of the right hand, and draw it off; but in so doing allow it to slip gently down into the palm of the left. Bring the folded edge of the handkerchief over the coin and wrap up the latter in it, as nearly as possible in the position it would have occupied had your pretence been reality. Give the handkerchief with the coin to someone to hold, with a request that it be grasped tightly. The coin will be felt within, and it will not be suspected that it is in reality outside the handkerchief, ensconced in a double fold.

The Mysterious Addition

This is a trick of almost childish simplicity, depending upon an elementary arithmetical principle. We have known it to occasion great perplexity, even to more than ordinarily acute persons.

Take a handful of coins, and invite another person to do the same and to ascertain privately whether the number taken is odd or even.

Request the company to observe that you have not asked the spectator a single question, but that you are able, notwithstanding, to divine and counteract this person's most secret intentions, and that you will, in proof of this, yourself take a number of coins, and add them to those the spectator has taken, at which point, if his number was odd, the total shall be even; and if the number was even, the total shall be odd.

Requesting the person to drop his coins into a paper bag or other container, held on high by one of the company, drop in a certain number on your own account. Now ask whether the spectator's number was odd or even; when the coins are counted, the total number will prove to be, as you predicted, exactly the reverse. The experiment is tried again and again, with different numbers, but the result is the same.

The secret lies in a simple arithmetical fact: if you add an odd number to an even number the result will be odd; if you add an odd number to an odd number the result will be even. You have only to take care, therefore, that the number you yourself add, whether large or small, shall always be odd.

The Coin that Got Away

This is a trick of genuine sleight-of-hand, in which one coin will "change" into another while being held tightly by a spectator. It will test your expertise in two or three different passes.

Having beforehand palmed a quarter in your right hand, borrow from one of the company a half-dollar (this trick may be performed with a nickel and quarter rather than quarter and half-dollar), requesting the owner to mark it in such manner that he may be able to identify it.

Make him stand up facing you, your own right side and his left being toward the audience. Taking the marked half-dollar between the fingers and thumb of the right hand (the back of which, from your position, will be toward the spectators), ask him whether he is nervous, whether he can hold tight, and so on. On receiving satisfactory replies, state that you are about to put him to the test, and request him to hold out his right hand, telling him that you are about to count to three, and that at the word *three* you will drop the coin into his hand which he is to close tightly upon it.

Accordingly count, "One! Two! Three!" each time making a motion as if dropping the half-dollar into his hand, and at the word *three* actually do drop it; he'll close his hand upon it, as directed, but you won't be satisfied. "That won't do," you exclaim. "You are not half quick enough—you allow all the electric fluid to escape. We'll try once more, and please be a little quicker in your movements. Give me the coin again. Now, then are you ready? One! Two!! THREE!!!" Give the words with great energy. As you say "three," stamp your foot, and apparently again drop the half-dollar, but really drop the quarter instead by one of the changes described above. He'll be sure this time to close his hand very quickly, and, having no reason to the contrary, will naturally believe that it is the half-dollar he holds, your previous feint (when you did actually drop the half-dollar) being specially designed to lead him to that conclusion.

Next, request him to hold the closed hand high, that all may see it. This will draw the general attention to him, and away from yourself, and enable you to get the half-dollar securely in the classic palm position. You continue, "You did better that time. Now, what will you bet me that I cannot take that half-dollar out of your hand without your knowing it?" Whether he admits or defies your power, the course of the trick will be the same.

"Well," you say at last, "you seem so determined that I am almost afraid to take the whole of the half-dollar away from you, I think I'll have to be content with twenty-five cents. Allow me to touch your hand with my wand." You do so, and on opening his hand he'll discover that the half-dollar has changed into a quarter.

Thank him for his assistance, hand him the quarter, and dismiss him to his seat. Naturally enough, he'll object to accepting the quarter in place of his half-dollar. Pretend at first not to understand him, but, as if suddenly enlightened, exclaim, "Oh, the half-dollar, you want the half-dollar? Well," you say, indicating the quarter, "that *is* the half-dollar. At present it is under an electric influence, but you have only to wait till that goes off (it won't take more than three weeks or so), when it will resume its former appearance. You don't believe me, I see; but I can easily convince you by discharging the electric fluid, when the change will take place at once. Watch!" Now take the quarter between the thumb and second finger of the left hand and perform one of the changes described, making a gentle rubbing movement with the fingers and thumb of the right hand before you open that hand and disclose the restored half-dollar. "Not bad," you say, thrusting both hands into your jacket pockets (leave the quarter in the left pocket, but retain the half-dollar in the right hand). "Oh, I'm sorry, this *is* your coin." Bring the right hand forward with the coin in it, pointing to the coin with the now-empty left hand. Make the classic palm pass, as if you transferred it to the left hand. Make a motion with the left hand, as if handing the coin, and say to the owner, "Will you be good enough to examine the half-dollar, and see that it is the same you marked?" He'll naturally hold out his hand for the coin, which he'll believe to be in your left hand, and which you'll pretend to give him; but it will have vanished. "Well," you say, "is it the same half-dollar?" Probably looking rather foolish, he'll reply that he has not got it. "Not got it!" you say; "Why, I just gave it to you. I passed it into your pocket. Look for yourself." He'll begin to search his pockets. "You are trying the wrong one," you say; "This is the pocket." As if desiring merely to assist his search, you'll plunge, into any pocket he has not yet tried, your right hand (in the palm of which the coin was left after the pass), and, letting the coin drop to the fingertips, take it out as if it were already in the pocket, as nine-tenths of the audience will believe it to have been.

It may be well to mention that it is generally desirable to borrow from the audience, when you can, any indifferent article used in a trick (e.g., a coin, a watch, a scarf or handkerchief), as you thereby seem to give a guarantee for the absence of preparation. Articles so borrowed are taken upon trust, so to speak, and by making a secret exchange you may still use a prepared substitute, which will escape the close scrutiny to which any article confessedly provided by yourself would be subjected.

Coins through Space

Two marked coins, wrapped in separate handkerchiefs, come together in one of them.

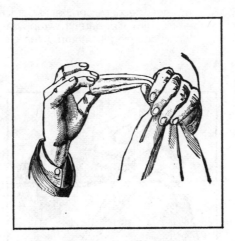

Needed for this trick are two handkerchiefs, a quarter, and two nickels. Palm in your right hand one of the nickels, and throw over the same hand one of the handkerchiefs. This will effectually conceal the substitute nickel, which you may now take between the finger and thumb.

You are now ready to begin. Show the quarter and nickel, borrowing them from the spectators if you wish, and have them marked for future identification. Holding the handkerchief spread out upon the open right hand, take up with the left hand the marked nickel and place it on the handkerchief, as if to wrap it therein, but at the same time with the third finger push a fold of the handkerchief under the substitute nickel in your right hand. Now invert the handkerchief over your left hand for a minute, allowing the marked nickel to drop back into that hand, and at the same time twist the fold already mentioned around the substitute. The audience will see the shape of a coin wrapped up in the handkerchief, and naturally believe that it is that of the marked nickel which you have apparently placed inside it. In reality, it is that of your own nickel, wrapped merely in an outside fold. Now hand the handkerchief to someone to hold, requesting that the coin be grasped and held tightly.

The marked nickel, it will be remembered, remains in your left hand, and the marked quarter on the table. As you go to take up the quarter, transfer the nickel to your right hand, and palm it; then pick up the quarter, holding it at the tips of the fingers. Spread the second handkerchief on the open palm of the left hand. Bring the quarter down smartly upon it, and by the same movement let the nickel fall from the palm onto the handkerchief. The two coins will now be lying (covered by the right hand) on the handkerchief, a couple of inches apart. Close the left hand on both coins, and turn the hand over, so that the edges of the handkerchief hang down. With the right hand grasp the handkerchief five or six inches below the coins. Take one of the coins through the handkerchief between the finger and thumb of the left hand, letting the other fall loose inside the handkerchief, which you then invite someone to hold in like manner, but in a horizontal position. This position is adopted in order that the two coins may not, by any accidental chink, prematurely disclose the fact that both are already in the handkerchief.

Now announce that you are about to make both coins pass into one handkerchief. Advancing to the person who holds the first handkerchief, request him, still maintaining his hold, to remove his hand four or five inches below the coin, to give you room to operate. First showing that your hand is empty, gently rub the substitute nickel through the handkerchief between your finger and thumb, when, being only wrapped within a fold, it will quickly fall into your hand (No one ever thinks of inquiring at this point whether it is the marked one or not.) Taking it in the left hand, in position for the French drop, say to the person holding the second handkerchief, "Having extracted this nickel from the one handkerchief, I will now pass it into the other. I won't even touch the handkerchief, but will simply take the coin in my hand, and say, 'Pass!' Will you be good enough, at the word *pass*, to let go of the coin you are holding, but still keep hold of the handkerchief with the other hand?" Appearing, by the French drop, to take the nickel in the right hand, you open that hand with a quick motion toward the handkerchief, saying, "Pass!" The person holding the handkerchief will loose his hold, as directed, when the two coins are heard to chink together, as though the second coin had just arrived in the handkerchief, and on examination they are, of course, found to be those marked.

We may here describe another and still neater mode (the invention, we believe, of Robert-Houdin) of apparently wrapping a coin securely in a handkerchief, though really only covering it with an outer fold.

Holding the coin upright between the fingers and thumb of the left hand, throw the handkerchief over it. Having shown that it is fairly covered, remark, "But perhaps you may think I have changed the coin. Allow me to show you that I have not." With the right hand, palm upward, take the coin through the handkerchief, between the first and second fingers of that hand, For a moment let go with the left hand (but without removing it from under the handkerchief). Turn over the right hand toward yourself, and again seize the coin with the left hand; but this time nip the opposite edge of the coin to that which it first held, and through the double thickness of the handkerchief. Remove the right hand from the coin, and with it raise the outer edge of the handkerchief and show the coin. Then let the edges of the handkerchief fall. Apparently the coin is underneath, and in the center of the handkerchief; but in reality it is outside, lying in a slight fold on the side away from the spectators.

The above description sounds intricate, but, if carefully followed with the coin and handkerchief will be found perfectly simple in practice. It is worthwhile taking some pains to acquire this sleight, as it is of great value in coin tricks.

Inside Outside Coins

Four coins wrapped in a handkerchief held by a spectator vanish, reappearing from the bottom edge of his trouser leg.

Begin by borrowing four marked half-dollars, quarters, or nickels, and a silk or cotton handkerchief or scarf. Then request the assistance of a very strong man. This gives an opportunity for a little fun in the selection. Having at last found a volunteer to your liking, seat him on a chair facing the company.

Spreading the handkerchief on your left palm, and placing the four coins upon it, close your hand upon them through the handkerchief, and hand them to him, requesting him to hold them firmly. Then, as if suddenly recollecting yourself, say, "Pardon me, I have omitted one little detail which is rather important. Give me the handkerchief again for one moment, please. I ought to have shown you that there are no holes in it." (The last sentence should not be pronounced until you have gained possession of the handkerchief, as the company might possibly declare themselves satisfied of the fact without examination, which would not answer your purpose.) The handkerchief being returned to you, you spread it out to show that it is free from holes, coming among the audience to do so, and appearing to lay great stress upon the fact.

Again spreading it over your left hand, count the coins one by one upon it; then giving a glance round at the company, say, as you quickly return to your stage area, "You have all seen that the four coins are fairly wrapped in the handkerchief," or make any other remark in order to draw the general attention, as a sharp, quick remark almost always will, to your face and away from your hands. At the same moment, move the left thumb over the face of the coins, thereby covering them with a fold of the handkerchief, and seize them, through the fold thus made, between the thumb and fingers of the right hand, immediately withdrawing the left hand.

The coins will now be held in the right hand, the handkerchief hanging down loosely around them. To anyone who has not watched your movements with more than ordinary vigilance, it will appear that the coins are within and under the handkerchief, though they are, in reality, wrapped in an external fold.

Giving them a twist round in the handkerchief, hand it to the person assisting you, asking him to say whether the money is still there, to which he'll naturally reply in the affirmative. Then tell him to grasp the handkerchief with both hands three or four inches below the coins, and to hold as tightly as he possibly can. Placing your wand under your right arm, and taking hold of the coins (through the handkerchief) with both hands, the right hand undermost, begin to pull against him, making a show of pulling with great force, and remarking that you are very glad it is not *your* handkerchief, that you should not have thought he was so strong, etc.

Meanwhile, and while the company are enjoying the discomfiture of the owner of the handkerchief, untwist the latter, and secretly get the money out of the fold into your right hand, and palm it therein. Give one last pull with your left hand, and let go smartly, observing that you fear you must give it up, and own yourself conquered. Take your wand in your right hand; this will make it seem natural for you to keep that hand closed, and will materially aid in concealing the fact that the money is therein. Your antagonist, or the spectators for him, will by this time have discovered that the money has vanished; but pretend to be unconscious of the fact, and request him to give it back, that you may return it to the owners. He'll naturally declare that he has not got it. With all the seriousness that you can command, insist that he has it, and that he must restore it. On his continued denial suggest that he should search his pockets, which you tap, one after another, with your wand, each giving a metallic sound as if containing money; but the coins will still not be found. At last, after all his pockets have been tried in vain, you, as if upon a sudden thought, will tap the leg of his trousers, the metallic chink still following every tap of the wand till you have nearly reached his feet, when you exclaim, "Yes, there it is. Will you please put your foot on that chair?" When he does so, quickly transfer your wand to the left hand, and with the fingers of the right turn up the edge of the trouser, giving at the same time a slight shake, at which time the four coins will be seen to fall out, to the great surprise of the victim.

This effect is produced as follows: The coins being in your right hand, you introduce them with the second, third, and fourth fingers under the edge of the trouser; then, with the first finger and thumb which are left outside, you nip them through the cloth, and hold them an instant till you have withdrawn the remaining fingers, when with a slight shake you let them fall.

The metallic chink on tapping the pockets may be produced in two ways. One method is to use a hollow metal wand, painted to match the one you ordinarily use, and containing throughout its length a loose piece of thick wire, which, striking against the sides of the tube, exactly imitates the chink of money. The other mode is to use merely the ordinary wand, allowing the end that you hold to chink against the money held in the same hand. With a little practice the effect is equally deceptive as with the special wand.

The Coin in the Orange

A vanished coin is found inside an orange.

For this excellent trick a little previous preparation is necessary. A slit (an inch and a half deep, and just large enough to admit a quarter) is made in each of two oranges, and in one of them a quarter (which for distinction we will call No. 1) is placed. These are in readiness behind the scenes, or so placed as to be out of sight of the audience.

You, the performer, palm in either hand a second quarter (No. 2), and, advancing to the audience, borrow from one of them a quarter, first marked by the owner (this last we will call No. 3). Invite special attention to the fact that throughout the experiment you are about to perform, the coin will never be removed from their sight, and accordingly place it (really substituting, by one or other of the changes, quarter No. 2) in full view on the table. Then go out to fetch an orange, and take the opportunity of slipping the marked quarter (No. 3) into the vacant one. Bring forward *this* orange publicly, and place it on your table at your *right* hand. Next, take the second orange and place it on the *left*-hand side of the table. Now (standing behind the table), ask into which orange, the right or the left, you should pass the coin.

As the right of the audience is your left, you are at liberty to interpret the answer in whichever way you think proper, and you should do so in such manner as to designate the orange containing the nonmarked quarter, No. 1. Thus, if the audience say "left," answer, "On my left? Okay." If they choose "right," say, "On your right? Okay." Not one person in a thousand will detect the equivoque.

Taking up quarter No. 2 from the table, and holding it in your left hand, pretend by the French drop to take it in your right, and thence to pass it into the orange, meanwhile dropping it from your left hand onto the *servante*. Showing your hands empty, cut open the orange, and exhibit the quarter (No. 1) therein contained.

Before giving the audience time to examine it for the mark, hear, or pretend to hear, a murmur among them to the effect that that was not the orange chosen. "Pardon me," you say, "some of you seem to think that I had a special reason for preferring this particular orange. I gave you absolute freedom to choose which you liked, and I understood you to say that you chose this one. However, in order to satisfy everyone, I will repeat the trick with the other orange."

Taking up the second orange, thrust the knife through it, in the slit already made, and give the knife thus loaded to someone to hold. Then, standing at some distance from it, take up quarter No. 1, and, getting rid of it by one or other of the passes previously described, make a motion as of throwing it toward the orange. Now request the person holding the orange to cut it open; the genuine quarter, No. 3, will be found therein, and duly identified.

Occasionally, a difficult spectator may insist upon the wrong orange (i.e., that containing the genuine coin) being cut open first. As you have offered the audience the choice, you cannot well resist this; but it makes very little difference. In accordance with the general desire, cut open the orange, and show the coin (No. 3), drawing particular attention to the mark. Its identity being fully established, offer, for the general satisfaction, to pass the same coin into the second orange. Being satisfied that it was the genuine coin in the first case, the audience will the more readily believe that it is so in the second; but in this case you should cut open the second orange yourself, as it will be necessary to again substitute the genuine quarter before you hand the coin to be examined.

A marked coin may be found in the center of an orange chosen at random through the use of a knife prepared in advance. The coin can be stuck with wax to one side of the blade. Take up the knife (taking care to keep the side on which the coin is away from the spectators), and cut open the orange. Cut about halfway down with the *point*, and then finish the cut by drawing the whole length of the blade through the opening thus made. This will detach the coin, which will fall between the two halves of the orange, as though it had all along been contained therein. Wipe it with a handkerchief to remove the juice of the orange from it, and hand it for identification. An apple can be used in place of the orange.

The Multiplication of Money

This is an old and favorite trick. It may be performed with half-dollars, quarters, nickels, dimes, or pennies, as may best suit your convenience. Whichever you use, prepare for the trick by secretly palming in the right hand such number (say three) as you intend to magically add.

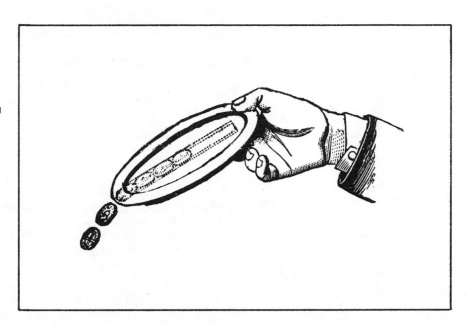

Advance to the audience, the loan of ten or a dozen of the coins (the precise number is immaterial), at the same time request someone of the company to collect them and bring them to you. Let's say this person collects twelve. Request him to count them openly upon the table, that all may be able to verify their number. This being done, invite a second person also to step forward and assist. Picking up from the table the same number of coins as you have concealed in your palm, give them to one of the two persons (whom we will call *A*) to hold. Then, taking up the remaining coins, request the second person (whom we will call *B*) to take charge of them. When *B* holds out his hand to receive them, let fall with them the palmed coins, so that *B* really receives twelve, though he believes there are only nine. Make *B* close his hand, and hold it high above his head.

Then ask *A* for the coins you entrusted to him. When returned, take them between the second finger and thumb of the left hand, and pretend by the French drop to transfer them to the right, really getting rid of them at the earliest opportunity on the *servante* or in one of your pockets. Announce that you are about to pass them invisibly into the hand of *B*, and after the necessary amount of magical gesture, open your hand, and show that they have vanished; and *B*, on examing his stock, will find that the supposed nine have increased to twelve.

It is a very good plan in performing this trick for the performer to collect the coins from the company in a plate, the coins to be added being held in the same hand that carries the plate, when, the thumb being naturally above and the fingers below, the coins are effactually concealed. After the collected coins have been counted, the performer, taking the plate in the other hand, pours them from it into the hand that already holds the concealed coins, thus bringing them together easily and naturally.

A further improvement may be made in the trick by using, in place of an ordinary plate, a special plate or tray, generally made of metal or plastic. The speciality of this plate (which is known as the "money plate" or "multiplying money tray") consists in a flat space running along its bottom, between its upper and under surface, just wide enough and deep enough to hold concealed a row of coins, and closed at the one end, but open at the other, the opening being concealed by the edge of the plate.

Prepare the plate beforehand by placing in the concealed space three, four, or six coins, and place it on your table. When you first take it up, take hold of it *near the opening*, when you may, of course, handle it as freely as you please, as the mouth of the passage being upward the coins cannot possibly fall out. Letting the plate-hand downward in a perpendicular position, and passing it carelessly from hand to hand, the audience cannot help observing that you have nothing concealed in your hands.

Then collect (or count out, if already collected) the money in the plate, and, after taking away and handing to A a number equal to the coins concealed, pour the remainder direct from the plate into the hands of B—first, however, so reversing the position of the plate (which you may do by merely transferring it from one hand to the other).as to turn the opening of the passage away from you. When you now slope the plate to pour the remaining coins into B's hands, the money in the concealed passage will naturally pour out into them, thus making the required addition with hardly a possibility of detection.

It is a good plan to perform the trick first without, and then repeat it with, the aid of the money plate, making a great point in the second instance of the fact that you do not even touch the money, and accounting for the use of the plate as designed to preclude all possibility of the use of sleight-of-hand, or any other mechanical mode of deception.

The spectators, having already seen you perform the trick without the aid of the plate, are precluded from supposing that this latter has any special connection with the secret; and seeing clearly that you have in this instance no coins concealed in your hands, naturally conclude that the same was the case on the former occasion. Thus the repetition of the trick, instead of assisting them to a solution, rather increases the mystery.

Double Impossible Vanish

This is not to be regarded as an independent trick, but may be introduced by way of flourish or by-play in the course of some more important illusion.

Take the coin between the fingers and thumb of right hand, and thence apparently transfer it to the left; but really classic palm it in the right. Rub the ball of the left wrist with the tip of the right-hand middle finger; then, opening the left hand, show that the coin has vanished. Bring the open right hand with a quick semi-circular sweep over the left, and in so doing drop the coin from the one palm to the other, and close the left hand. Repeat the rubbing gesture. Again open the left hand, and show that the coin has returned to it.

Thus nakedly described, it would seem that so simple a sleight could hardly produce any illusion, but such is not the case. No outsider seems even to suspect that the coin remains at the outset in the open right hand, and that the careless sweep of this latter over the left palm covers the transfer of the coin.

The Fadeaway Coin

This is another "flourish." The performer takes a coin in the right hand, and bending the left arm, pretends to rub the coin into the left elbow. The coin drops on the floor, but he picks it up and tries again. Again it drops, and again he picks it up, but this time with the left hand, whence he takes it, apparently, with the right, but really, by means of the French drop, leaves it in the left hand. The fingers recommence the rubbing of the elbow, as though they still held the coin; but meanwhile the left hand, which is brought by the bent position of the arm close to the neck, drops the coin inside the performer's collar, to be regained at pleasure. Meanwhile the performer continues the rubbing, presently removing the fingers and showing that, apparently, the coin has passed into the elbow, both hands being obviously empty.

COIN TRICKS REQUIRING SPECIAL APPARATUS

A great many mechanical contrivances and specially prepared coins are available from magic *depôts*. The student is urged not be dependant on these devices as a replacement for the exercises in sleight-of-hand necessary to the conjurer when manipulating coins.

Heads or Tails?

This is a pretty little trick of an unpretending nature but of very good effect, especially if introduced in a casual and apparently *extempore* manner.

As the performer, borrow or produce from your own pocket four coins. Placing them upon the table, request someone to make a pile of them, all one way, say "tail" upward. Next request the same or another person to turn over the pile so made, without disturbing the relative position of the coins, and announce with an air of supernatural knowledge that they will now all be found "head" upward. This appears so ridiculously obvious that the audience will naturally observe (with more or less straightforwardness of expression) that "any fool could tell that."

"Pardon me," says the performer, "it is not quite such a simple matter as you think. I very much doubt whether any of you could do as much. I will place the coins again; watch me as closely as you please. I will place them as before—tail, tail, tail, tail. Is that fairly done? Now I will turn them over." He does so, letting the tips of his fingers rest upon them. "What are they now?" A general chorus replies, "All heads, of course!" But on examination it is found that only three are "heads," and one a "tail."

Again he arranges them, placing them this time alternately—head, tail, head, tail. He turns them over. The natural order (beginning from below) would again be head, tail, head, tail; but they are found to be head, tail, tail, tail. Again he places them, tail, tail, tail, head. When turned over they should be tail, head, head, head, but are found to be tail, head, tail, head.

The secret lies in the use of a prepared coin, consisting of similar halves (in the case above described, two "tails") soldered together, so as to be "tail" on either side.

This the performer palms in his right hand. After first going through the operation with the genuine coins, as above, he picks them up with his left hand and apparently transferring them to the right, really transfers three of them only. He then performs the trick with these and the prepared coin, when the apparently miraculous result above described becomes a matter of course.

It is best not to repeat the trick too often, and a little practice is necessary in order to be able to return the three genuine coins neatly to the left hand (in which the fourth borrowed coin must be retained throughout the trick), at the same time secretly retaining your own. It is a frequent occurrence for one or other of the company, imagining some natural principle, to request to be allowed to try for himself. It is obvious that, under such circumstances, it would not do to hand him the prepared coin, and hence the necessity for some quick and natural method of again getting the four genuine coins together.

The trick may be brought to an effective conclusion as follows: After you have got rid of the double-faced coin, you may continue with, "Perhaps it is a little too complicated for you with four coins; suppose we try it with one only, and I won't even turn it over."

Placing one of the genuine coins on the middle of the right palm, which you hold out horizontally before you, draw special attention to the fact that the coin is (say) "tail" upward. Quickly covering it with the other hand, ask, "What is it now?"

"Tail," will be the reply.

"Wrong again!" you'll say, and, lifting up the hand, show that the coin has this time vanished altogether.

This mysterious disappearance is effected as follows: When you apparently cover the coin with the left hand, bring the hands together with a quick lateral motion as though sliding the one across the other. This shoots the coin from the palm down the opposite sleeve, the motion being so quick that the keenest eye cannot detect it. This little sleight is by no means difficult, and is well worthy of acquirement, as it may be introduced with equal effect in many tricks.

The Stack of Quarters

The principal apparatus consists of half-a-dozen quarters, of which the center portion has been cut out, leaving each a mere rim of metal. Upon these is placed a complete quarter, and the whole are connected together by a rivet running through the whole thickness of the pile. When placed upon the table, with the complete coin upward, they have all the appearance of a pile of ordinary quarters, the slight lateral play allowed by the rivet aiding the illusion. A little leather cap of such a size as to fit loosely over the pile of quarters, with an ordinary die such as backgammon is played with, complete the necessary requirements.

 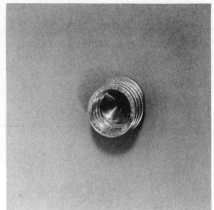

Begin by drawing attention to your magic cap and die, late the property of the king of the fairies. In order to exhibit their mystic powers, request the loan of half-a-dozen quarters (the number must, of course, correspond with that of your own pile), and, while they are being collected, take the opportunity to slip the little cap over your prepared pile, which should be placed close at hand behind some small object on the table, so as to be unseen by the spectators. Pressing the sides of the cap, lift the pile with it, and place the whole together in full view, in close proximity to the die.

The required quarters having been now collected, beg all to observe that you place the leather cap (which the spectators suppose to be empty) fairly over the die. Taking the genuine coins in either hand, pretend, by one of the passes, to transfer them to the other. Holding the hand that is now supposed to contain the coins immediately above the cap, announce that they will at your command pass under the cap, from which the die will disappear to make room for them. Saying, "One, two, three, pass!" open your hand, and show that the coins have vanished. If you use a regular table, you may place them on the *servante* and show both hands empty; and then, lifting up the cap, show the hollow pile, covering the die, and appearing to be genuine coins. Once more covering the pile with the cap, announce that you will again extract the coins, and replace the die; and to make the trick still more extraordinary, you will this time pass the coins right through the table. Placing the hand that holds the genuine coins beneath the table, and once more saying, "One, two, three, pass!" chink the coins, and bringing them up, place them on the table. Again picking up the cap, but this time pressing its sides, lift up the hollow pile with it, and disclose the die. Quickly transfer the cap, without the pile, to the other hand, and place it on the table, to bear the brunt of examination, while you get rid of the prepared coins.

The trick may be varied in many ways, according to the ingenuity of the performer.

The Rattle Box

This is a useful and ingenious little piece of apparatus. It is an oblong wood box, with a sliding lid. Its dimensions are about three inches by two, and one inch in depth externally; internally, it is only half that depth, and the end piece of the lid is of such a depth as to be flush with the bottom. Thus, if a coin be placed in the box, and the box held in such a position as to slant downward to the opening, the coin will of its own weight fall into the hand that holds the box, thus giving the performer possession of it without the knowledge of the audience.

Between the true and the false bottom of the box is placed a slip of zinc, which, when the box is shaken laterally, moves from side to side, exactly simulating the sound of a coin shaken in the box. In its normal condition, however, the slip of zinc is held fast (and therefore kept silent) by the action of a spring also placed between the two bottoms, but is released for the time being by a pressure on a particular part of the outer bottom at the end of the box held with the fingers. The fingers squeeze the end of the box and shake the box. A casual inspection of the box suggests nothing, save perhaps that its internal space is somewhat shallow in proportion to its external measurement.

The mode of using it is as follows: The performer invites any person to mark a coin, and to place it in the box, which he holds for that purpose as represented in the illustration; the coin is thus no sooner placed in the box than it falls into his hand. Transferring the box to the other hand, and pressing the spring, he shakes it to show by the sound that the coin is still there; then, leaving the box on the table, he prepares for the next phase of the trick by secretly placing the coin, which the audience believe to be still in the box, in any other apparatus in which he desires it to be found in, or make such other disposition of it as may be necessary. Having done this, and having indicated the direction in which he is about to command the coin to pass, he once more shakes the box to show that the coin is still inside. Then, with the mystic word, *Pass!* he opens the box, which is found empty, and shows that his commands have been obeyed.

The Money-Box

The money-box is for the vanishing of money. It is a short cylinder, sealed at the bottom and with merely a slit in the top, just large enough to admit the coin, which, once dropped in, cannot be got out again without a knowledge of the secret.

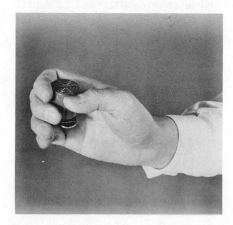

The money-box consists of two tubes, one within the other. When shaken the tubes move apart, thereby disclosing an opening of the inner tube which allows the coin to slip out of the box into the hand. Some little practice is required to use the money-box with dexterity. You should hold it tightly by the middle between the finger and thumb of your right hand, taking care that the side on which the secret opening is shall lie toward the inside of the hand. As you drop the coin through the slit, press lightly on the top with the fingers of the left hand, and at the same time push upward with the right hand. If you prefer to use one hand only, press downward on top with the first finger, at the same time pressing upward with the second finger and thumb to close the box.

Handkerchief Money Vanish

This is another appliance for vanishing a coin. It is an ordinary handkerchief of silk or cotton, in one corner of which, in a little pocket, is sewn a coin, say a dime or a penny, or any substitute which, felt through the substance of the handkerchief, shall appear to be such a coin.

The mode of using it is very simple. Holding the handkerchief by the corner in which is the coin, and letting it hang loosely down, you as performer borrow a similar coin, and, after carelessly shaking out the handkerchief to show that all is fair, place, to all appearance, the borrowed coin in the center (underneath), and give the handkerchief to someone to hold. In reality, you have only wrapped up the corner containing the substitute coin, and have retained the genuine one for your own purposes.

When it is desirable to make it appear that the coin has left the handkerchief, simply take it from the person holding it and give it a shake, at the same moment rapidly running the edges of the handkerchief through your hands, till the corner containing the coin comes into one or the other of them.

The Devil's Hank

This is an improvement on the above, and possesses a much wider range of utility, inasmuch as it really does cause the disappearance of any article placed under it, and is available to vanish not only a coin, but a card, an egg, or any other article of moderate size.

It consists of *two* patterned handkerchiefs stitched together all round the edges, and with a slit of about four inches in length cut in the middle of one of them. The whole space between the two handkerchiefs thus forms a kind of pocket, of which the slit above mentioned is the only opening. In shaking or otherwise manipulating the handkerchief, the performer takes care always to keep the side with the slit away from the spectators.

When you desire by its means to cause the disappearance of anything, carelessly throw the handkerchief over the article, at the same time secretly passing the latter through the slit in the underside, and hand it thus covered to someone to hold. Then, taking the handkerchief by one corner, request the holder to let go; the object will be retained in the space between the two handkerchiefs, but will appear to have vanished into empty air.

This is an appliance that no conjurer should be without. It may be purchased ready-made at any of the *depôts* for magical apparatus, or may be of home-manufacture, which in this case (contrary to the general rule) is not unlikely to produce the better article.

The Nest of Boxes

This consists of a number, generally six, but sometimes more, of circular wood or plastic boxes, one within the other, the smallest being just large enough to contain a coin. The series is so accurately made that by arranging the boxes in due order, one within the other, and the lids in like manner, you may, by simply putting on all the lids together, close all the boxes at once, though they can only be opened one by one.

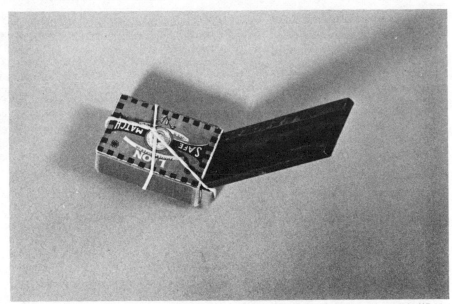

One version of nest of boxes with match box. The coin is introduced into the box down a metal slide. When the slide is removed, note how elastic band apparently holds box closed.

These are placed, the boxes together and the lids together, anywhere so as to be just out of sight of the audience. If on your table, they may be hidden by any more bulky article. Having secretly obtained possession, by either of the means before described, of a coin that is ostensibly deposited in some other piece of appartus, e.g., the rattle box, seize your opportunity to drop it into the innermost box, and to put on the united lids. Then bring forward the nest of boxes (which the spectators naturally take to be one box only), and announce that the coin will at your command pass from the place in which it has been deposited into the box that you hold in your hand, and which you forthwith deliver to one of the audience for safekeeping.

Touching both articles with the mystic wand, invite inspection of the first to show that the money has departed, and then of the box, wherein it is to be found. The holder opens the box, and finds another, and then another, and in the innermost of all the marked coin. Seeing how long the several boxes have taken to open, the spectators naturally infer that they must take as long to close, and (apart from the other mysteries of the trick), are utterly at a loss to imagine how, with the mere moment of time at your command, you could have managed to insert the coin, and close so many boxes.

Nests of square boxes with hinged lips and self-closing locks are made on the same principle. These are designed for larger articles, and greatly vary in size and price.

Coin in the Ball of Wool

An easy and effective mode of terminating a money trick is to pass the marked coin into the center of a large ball of wool, the whole of which has to be unwound before the coin can be reached.

The modus operandi, though perplexing to the uninitiated, is absurdly simple when the secret is revealed. The only apparatus necessary over and above the wool (of which you must have enough for a good-sized ball), is a flat metal tube, three to four inches in length, and just large enough to allow a quarter or half-dollar to slip through it easily. You prepare for the trick by winding the wool on one end of the tube, in such manner that when the whole is wound in a ball, an inch or so of the tube may project from it. This you place in your pocket, or anywhere out of sight of the audience. You commence the trick by requesting someone to mark a coin, which you forthwith exchange, by one or other of the means already described, for a substitute of your own, and leave the latter in the possession or in view of the spectators, while you retire to fetch your ball of wool, or simply take it from your pocket.

Before producing it, you drop the genuine coin down the tube into the center of the ball, and withdraw the tube, giving the ball a squeeze to remove all traces of an opening. You then bring it forward, and place it in a glass goblet or tumbler, which you hand to a spectator to hold. Taking the substitute coin, you announce that you will make it pass invisibly into the very center of the ball of wool, which you accordingly pretend to do, getting rid of it by means of one of the passes already described. You then request a second spectator to take the loose end of the wool, and to unwind the ball; when that is done, the coin will fall out into the glass.

The only drawback to the trick is the tediousness of the process of unwinding. to obviate this, some performers spin the wool on their wands, which materially shortens the length of the operation.

The Shower of Money

The magical phenomenon known under this name surpasses the philosopher's stone, in the pursuit of which so many of the wise men of old expended their lives and fortunes. The alchemist's secret aimed only at producing the raw material, but the magician's quick eye and ready hand gather from space money ready coined. Unfortunately, the experiment is subject to the same drawback as the more ancient process—namely, that each dollar produced costs precisely one dollar, leaving hardly sufficient profit to make this form of money-making renumerative as a commercial undertaking.

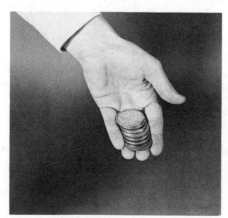

Coins held in left hand.

Left hand holds coins against inside of pail ready to drop one at a time.

The effect of the trick is as follows: The performer produces a metal ice-bucket, top hat, or other container, which he holds in his left hand. Turning up his sleeves, he announces that he requires a certain number, say ten, of silver dollars or half-dollars. The spectators put their hands in their pockets with the idea of contributing to the supposed loan; but the professor, anticipating their intention, says, "No, thank you; I won't trouble you this time. There seems to be a good deal of money about tonight; I think I will help myself. See, here is a half-dollar hanging to my elbow. Here is another climbing the wall. Here is another just settling on this lady's hair. Excuse me, sir, but you have a half-dollar behind your ear," and so on. At each supposed new discovery the performer takes with his right hand, from someplace where there clearly was nothing an instant before, a half-dollar, which he drops into the container held in his left hand, finally turning over the container and pouring the coins from it, to show there has been "no deception."

The explanation is very simple, the trick being merely a practical application of the art of palming, though its effect depends on the manner and address of the operator even more than on his skill in sleight-of-hand. The performer provides himself beforehand with ten half-dollars. Of these the palms two in his right hand, and the remainder in his left. When he takes the container, he holds it in the left hand, with the fingers inside and the thumb outside, in which position it is comparatively easy to drop the coins one by one from the hand into the hat.

When he pretends to see the first half-dollar floating in the air, he lets one of the coins in his right hand drop to his fingertips, and, making a clutch at the air, produces it as if just caught. This first coin he really does drop into the container, taking care that all shall see clearly that he does so. He then goes through a similar process with the second; but when the time comes to drop it into the container, he merely pretends to do so, palming the coin quickly in the right hand, and at the same moment letting fall into the container one of the coins concealed in his left hand.

The audience, hearing the sound, naturally believe it to be caused by the fall of the coin they have just seen. The process is repeated until the coins in the left hand are exhausted. Once more the performer appears to clutch a coin from space, and showing for the last time that which has all along been in his right hand, tosses it into the air, and catches it visibly in the hat. Pouring out the coins on a tray, or into the lap of one of the company, he requests that they may be counted, when they are found to correspond with the number that he has apparently collected from the surrounding atmosphere.

Some performers, by way of bringing the trick to a smart conclusion, after they have dropped in all the coins, remark, "The container begins to get heavy," or make some similar observation, at the same time dipping the right hand into the hat, as if to gauge the quantity obtained; and, giving the money a shake, bring up the hand with four or five coins clipped breadthwise against the lowest joints of the second and third fingers. Then pretend to catch in quick succession that number of coins, each time sliding one of the coins with the thumb to the fingertips, and tossing it into the container.

It is obvious that, in the above form of the trick, the performer cannot show the inside of his hands; and it is not uncommon to find an acute observer so far hit upon the true explanation, as to express audibly a conjecture that the money that the performer catches is really the same coin over and over again. There are, however, a number of coin slides and coin clips that allow the performer to replenish his supply of coins and also show his hand empty. These devices hold a number of coins and may be pinned at the lower edge of the jacket where they may be stolen when needed. It is best to begin the trick in the ordinary manner, and after having produced three or four coins in this way, to overhear, or pretend to overhear, a suggestion that the coin is all the while in your hand. Ostentatiously throwing the coin with which you have so far worked into the container, you draw special attention (not in words, but by gesture) to your empty hand (the left hand is never suspected), and then have recourse to the hidden load of coins.

A piece of conjuring apparatus known as a *coin wand* may also be effectively introduced in the trick. This is a wand made of a brass tube about twelve inches in length and five-eighths of an inch in diameter. On one side of it, and so placed as to be just under the ball of the thumb when the wand is held in the hand, is a little stud, which moves backward and forward for a short distance. When this stud is pressed forward, a half-dollar appears on the opposite end of the wand, retiring within it when the stud is again drawn back. The half-dollar is a genuine one, but is cut into three portions after the fashion of the folding coin used in the Coin in the Bottle trick, (which will be described next).

After having caught in the ordinary manner such number of coins as he thinks fit, the performer pretends to perceive that the audience suspect that the coins are in some manner concealed in his right hand. To show that this is not the case, he offers to catch a few coins on the top of his wand instead of in his hand, and finishes the trick by producing two or three on the wand accordingly. It is desirable, on each occasion of pressing forward or withdrawing the stud, to place the opposite end of the wand in such a situation as to be a little shielded from the eyes of the spectators, so that they may not see the actual appearance of the coin. A very slight "cover" will be sufficient. The end of the wand may be placed within a person's open mouth (and withdrawn with the half-dollar thereon), within a pocket, or the like. Where no such cover is available, a quick semi-circular sweep should be made with the wand as the coin is protruded. The wand is then tapped on the edge of the container, the coin withdrawn into the wand, and one of the supply in the left hand dropped into the container simultaneously.

Whenever you can, as in this instance, produce the same result by two wholly different methods, the effect on the audience is most bewildering. Their conjectures as to the explanation of the first method being inadmissible as to the second, and vice versa, the more they puzzle over the matter, the further are they likely to be from a correct solution.

The Coin in the Bottle

The bottle used is an ordinary narrow-necked bottle, without any speciality. The secret lies in the coins used, which are of the kind known as "folding" coins. The coin, say a half-dollar, is placed on a lathe, and a deep groove cut all round its outer edge. This done, the coin is cut into three parts. The three parts are now joined together again by means of a tiny rubber band, inserted into the groove, and so encircling the coin. The coin thus reconstructed will fold into one-third of its diameter, and in its folded condition may be passed into a narrow-necked bottle, but again expands and resumes its shape the moment it has passed the neck. If well made, the cuts in the coin are scarcely perceptible, and if the bottle is shaken a little as it is passed before the eyes of the audience, there will be little fear of their detecting that the half-dollar is not an ordinary coin. Folding coins are available from magic suppliers at surprisingly modest cost.

The Multiplying Coins

The coin in this case (say a half-dollar) is of special construction. It in reality consists of two coins. One of them is hollowed out on one side, so as to leave a mere shell. The other is simply reduced a little in circumference, so as to fit easily within the first, in which condition the two look like one coin only.

Shell coin rests on top of regular coin.

With the aid of the double coin, or still better a couple of such coins, sundry good close-up tricks can be performed. For instance, the performer, having borrowed a half-dollar, takes his stand behind his table, on which, behind a book or other object (the smaller and shallower the better), he has placed two of these double coins. Borrowing a half-dollar, he takes it in the right hand, and thence apparently transfers it to the left, with which he has just secretly picked up one of the "doubles." While exhibiting the latter, he quietly drops the right hand, and lays the borrowed coin behind the book.

After a few remarks as to the curious way in which money begets money, he says, "This half-dollar, placed out at compound interest at five percent, would double itself in fifteen years or so; but you might not care to wait fifteen years to see the process. With the aid of a little magic, I think we may be able to produce the effect a little quicker. Watch me carefully, please. Here is a half-dollar, and you can see for yourselves that, with that exception, my hands are absolutely empty. Now I am going to begin to make money. I take the coin, so, give it a little gentle pressure, and its value is doubled. In fact, the coin has become two," which he shows, accordingly, one in each hand.

Some little practice is necessary in order to mainipulate the double coin with neatness. It should be taken between the first and third fingers of the right hand, the back of the hand toward the spectators, the shell portion also toward the spectators, and the thumb supporting the solid coin from behind. By relaxing the pressure of the thumb and at the same time tilting the double coin a little, the solid coin falls back on the thumb-tip, from which position it may be brought into view to right or left as may be necessary. Even when both hands are used, the developing process is still the same.

The trick, however, is not yet over. Holding the coin and shell side by side between the forefinger and thumb of the right hand, the performer drops the left hand to the table and picks up the second "double." He then makes believe to transfer one of the coins in the right hand to the left, but actually draws back the solid coin into its shell, and shows the double in the left hand. He has now (apparently) one coin only in each hand, and takes the opportunity to carelessly show back and front, which he could not do when the one double represented two coins. Bringing the hands together, he again slips out the right-hand solid coin from its shell, and shows that the two coins have become three; then does the same with the left hand, and shows them as four.

Remarking, "It's a poor rule that won't work both ways," he slides back the left-hand solid coin into its shell, and shows it as one. So far all is tolerably plain sailing, but the next movement will require some practice in order to execute it neatly. Bringing the hands together, he again draws the left-hand solid coin out of its shell, at the same time letting the other double slip back into the right hand. The spectators, seeing the solid coin and shell in the left hand, naturally take them to be the same two coins they have just seen. The operator draws attention to them by remarking, "Now, I want you to watch these two coins with especial vigilance; for the next change will be still more remarkable. I shall do nothing to them, I will not even touch them with the other hand. I simply say, 'One, two, three—go!' and the two coins are again only one," which he shows them to be. This harangue, followed by the visible change of the two coins to one, draws the general attention to the right hand. Meanwhile, the left hand drops carelessly to the surface of the table, lays down the double thereon, and picks up and palms in its stead the original borrowed coin. No sooner has the performer shown the united double in the right hand than he makes the gesture of transferring it to the left, really palming it in transit, and showing in its place the borrowed coin, and handing the latter for examination.

Caps and Pence

Two double coins are used, and in addition two little brass or silver covers, just large enough to go over a pile of half-dollars or British pence, ten or a dozen in number. The two "doubles" are used in conjunction with five ordinary coins, the latter being in the center, with a double at top and a double at bottom. The "double" must in each case have its "shell" uppermost.

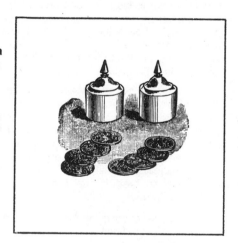

These being concealed in the performer's left hand, he borrows eight half-dollars, collecting them on a tray held in the same hand, the use of the tray effectually masking the presence of the concealed coins. When he has obtained the required number, he forms a pile with them on the tray; takes them in the right hand, and apparently transfers them to the left, showing in their place the prepared pile already there; then places this latter on the table, meanwhile dropping the borrowed coins on his *servante* or in his jacket pocket. (The prepared heap contains *seven* coins only, but there is not the smallest fear of anyone perceiving that there is one short of the number borrowed.) He next exhibits the little metal covers, giving them freely for examination, and calling special attention to the fact that there is no possible mechanism or secret compartment about them. When they are returned, he begins his commentary, to something like the following effect:

"Ladies and gentlemen, I have here eight coins, and two small covers. You will observe that the covers are empty, likewise my hands; that I have no coin or anything else concealed in them. I propose to divide these eight coins into two equal portions, four coins in each, and place one of these covers over each heap. Make sure, please, that I do so fairly. One, two, three, four!"

He counts the coins one by one from the top of the heap, laying each slightly overlapping the last, at a few inches distance from the main pile. The double which was previously at top is thus brought to the bottom of the new heap. He now counts the remaining coins in like manner, "One, two, three, four!" but, lifting them slightly between the second finger and thumb, and commencing with the bottom coin, the "solid," which the lifting movement causes to drop out of its shell. The two groups of coins are now layed out in two rows, each coin overlapping the one ahead of it toward the spectators; the undermost coin of the right-hand heap is a double, and the two undermost coins of the left-hand heap are a shell and a solid respectively.

"You can see for yourselves that I have fairly divided the eight coins. There are four in each group, no more, no less. I will cover each of these groups of four with one of these little covers." (He does so, gathering the four coins into a heap with the edge of the cover, and then dropping the cover over it.) "I am now going to attempt a very difficult experiment. I am going to command one of these coins to leave the left-hand heap, and join the right-hand heap. One, two, three—pass!"

He lifts the right-hand cover. Four coins alone are visible, but the spectators cannot be sure, at a few feet distance, whether there are four or five. The performer begins to count them, and, as before, in the act of spreading them, lifts off the shell of the last coin, so as to make it appear as two coins. Count them, "One, two, three, four, *five!*" The condition of the heap is now as follows, the coins overlapping from the bottom upward:

Ordinary
Ordinary
Ordinary
Shell
Solid

"And here," he continues, lifting the second cover, "we have only three coins," as they now appear to be, the application of the cover naturally bringing the shell coin immediately over the solid, when it drops into position, and the two become one. These three he transfers, beginning from the top, to the top of the larger heap, completing the count by saying, "Six, seven, eight!"

The total heap is now as follows:

Double
Ordinary
Ordinary
Ordinary
Ordinary
Ordinary
Shell
Solid

"Let us see," he continues, "whether we can carry the process a step further. We will now make a heap of five on one side, and three on the other." He accordingly counts off five coins one by one from the top, making a fresh heap as follows, with the double at bottom:

Ordinary
Ordinary
Ordinary
Ordinary
Double

The three remaining are, it will be remembered:

Ordinary
Shell
Solid

"Again I replace the covers, and order a coin to pass from the smaller to the larger heap. One, two, three—pass! I am obeyed, you see." (He takes off the right-hand cover, developing the double as before.) "Here we have one, two, three, four, five, *six* coins. And here, under the other cover, are only two," as they now appear to be. These two he adds to the larger heap, so as again to bring the double uppermost.

"I will even allow anyone present to hold the coins himself, and still I can produce the same result. Who will volunteer? Thank you, sir. May I ask you to extend your arms, so that the hands may be as far apart as possible, and to open your hands, keeping the palms perfectly flat. First, the right hand. One, two, three, four, five, six!" He counts off six coins from the top of the heap on to the open palm, the double, as before, being undermost, then places the remaining two (the shell and solid), without reversing their order, on the opposite palm. "Now for the covers. I tell you what, I will not even cover the coins, I will simply ask you to close your hands. Make sure, please, before you close them, how many coins you have in each. Six coins in the right hand, and two in the left. Close the hands, please. One more coin, pass!" waving the wand from the left hand toward the right. "Open your left hand, please. You have now only one coin in the left hand," which is seen to be the case, for the act of closing the hand has caused the shell and solid to coalesce. This coin the performer at once takes away, and lays on the table. "Now open the other hand, please." He spreads the coins after the usual manner, and counts, "One, two, three, four, five, six, *seven!*" Then runs them together again, and places the heap on the table, adding on the top the double already there.

"Once again I will show you the same effect, not even covering the coins at all. One coin shall travel visibly from my hand, and go back to the heap. If you watch carefully, you will no doubt be able to see it go."

The heap on the table, now arranged vertically, one coin upon another, is as follows:

Double
Ordinary
Ordinary
Ordinary
Ordinary
Ordinary
Double

He takes off with the left hand the upper shell only; takes it apparently in the right, by the French drop, really leaving it in the left, which forthwith drops out of sight, then saying for the last time, "Pass," opens the right hand and shows it empty, then counts the coins as before, developing the double at their base, and shows that the full tale of eight is there. He then once more "changes" the heap for the borrowed coins, and returns the latter to their owners,

TRICKS WITH WATCHES AND RINGS

An Hour in Mind

Taking a watch in one hand and a pencil in the other, propose to your audience to give a specimen of your powers of divination. For this purpose request anyone present to write down, or, if preferred, merely to think of, any hour he pleases. This having been done, proceed, without asking any questions, to tap with the pencil different hours on the dial of the watch, requesting the person who has thought of the hour to mentally count the taps, *beginning from the number of the hour he thought of*. (Thus, if the hour he thought of were nine, he must count the first tap as ten, the second as eleven, and so on.) When, according to this mode of counting, the number twenty is reached, he is to say, "Stop," at which point your pencil will be found resting precisely upon that hour of the dial the spectator thought of.

This capital little trick depends upon a simple arithmetical principle; but the secret is so well disguised that it is very rarely discovered. All you as a performer have to do is count in your own mind the taps you give, calling the first "one," the second "two," and so on. The first seven taps may be given upon any figures of the dial indifferently; indeed, they might equally well be given on the back of the watch, or anywhere else, without prejudice to the ultimate result. But the eighth tap must be given invariably on the figure twelve of the dial, and thenceforward the pencil must travel through the figures in order counterclockwise: eleven, ten, nine, and so on. By following this process it will be found that at the tap which, counting from the number the spectator thought of, will make twenty, the pencil will have traveled back to that very number. A few illustrations will make this clear. Let us suppose, for instance, that the hour the spectator thought of was twelve. In this case he will count the first tap of the pencil as thirteen, the second as fourteen, and so on. The eighth tap in this case will complete the twenty, and the reader will remember that, according to the directions we have given, he is at the eighth tap always to let his pencil fall on the number twelve; so that when the spectator, having mentally reached the number twenty, cries, "Stop," the pencil will be pointing to that number. Suppose, again, the number thought of was eleven. Here the first tap will be counted as twelve, and the ninth (at which, according to the rule, the pencil will be resting on eleven) will make the twenty. Taking again the smallest number that can be thought of, one, here the first tap will be counted by the spectator as two, and the eighth, at which the pencil reaches twelve, will count as nine. Henceforth, the pencil will travel regularly backward round the dial, and at the nineteenth tap (completing the twenty, as counted by the spectator) will have just reached the figure one.

The arithmetical reason for this curious result, though simple enough in itself, is somewhat difficult to explain on paper, and we shall therefore leave it as an exercise for the ingenuity of our readers.

The Flying Ring

The majority of ring tricks depend upon the substitution at some period of the trick of a dummy ring for a borrowed one, which must be so nearly alike as not to be distinguishable by the eye of the spectator. This end is secured by using wedding-rings, which, being usually made plain, are all sufficiently alike for this purpose. You may account for your preference of wedding-rings by remarking that they are found to be imbued with a mesmeric virtue that renders them peculiarly suitable for magical experiments; or give any other reason, however absurd, so long as it is sufficiently remote from the true one. As, however, many people have a sort of superstitious objection to removing their wedding-rings, even for a temporary purpose, it will be well to provide yourself with an extra one of your own, so as to meet a possible failure in borrowing.

There is a little appliance, exceedingly simple in its character, that may be used with advantage in many ring tricks. It consists of a plain gold or gold-plate ring, attached to a short piece of strong white or gray thread. This again is attached to a piece of elastic cord, fastened to the inside of the coat sleeve of the performer, in such manner that, when the arm is allowed to hang down, the ring falls a couple of inches short of the edge of the cuff. It is obvious that if a ring so prepared be taken in the fingers of the hand to whose sleeve it is attached, it will, on being released, instantly fly up the sleeve. This renders it a useful auxiliary in any trick in which the sudden disappearance of such a ring is an element, and a little ingenuity will reveal numerous modes of making it so available.

One of the simplest modes of using it is as follows: Producing a small piece of paper to which you direct particular attention, you state that a wedding-ring wrapped up therein cannot be again extracted without your permission. A wedding-ring is borrowed in order to test your assertion, and you meanwhile get in readiness the flying ring, which is attached, we will suppose, to your left sleeve. Receiving the borrowed ring in your right hand, apparently transfer it to the other hand (really palming it between the second and third fingers, and at the same moment exhibiting your own ring), and immediately afterward drop the borrowed ring into the jacket pocket on that side. You must take care to stand so that the back of your left hand is toward the spectators, in order to hide from them the thread lying along the inside of your hand. Spreading the paper on the table, and placing the ring upon it, you fold the paper over it, beginning with the side away from you, and pressing it so as to show the shape of the ring through it. As you fold down a second angle of the paper you release the ring, which forthwith flies up your sleeve. You continue to fold the paper, and repeating your assertion that no one can take the ring out without your permission, hand it to a spectator, in order that he may make the attempt. On opening the paper he finds that you were very safe in asserting that he could not take the ring out of it, inasmuch as the ring is no longer in it.

Having gained possession of the borrowed ring, you may reproduce it in a variety of different ways, according to your own fancy and invention. For instance, you may place the original ring in the nest of boxes, to be discovered therein once it is seen to have disappeared from the folded paper.

Ring through Handkerchief

This is but a juvenile trick, but we insert it for the sake of completeness. It is performed with the aid of a piece of wire, sharpened to a point at each end, and bent into the form of a ring.

As performer, you, having this palmed in your right hand, bring forward a ring and a handkerchief. Holding the ring between the fingers of your right hand, you throw the handkerchief over it, and immediately seize with your left hand, through the handkerchief, apparently the ring, but really the sham wire ring, which you adroitly substitute. You now request one of the spectators to take hold of the ring in like manner, taking care to make the person hold it in such a way that it will not be possible to feel the opening between the points, which would betray the secret. The ring thus being held, and the handkerchief hanging down around it, a second spectator is requested, for greater security, to tie a piece of tape or string tightly round the handkerchief an inch or two below the ring.

Then take the handkerchief into your own hand, and throwing the loose part of the handkerchief over your right hand, so as to conceal your mode of operation, slightly straighten the sham wire ring, and work one of the points through the handkerchief, so getting it out, and rubbing the handkerchief with your finger and thumb in order to obliterate the hole made by the wire in its passage. Now palm the sham wire ring, and produce the real one, which has all along remained in your right hand, requesting the person who tied the knot to ascertain for himself that it has not been tampered with.

Solid Penetrates Solid

A ring passes through the table. The necessary apparatus consists of an ordinary glass tumbler and a handkerchief, to the middle of which is attached, by means of a piece of ribbon about four inches in length, a substitute ring of your own.

Borrowing a ring from one of the company, you announce that it will at your command pass through the table; but as the process, being magical, is necessarily invisible, you must first cover it over. Holding the handkerchief by two of the corners, you carelessly shake it out (taking care to keep the side the suspended ring is on toward yourself), and wrapping in it apparently the borrowed, but really the suspended ring, you hand it to one of the company, requesting him to grasp the ring through the handkerchief, and to hold it securely.

A word of caution may here be given, which will be found more or less applicable to all magical performances. Have the room in which you perform as brilliantly lighted as you please, but take care to arrange the lights, or to place yourself, so that all the lights may be in front of you, and none behind you. The trick we are now describing affords a practical illustration of the necessity for this. If you have any light behind you, the handkerchief, as you shake it to show that it is not prepared, will appear semitransparent, and the spectators will be able to see the suspended ring dangling behind it. For a similar reason, you should always endeavor to have a dark background for your performances, so that any thread or the like that you may have occasion to secretly use will then be invisible at a short distance, while against a light background would be instantly noticeable.

But to return to our trick: We left one of the spectators tightly holding the suspended ring, covered by the folds of the handkerchief. Your next step is to request the audience to choose at what particular spot in the table the ring shall pass through it. When they have made the selection, you place the tumbler upon the spot chosen, and request the person having charge of the ring to hold his hand immediately over the glass, around which you drape the folds of the handkerchief.

"Now," you say, "will you be kind enough to drop the ring in the glass." He lets go, and the ring falls with an audible "ting" into the glass. "Are you all satisfied," you ask, "that the ring is now in the glass?" The reply will generally be in the affirmative; but if anyone is skeptical, you invite that person to shake the glass, still covered by the handkerchief, until the ring is heard to rattle within.

You next introduce a container of some sort (a wicker basket, a hat, a plastic bowl, a paper sack), which you take in the hand that still retains the genuine ring, holding it in such manner that the tips of the fingers are just inside the container, the ring being concealed beneath them. In this condition you can freely exhibit the inside of the container, which is seen to be perfectly empty. You now place the container under the table, mouth upward, relaxing as you do so the pressure of the fingers, and allowing the coin to slide gently down into it. Leaving the container under the table, which should be so placed that the spectators cannot, as they stand or sit, see quite into it, you take hold of the extreme edge of the handkerchief, and saying, "One, two, three, *pass!*" jerk it away, and request someone to pick up the container, and return the borrowed ring to the owner.

Ring on Wand

In this trick, the handkerchief prepared with the ring attached for the purpose of the last illusion may be again employed, though some use for the present purpose a handkerchief with a ring stitched in one corner. In our opinion, the suspended ring is preferable, and we shall describe the trick accordingly. The only other requisite will be the magic wand, or any short stick or rod of such diameter that a finger-ring may slip easily upon it.

Having borrowed a ring, proceed to wrap it (in reality the substitute) in the handkerchief, and hand it to someone to hold. The borrowed ring, of course, remains in your hand. Picking up the wand with your other hand, transfer it to the hand containing the ring. Taking hold of it by the extreme end, pass the ring over it, which a very little practice will enable you to do without the smallest difficulty.

Then say, "I am about to order the ring Mr. So-and-so is holding to leave the handkerchief, and pass on to this wand. For greater security, I will ask two people present to hold the ends. Are there any volunteers for this purpose?" Two candidates having come forward, you place yourself facing the person who is holding the ring in the handkerchief, at the same time sliding your hand with the ring to the center of the wand, and holding the latter in a horizontal position across your body.

Now invite the two volunteers each to take hold of one end, pretending to be very particular that the wand should be perfectly horizontal, this giving you an excuse for keeping your hand upon it, sliding it backward and forward, and raising now one end, now the other, till the level is such as to satisfy your correct eye. When at last you are satisfied, ask the person in charge of the ring to step forward, so as to bring it immediately above the wand, over which you immediately spread the handkerchief, letting the edges fall on either side of the wand.

As soon as the wand is covered, you can of course remove your hand. Then, taking hold of one corner of the handkerchief, request the holder of the ring to let go at the word *three*, and saying, "One, two, three, *pass!*" draw away the handkerchief sharply, which, brushing against the genuine ring, will set it revolving rapidly, as though it had just passed on to the wand.

Some professors introduce the "flying ring" in the performance of this trick, thus dispensing altogether with the handkerchief. The slight variations in working thereby rendered necessary will readily suggest themselves without further explanation.

TRICKS
WITH
HANDKERCHIEFS

We have already discussed a good many tricks in which handkerchiefs are employed in one way or another. The present chapter will be devoted to those feats in which the handkerchief forms the sole or principal object of the illusion. In "knot" tricks you should, if possible, use a silk handkerchief, which, from its softer nature, will be found more tractable than cotton.

We will begin by describing a couple of little "flourishes," which may be incidentally introduced in the performance of more ambitious tricks, and which will sometimes be found useful in occupying the attention of the audience for a moment or two while some necessary arrangement is being made behind the scenes for the purpose of the principal illusion.

The No-Knot Hank

Take up a handkerchief and pull it this way and that, as if to ascertain its fitness for the purpose of the trick. Finally twisting the handkerchief into a sort of loose rope, throw the two ends one over the other, as in the ordinary mode of tying, and pull smartly; but instead of a knot appearing in the middle of the handkerchief, as would naturally be expected, it is pulled out quite straight.

"This is a very curious handkerchief," you remark; "I can't make a knot in it." The process is again and again repeated, but always with the same result.

The secret is as follows: The performer, before pulling the knot tight, slips the left thumb, as shown in the illustration, beneath such portion of the "tie" as is a continuation of the end held in the same hand. The necessary arrangement of the hands and handkerchief, though difficult to explain in writing, will be found quite clear upon a careful examination of the illustration.

The Vanishing Knot

For this trick you must use a silk handkerchief. Twisting it rope-fashion, and grasping it by the middle with both hands, you request one of the spectators to tie the two ends together. He does so, but you tell him that he has not tied them half tight enough, and you yourself pull them still tighter. A second and a third knot are made in the same way, the handkerchief being drawn tighter by yourself after each knot is made. Finally, taking the handkerchief, and covering the knots with the loose part, you hand it to someone to hold. Breathing on it, you request him to shake out the handkerchief, at which time all the knots are found to have disappeared.

When apparently tightening the knot, you in reality only strain one end of the handkerchief, grasping it above and below the knot. This pulls that end of the handkerchief out of its twisted condition in the knot into a straight line, round which the other end of the handkerchief remains twisted—in other words, converts the knot into a slip-knot. After each successive knot you still straighten this same end of the handkerchief. This end, being thus made straight, would naturally be left longer than the other which is twisted round and round it. This tendency you as performer can counteract by drawing it partially back through the slip-knot at each pretended tightening. When you finally cover over the knots, which you do with the left hand, hold the straightened portion of the handkerchief, immediately behind the knots, between the first finger and thumb of the right hand, and therewith, in the act of covering over the knots, draw this straightened portion completely out of the slip-knot.

Some performers (among whom we may mention Herrmann) make this feat still more effective by borrowing half a dozen handkerchiefs and scarves, and allowing them all to be tied end to end by the spectators. After each knot the professor pretends to examine it, asking, "What kind of a knot do you call this?" and meanwhile pulls it into the required condition. The joined handkerchiefs are then placed one upon the other on a chair and are immediately afterward shown to be separate.

The student must be on his guard against one particular kind of knot, which cannot be pulled into the condition above named. We allude to the very common mode of tying, in which the two ends to be tied are placed side by side, and tied simultaneously in a single knot. The employment of this kind of knot may generally be avoided by holding the two ends to be tied at a tolerably wide angle, so that they cannot very well be drawn parallel. If, however, a spectator appears determined to tie this particular knot, it is better to allow him to do so, and then remark, "As the knots are tied by yourselves, ladies and gentlmen, you can have little doubt that they are all fair. However, for the greater satisfaction of all present, I will ask some gentleman to be good enough to untie one of them, which will give a fair criterion of the time it would take, in a natural way, to get rid of the remainder." So saying, you hand the knot in question to be untied, and in subsequently giving the ends to be again joined select a more accommodating person to tie them.

The Instant Knot

The performer takes a small handkerchief by two opposite corners, one in each hand, and rolls it into a loose "rope." Remarking that merely blowing on its center will produce a magical knot upon it, the conjurer blows upon it accordingly. There is an almost imperceptible wave of movement along the handkerchief, and instantly a large knot appears on its center.

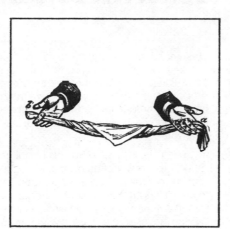

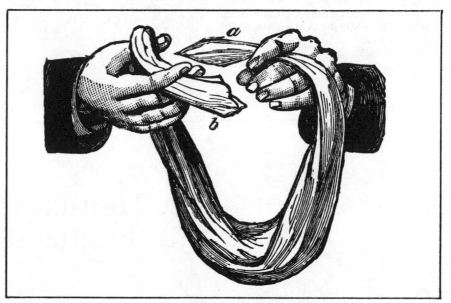

This effect depends mainly on the manner in which the handkerchief is held, though a good deal of practice will be necessary before the tying movement will be as invisible as above described. The handkerchief is taken as shown in the illustration. On a casual examination it might seem that both ends are held in the same manner, but such is not the case. Each end is held between the first and second fingers, but in the case of the right hand the end passes in front of the second, third, and fourth fingers, and thence to the back of the hand. The end in the left hand passes *behind* the second, third, and fourth fingers, and thence, between the first and second fingers, to the front of the hand.

Such is the position in which the handkerchief is first shown. In the act of blowing, the performer swiftly brings the hands together, and separates them again. The act takes but a moment, but in that moment the trick is done.

As the hands approach each other the performer slips the thumb of the right hand under the handkerchief, and brings it opposite the middle finger, at the same time turning the hand slightly over. The thumb of the left hand in like manner approaches the middle finger of that hand. The position of the hands, when the two come together, is therefore as shown in the illustration, the end originally held by the right hand falling naturally into the forceps formed by the thumb and middle finger of the left hand, and the end originally in the left hand falling in like manner between the thumb and middle finger of the right hand. The thumb and finger in each case nip the handkerchief. The hands are drawn rapidly apart, and the knot is formed.

Stretching a Handkerchief

Having borrowed or produced a handkerchief for the purpose of some trick, you find, or pretend to find, that it is not quite large enough. You make a show of being about to return it, and to borrow another, but change your mind, and say you will make it do, if the owner will not object to your making it "a little larger." Permission having been granted, you take it by two opposite corners, twist it ropewise, and presently begin, with much affectation of stretching, to pull it out longer. Strange to say, its length is actually seen to increase inch by inch, until it is some forty or fifty percent greater than it was at first.

This very effective illusion rests upon an extremely slight foundation. Few people realize how long even a comparatively small handkerchief is *diagonally*. Readers acquainted with the forty-seventh proposition of Euclid will be able to work out the proposition for themselves, but we may state, by way of illustration, that a handkerchief twenty-four inches square measures, when merely laid flat, two feet, ten inches across its diagonal, and that this length may, by stretching, be increased to over three feet.

In taking up and twisting the handkerchief, you as performer must manage to gather up a few inches of "slack" into each hand, though if this is deftly done, not one in ten of the audience will suspect that the handkerchief is not already stretched to its full length. You throw the handkerchief over and over with a sort of skipping-rope movement, thereby twisting it into a loose rope, at the same time releasing little by little the reserve portion in your hands. To the eye of the spectator it will seem that the handkerchief is growing longer and longer, the elongation only terminating, apparently, when it has reached the full stretch of your arms.

You should make a pretense of great exertion, as if the handkerchief were really stretched by strong muscular effort. Further, however much of the slack of the handkerchief is gathered up in the hands, the extreme corners should always remain visible; this being accepted as a proof, by the uninitiated, that the whole of the handkerchief is seen.

The Handkerchief Vanishes: Silk-Flight Sleights

There are numerous ways of causing the sudden disappearance of a handkerchief, some by pure sleight-of-hand, others by means of mechanical aids.

Nothing is more effective, if the handkerchief be small enough, than simply palming—the handkerchief being rapidly rolled between the hands into a compact ball, "passed" professedly from right to left, but really retained in the right hand, either in the hollow of the palm or clipped against the lower joints of the second and third fingers, whence it can be reproduced at pleasure.

Some little practice is needed to roll the handkerchief into a compact ball that will be manageable in use and will not expand and show loose corners at an inconvenient moment. The chief point is to take care that three of the corners are folded into the center at a comparatively early stage, while the fourth acts as a wrapper for the rest, and keeps all snug.

I have known performers to have a small pin stuck in the vest, and in the course of their preliminary manipulations transfer this to one corner of the handkerchief. This corner is the last to be folded, and the pin thrust into the ball makes all secure. This, however, is an expedient which should be quite unnecessary to a first-rate palmer; and it is open to objection as tending to impede the reproduction of the handkerchief, a good deal of the effectiveness of such reproduction (if produced from the hand itself) depending upon its rapid unfolding, the sudden increase of its apparent bulk rendering it apparently impossible that it could have been concealed in the hand. To facilitate such rapidity of reproduction, it is well to tuck the last corner, with the extreme angle first doubled down, between the first and second fingers. When it is desired to reproduce the handkerchief, a slight relaxation of pressure, accompanied by a quick jerk, at once casts it loose again, all but the corner nipped between the fingers as above.

If the handkerchief to be dealt with is silk, it is a good plan to have a few balls of shot sewn into the corner that is retained. The fingers "bite" on the bulge thus created, while the smooth surface of the silk alone would give them little or no hold.

Another "vanish" for a handkerchief is as follows: The performer, standing three-quarter-face to the audience, right side toward them, takes the handkerchief in the right hand, and with it makes a quick "down-and-up" movement, as if throwing it to the ceiling. Meanwhile, the left arm crosses behind the body, and the left hand takes the handkerchief from the right as it reaches the lowest point, and slips it into a pocket. The right hand makes its upward movement empty, the effect being as if the handkerchief, thrown upward, had vanished into space. I have seen this sleight executed by a French artist with singularly illusive effect, but have never met with it among English conjurers.

Silk-Flight Apparatus

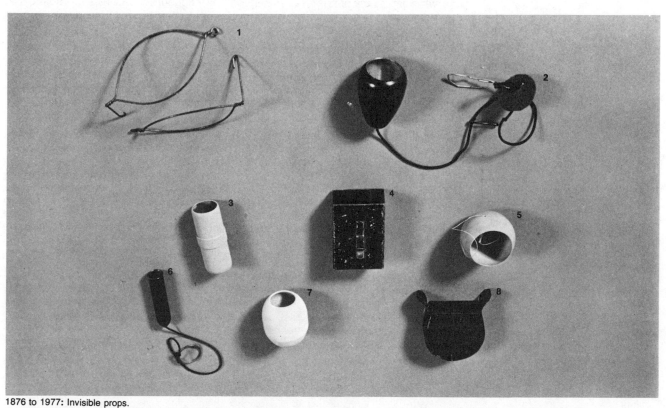

1876 to 1977: Invisible props.
1. Ingenious clip to hold a packet of spring flowers. **2.** Pull for handkerchief vanish. **3.** Dye tube for color-changing handkerchief. **4.** Box with finger clip for silk production or vanish. **5.** Stilwell ball with loop of thread to hang over thumb for silk production or vanish. **6.** Pull to vanish pencil or cigarette. **7.** Stilwell ball for silk production, vanish, or color change. **8.** Heel box for silk production with sharp pin attached to hook to clothes. (Apparatus from the collection of Richard Robinson.)

Passing to methods involving the use of mechanical aids, one of the most perfect is by means of the apparatus known as the *Buatier pull,* Buatier de Kolta being the ingenious performer to whom the craft is indebted for its invention.

As applied to handkerchiefs, it consists of a cylindrical metal cup, 1 to 1¼ inch in diameter, and 2½ to 3 in length, tapering at the closed end, and attached at the closed end to a silk cord, which passes up (say) the left sleeve, behind the back, and down the opposite sleeve of the performer, where it is held fast to the right wrist. The length of the cord is so adjusted that when the arms hang down at full length by the side of the body, the cup lies about halfway up the left forearm, though by bending the arms, and so slackening the cord, it may be brought into the hand at pleasure. When it is desired to use the Buatier "fake" to cause the disappearance of a handkerchief, the cup is got into the hand and palmed, the performer standing (in the case supposed of the cup being in the *left* sleeve) with the left side toward the audience. Taking the handkerchief, the conjurer begins apparently to rub it between the hands, gradually working it, by means of the second finger of the more remote hand, into the cup, calling attention the while to its gradual disappearance. When the whole of the handkerchief is safely stowed within the cup, he gives a forward lunge with both arms, and at the same time relaxes his hold on the cup. The extension "pulls" the cord, and the cup is drawn up the sleeve, enabling the performer to show both hands completely empty.

The cup may be placed within either the right or left sleeve, as may best suit the personal idiosyncrasies of the performer; and may vary in shape or size, according to the object for which it is intended to be used. The cup is often replaced with either a metal clip to which a length of rope or ribbon can be attached, an adjustable loop of cord through which several silks can be secured, or other device, depending on the object to be vanished.

It is a curious fact, and illustrates the proverbial irony of fate, that one of the latest and most artistic of conjuring devices should be a practical realization of the "up his sleeve" theory, which has in all ages been accepted by the vulgar as the explanation of the great bulk of magical disappearances, though in ninety-nine cases out of a hundred the sleeve had absolutely nothing to do with the matter. Thus "the whirligig of Time brings in his revenges." The innocent sleeve, unjustly credited with a thousand uncommitted sins, has at length turned upon its maligners, and no doubt laughs in itself to think how neatly it outwits them.

Here, however, those who saw Buatier's performances might interpose an objection. "But surely," such an observer might exclaim, "Buatier vanished a handkerchief with his arms bare to the elbow? What becomes of the sleeve theory in that case?" The aim of every true conjurer is to be able to produce the same trick by several different methods, so that, if foiled or suspected in the use of one of them, he may be able to fall back upon another.

To produce the "bare-armed" vanish, the tin cup is again called into requisition, but in a different way. The cord is in this case a piece of stout elastic, and passes through a small ring sewn to (say) the left armhole of the performer's vest or at a similar point on the performer's shirt. Thence it passes behind his back (within the vest if he wears it), and round his waist on the opposite side, being finally tied at the belt loop on his right side. The length is so arranged that the cup shall be drawn close up to the armhole, with a fairly strong amount of tension, though it can be drawn out at pleasure to a distance of some eighteen or twenty inches from the body. The use of so long a piece of elastic (some three feet) is expressly designed to allow for free extension in this manner.

When the performer desires to use the apparatus, he takes an opportunity, in turning to his table, or the like, to get the cup into his hand. This done, the rest is easy. The handkerchief is worked into the cup as above described. When it is fairly home, the performer makes a forward and backward movement of the hands, and simultaneously with the latter relaxes his hold on the cup; it flies under the lapel of the coat, and up to the armhole, where it rests effectually concealed.

The exact shape of the apparatus is a matter of taste. Its original shape was that of a tube, open at one end, as described for the sleeve; but it is also made pear-shaped, with an opening (oval) at one side. The latter is, I think, in this case, the preferable pattern.

In order to facilitate the getting of the cup into the hand, I have found the following a useful plan: Firmly sewn to the bottom of the vest, at the point where the backing joins the front, I have a lady's black dress-hook, fixed point-downward, and slightly sloping toward the center of the body. The cup is beforehand drawn down to this point, and the elastic slipped under the hook. The cup is thus held perfectly secure, and in a very get-at-able position, while the mere downward pressure of the hand, in the act of palming it, instantly releases it from the hook.

Another Approach

There is yet another bare-armed "vanish" for which conjurers are indebted mainly to the fertile brain of Buatier de Kolta, which calls for a *hand-box,* or *hank-ball*. This is a palmable container open at one or both ends, large enough to contain one or two silks while small enough to be concealed in the hand. There are various aids attached to the container to make it easier to manipulate: spring clips that hold it to the flesh of the palm; thread that allows it to be suspended from the thumb; studs that can be secured between the fingers; or a soft wax smeared on the outside of the container that makes it stick to the front or back of the hand.

The container is concealed in the left hand. The right hand takes the silk and starts to work it into the closed left hand, in reality into the container. The container is then stolen into the right hand, the left hand kept close as if containing it; the effect to the audience is as if the handkerchief were merely rolled up and placed in the left hand. On opening the hand, the handkerchief is found to have disappeared, the performer having meanwhile plenty of opportunity to drop the concealed handkerchief, container and all, into a right-hand pocket.

To illustrate the capabilities of this apparatus, I cannot do better than describe one of Buatier's most popular sleight-of-hand feats, which he accomplishes with the use of a small container having a dab of soft wax (of good adhesive quality, such as "magician's wax") on the sides of the container.

The Dissolving Handkerchiefs

Buatier exhibits two handkerchiefs of very soft silk—one red, one blue—about fourteen inches square. Having shown that they are free from any special preparation, he throws them side by side over the back of a chair, and next calls attention to an ordinary soup plate, which he ultimately lays mouth downward on a table, first spreading newspaper beneath it to exclude the idea of any assistance from below. In the act of turning down the plate, he secretly introduces beneath it a couple of duplicate handkerchiefs rolled up into a very small compass, which was beforehand placed in readiness in a clip near the hem of his coat jacket or on his *servante*.

He announces that he proposes to pass the two handkerchiefs he has shown under the inverted plate, and asks whether he shall do so "visibly" or "invisibly." Whatever the reply, the procedure is the same. Turning up his sleeve to the elbow, and incidentally showing that his hands are empty, he takes one of the handkerchiefs from the back of the chair, and with it the little container, which, unknown to the audience, is stuck, by means of the wax, to the upper edge of the chair-back, the depth of the wood (three or four inches) effectually screening it from observation.

Standing with his right side to the audience, and holding container and handkerchief between his palms, he begins to work the handkerchief into the container, calling attention to its gradual disappearance. As soon as it is fairly in he thrusts one or two fingers of the hand nearest the audience into the mouth of the container, and with their aid transfers it to the back of the opposite hand, to which a good squeeze compels it to adhere.

Showing, with a careless gesture, that the handkerchief has completely disappeared, and that there is nothing in either hand, he steps up to the chair, and with the right hand takes the second handkerchief, and throws it over the other hand. This makes all safe, for the handkerchief just picked up falls over and conceals the container. He rubs this second handkerchief between his hands, under cover of so doing again getting the container between the palms, and working the handkerchief into it. He does not this time pass the box to the back of the left hand, but simply palms it in the right. From the position in which he stands, the audience see the back only of this hand, but the hands having been shown (as far as the palms are concerned) unmistakably empty on the first occasion, it never strikes anyone that they may now be otherwise, or that the omission to show the inside of both hands is intentional. Buatier does not allow them too much time to think over the matter, but at once turns up the soup plate and shows the duplicate handkerchiefs. These, when picked up again, serve to mask the presence of the hidden container in the right hand until it can be conveniently gotten rid of.

The above description will enable the reader to comprehend the modus operandi of the trick, but conveys only a faint idea of its illusive effect, the impression on the mind of the ordinary spectator being that he sees the handkerchiefs visibly dematerialize themselves between the hands of the performer. Their reappearance under the plate is a less striking phenomenon; given that the handkerchief just shown has really melted into thin air, it is taken for granted by the uninitiated that those subsequently produced from the plate must be the same.

The same feat is sometimes performed with the aid of a mechanical plate. The plate has a false bottom of metal or cardboard, painted on one side to match the plate, and covered on the other side with newspaper. The dummy handkerchiefs are in this case laid beforehand in the plate with the false bottom on the top of them. When the plate is inverted on the table, the false bottom falls out, and releases the handkerchiefs, the reverse side matching the piece of newspaper already lying on the table, and thus rendering it practically invisible. To an expert palmer, however, the use of such an appliance is a needless complication.

Inside the Box

A handkerchief, scarf, or other object is vanished and then caused to reappear in the innermost of a nest of boxes (which has throughout the entertainment been hung up in full view of the audience), the outermost of which is carefully corded and sealed.

The performer takes the box from where it is hanging and places it on the table. Cutting the cords and opening the box, the conjurer produces from it another, corded like the first. From this second box is produced yet another smaller box. This is handed to the owner of the handkerchief, with a request that she open it, and find her handkerchief inside.

The trick in this form is one of the very best exhibited on the stage, and yet, as indeed are most of the best feats, it is performed by the simplest possible means. The outer box is an ordinary wood box, honestly sealed and corded; but the second, though equally genuine in appearance, has no bottom, and the cord, though apparently quite complete, does not cross beneath the box, which is, in fact, nothing more than a wooden shell, or cover, with a lid on it. When the performer takes out this second box and places it on the table, he tilts it forward for a moment, and in that moment slips the nest of boxes (which is placed in readiness on the servante), underneath it, immediately afterward raising the lip, and taking out the nest, as if it had all along been contained therein.

It only remains to explain the mode by which the nest of boxes, with the handkerchief therein, is placed upon the servante. Some performers employ the rather too transparent expedient of making the assistant bring in, then and there, a small round table, behind which, on a servante of its own, is placed the closed nest of boxes. A better plan, where the size of the nest permits, is to have it placed open, before the performance commences, on the servante of the center table. It is then an easy matter for the performer to slip in the object, and close the boxes, the remainder of the trick proceeding as already described.

Some performers use for the purpose of this trick a special mechanical table, which, by means of a lifting apparatus, itself introduces the nest of boxes through a trap into the bottomless box, without the necessity of tilting the latter.

The Shower of Sweets

This is a trick that is sure to be well received by a juvenile audience. You come forward with an ordinary plate or tray, which you hand for examination and then place on the table. Next, borrow or produce a handkerchief. Laying it flat over the plate, lift it up by nipping the middle with your finger and thumb, letting the four corners hang down. Then stroke down the handkerchief with the other hand, under the pretense of mesmerizing it, when a shower of candies, chocolates, gum drops, etc., will pour down upon the plate. Again stroke the handkerchief, and again the shower will pour down; and the plate, being by this time full, will be handed round to the company to prove that in the quality of the sweets, at any rate, there is "no deception."

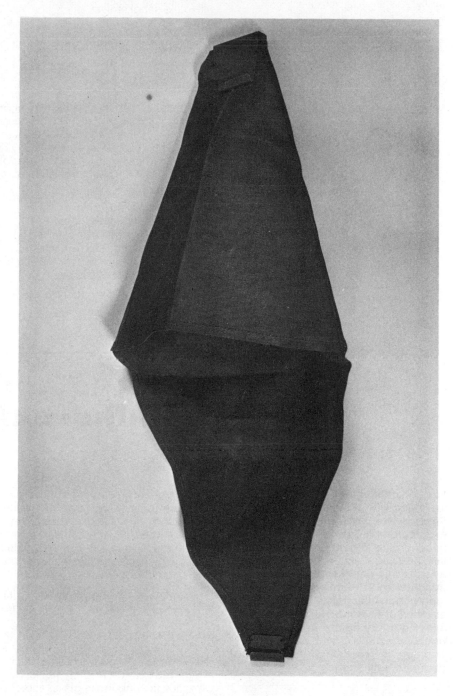

The secret lies in the use of a small cloth bag, shaped like an inverted letter V. The edges are turned in at the mouth, and through each hem is passed a straight piece of watchspring, one a little longer than the other. The natural tendency of these is to lie side by side, keeping the mouth of the bag closed; but if pressure be simultaneously applied to both ends of the springs, the longer one assumes the shape of a semicircle, thereby opening the bag. Through the opposite end of the bag is passed a pointed wire hook. The bag is beforehand filled with nuts or bonbons, and hung by the hook at the edge of the table on the side away from the spectators. Though the bag is mouth downward, the action of the spring keeps it closed, and nothing can fall out.

When standing behind the table, you draw the handkerchief over the plate, allow a portion of the back edge to hang over the edge of the table nearest yourself. When you pick up the handkerchief, which you do with your finger and thumb, take hold, through the handkerchief, of the upper part of the bag. The bag is thus lifted up within the handkerchief, but is concealed by the folds of the latter hanging down around it. The movement of the hand is stroking down the handkerchief presses the springs, and the bag opens, again closing as soon as the pressure is relaxed. When all the contents have fallen, drop the handkerchief, bag and all, on the table, while you advance to the audience with the results of the trick, and, on again picking up the handkerchief, let fall the empty bag upon the *servante*, or slip it into your pocket.

It will be observed that, in the form of the trick above described, the use of both hands is necessary—one holds the handkerchief, while the other, stroking it down, presses the springs, and causes the bag to open. There is an improved form of the bag, used and, we believe, invented by Robert-Houdin, that enables the performer, holding the handkerchief at arm's length, to perform the trick by mere word of command, without using the left hand at all.

The bag is in this case of the form shown in the illustration. No springs are used, but the bag, when filled, is closed by bringing up the flap and hooking the little ring at the tip of the flap over the hook, the bag thereby assuming the appearance as shown in the illustration. It is picked up within the handkerchief as described in the case of the spring bag; but when it is desired to produce the sweets, a slight inclination of the hook causes the ring to slip off and the flap to fall down, releasing the whole contents of the bag.

A larger version of this bag can be used to produce a rabbit or a dozen oranges.

The Egg and the Handkerchief

For this capital feat, generally identified with the name of Colonel Stodare, the following are required: a glass tumbler, two small handkerchiefs (generally of plain red silk, and about sixteen inches square), a larger silk handkerchief to which is attached, by a thread about four inches long, a blown eggshell (an eggshell emptied of its contents and the inside allowed to dry before use), and a hollow plastic egg with an oval opening on one side of it (a standard item at magic shops).

The performer comes forward, having in his right hand the glass and one of the red silk handkerchiefs. The larger silk handkerchief is thrown with apparent carelessness over the other hand, and upon it rests the blown egg, so placed that the thread may be out of sight, while beneath the egg, concealed in a fold of the handkerchief, lies the second red handkerchief, rolled up into as small a ball as possible. The plastic egg is, meanwhile, placed in the left-hand jacket pocket of the performer who introduces the trick as follows:

"I have here, ladies and gentlemen, a drinking glass, a couple of silk handkerchiefs, and an egg." He passes quickly in front of the audience, as though offering the articles for examination (taking care, however, to keep his right arm advanced toward the spectators, so that the glass and small silk handkerchief may bear the brunt of the inspection), and finally places the glass and small handkerchierf on a table or chair in full view. "Please watch," he continues, "that not one of the articles is removed from your sight, even for one moment. Now, please follow me closely. I will place the egg in the glass, and cover it over with this handkerchief." This he does by one movement, for as the egg is already lying on the handkerchief, a mere turn of the wrist places the egg in the glass, and at the same time lets fall the handkerchief over it; simultaneously, the smaller handkerchief, which was concealed in the larger, is released, and falls into the glass with the egg.

"You have all seen me place the egg in the glass" (at the same time shaking the glass, to show by the sound that the egg is still there), "which I will not again touch. I shall now take this small handkerchief" (the one that has remained on the table), "and standing as far away as possible, I shall command the handkerchief to dissolve and pass into the glass, and the egg which is now in the glass to come into my hands.

So saying, he holds up the handkerchief in such a manner as to show indirectly that he has nothing else in his hands. Taking a few steps, as though merely to get farther from the glass, and holding the handkerchief hanging down between the finger and thumb of the right hand, he drops the other hand to his side, and secretly takes from his pocket the hollow plastic egg which he palms, keeping the opening outward. He then, standing with his left side toward the spectators, joins his open hands, the handkerchief hanging down between them. Requesting the audience to watch closely, that they may be quite sure that there is no deception, he begins to wave his joined hands slowly up and down, the second and third fingers of the right hand (which, it will be remembered, is away from the audience) meanwhile gradually working the handkerchief into the hollow of the plastic egg. Every now and then he pauses to show that the handkerchief is gradually diminishing, and at last when it is wholly worked into the egg, opens his hands, and shows the egg lying in his palm, taking care, of course, that the opening is undermost.

To all appearance, the handkerchief has changed into an egg. "Here is the egg," he remarks; "Let us see if the handkerchief also has obeyed my bidding." So saying, he lays the egg, still with the opening downward, upon the table, and taking hold with the finger and thumb of the handkerchief that covers the glass, lifts it up daintily, carrying with it, concealed in its folds, the eggshell attached thereto, and leaving the duplicate red handkerchief lying in the glass.

It may sometimes, though not very often, occur that one or other of the spectators, suspecting some peculiarity about the egg, may ask to be permitted to examine it. This, of course, you cannot permit, while to refuse would destroy half the prestige of the illusion. Fortunately, there is a way out of the difficulty which absolutely enhances the effect of the trick.

"You would like to see the egg," you reply; "By all means. It is a special feature of my entertainment that all articles used therein will bear the strictest examination. Here is the egg." During these few words, you have taken up the sham egg with the fingers of your right hand, taking care, of course, to keep the opening away from the audience, and have thence apparently transferred it to your left, with which hand you offer it to the too-curious spectator. It is hardly necessary to remark that, in the apparent transfer of the egg to the left hand, you have really palmed it in your right; and as you extend the left hand to the spectator, you quietly drop it into your right jacket pocket or onto your *servante*.

As the inquirer holds out his hand to receive it, you say, "Please examine it closely," opening your empty hand over his own. "What! You haven't got it? Ah, that is *your* fault; you were not quick enough. I always find that this experiment makes the egg excessively volatile."

This unexpected *dènouement* never fails to raise a laugh against the individual who has sought to embarrass you, while the impromptu disappearance of the egg will be regarded by many as the most marvelous portion of the trick. The same expedient will be equally available to prevent the examination, at an awkward moment, of other small articles.

THE CUPS AND BALLS

The subject of the present chapter may be said to be the groundwork of all legerdemain, being, we believe, the very earliest form in which sleight-of-hand was exhibited. It is well worthy the attention of the student of modern magic, not only as affording an excellent course of training in digital dexterity, but as being, in the hands of an adept, most striking in effect. It is by no means uncommon to find spectators who have received more elaborate feats with comparative indifference become interested, and even enthusiastic, over a brilliant manipulation of the cups and balls

The prestige of the illusion is heightened by the simplicity of the appliances used, consisting merely of three metal cups about three inches high, usually in the form of a truncated cone, with a rim or shoulder round the base; the ordinary wand; four cork or rubber balls, three-quarters of an inch or a little less in diameter; three larger balls of about an inch and a quarter in diameter; and four more of such a size as to just fill the cups. The number of balls may vary according to the particular "passes" the performer desires to exhibit, but the above will be found sufficient for most purposes.

The performers of olden times were accustomed to use the *gibecière*, or apron with pockets, already mentioned, and to perform at a table having no specialty, save that it was a little higher than those in ordinary use; but at the present day the gibecière is entirely discarded, the *servante* of the table or the conjurer's jacket pockets answering the same purpose.

The whole art of cup and ball conjuring resolves itself into two elements: (1) the exhibition of a ball under a cup where a moment previously there was nothing; and (2) the disappearance of a ball from beneath a cup under which the audience have just seen it (or believe they have seen it) placed.

The routine is as follows: A cup is lifted, to show that there is nothing beneath it, and again replaced, mouth downward, on the table. A ball is taken in the right hand, transferred to the left, and thence ordered to pass under the cup. The hand is opened, the ball has vanished, and, on the cup being lifted, is found beneath it. Again, the ball, first exhibited in the right hand, is openly transferred, either directly under the cup, or first to the left hand, and then to the cup. All having seen it placed beneath the cup, it is now commanded to depart, and on again lifting the cup, it is found to have vanished. A ball placed under one cup mysteriously travels to be found under one of the other cups. The small balls placed under each cup, the performer lifts the cup to reveal balls three times the size of those originally placed thereunder. It will hardly be believed, until proved by experiment, of what numerous and surprising combinations these elements are capable.

The sleight-of-hand requisite for the cups and balls is technically divisible into four different acts or movements:

1. Palming the ball
2. Reproducing the palmed ball at the end of the fingers
3. Secretly introducing the palmed ball under the cup
4. Simulating the action of placing the ball under the cup

The modes of effecting these objects will be discussed in due order.

1. Palming the Ball

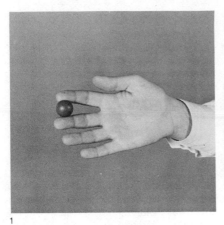

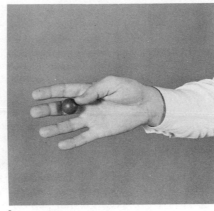

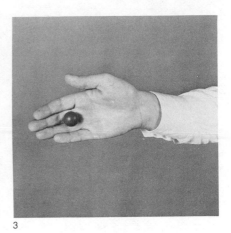

1   2   3

First Method

We use the generic term *palm* for the sake of convenience, though in this first method the ball is really concealed between the second and third fingers, and not in the palm.

Take the ball between the first finger and thumb of the right hand; slightly bend the fingers, and at the same moment roll the ball with the thumb across the first and second fingers, till it rests between the second and third fingers which should slightly separate to receive it, again closing as soon as it is safely lodged. The ball will now be clipped at the base of the second and third fingers and held in place by the flesh of those fingers. It will be found that the hand can be opened or closed with perfect freedom, and, indeed, be used in any manner, without being in the least hampered by its presence. The student should practice palming the ball in this manner both in the act of (apparently) transferring the ball to the left hand, and in that of (apparently) placing it under a cup lifted by the left hand for that purpose.

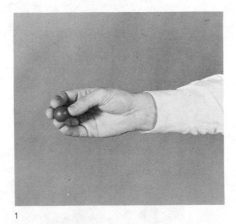

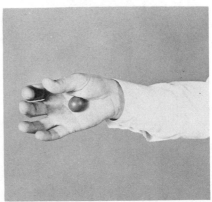

1   2

Second Method

The second method is to actually palm the ball, in the same manner as a coin. For this purpose the ball is, as before, taken between the first finger and thumb of the right hand, but is then made by the thumb to roll between the tips of the third and fourth fingers. Pretend to pass the ball to the other hand, but under cover of the move close the third and fourth fingers into the palm which places the ball in the exact position to be "palmed" and, again opening the fingers, leave the ball behind. With practice, two balls in succession may be palmed in this way, and then a third by the first method.

  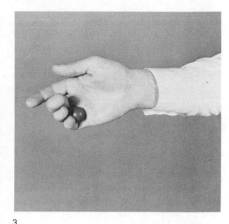

1   2   3

Third Method

The third method is that which was adopted by the celebrated Giovanni Bartolomeo Bosco, a most accomplished performer with the cups and balls. The ball is held between the thumb-tip and the first and second joints of the first finger. In the act of making the pass, the thumb releases the ball and it rolls across the third joint of each finger until finally stopped by a slight contraction of the little finger, or of the third and little fingers. This is perhaps the simplest of the three methods above, but extremely effective.

2. Reproducing the Palmed Ball at the End of the Fingers

The mode of doing this will vary according to the method by which the ball is palmed. If according to the first or third method, the ball is simply rolled back to the fingertips with the ball of the thumb, exactly reversing the process by which it was palmed. But if the ball was palmed by the second method, the third and fourth fingers must close upon the ball and grasp it between their tips, then extending outward with the ball when the thumb is enabled to reach it and to roll it to the fingertips in the manner just described.

3. Secretly Introducing the Palmed Ball Under the Cup

This is always done in the act of raising the cup (with the right hand, which palms the ball), for the ostensible purpose of showing that there is nothing underneath it.

The chief thing to be attended to is the position of the right hand (in which the ball is palmed by one or other of the methods above mentioned) in raising the cup. This should be done with the hand spread almost flat upon the table, and grasping the cup as low down as possible, between the thumb and the lowest joint of the forefinger. In the act of raising the cup, the fingers naturally assume a position whereby the ball is brought in close proximity to, and slightly under, the edge of the cup.

If the ball is palmed by the first method, all that is necessary in order to release it is a slight backward movement of the second finger and a forward movement of the third finger, made just before the cup again touches the table. This will be found to drop the ball immediately under the cup.

If the ball is palmed by the third method, its introduction under the cup is a still easier matter, as by the act of raising the cup it is brought directly underneath it, and is released by the mere act of straightening the third and fourth fingers. With this method the cup does not even have to be lifted from the table; the act of tipping it forward on its front edge makes enough room at the back for the ball to be introduced under the cup.

If the ball is palmed by the second method, it becomes necessary to close the third and fourth fingers slightly, grasp the ball, and bring it under the cup where it can then be dropped before the cup is replaced on the table.

It is advisable to attempt all three methods of palming the ball and all three methods of introducing the ball under the cup before deciding which palm and secret introduction is the easiest.

It is sometimes necessary to introduce a ball between two stacked cups. It will be remembered that each cup is made with a cylindrical rim or shoulder. The purpose of this shoulder is that, when two cups are placed one upon the other, there is a space between them sufficient to receive a ball. To further facilitate the introduction of the ball, the top of each cup is made concave.

When it is desired to introduce a ball between two cups, that object is effected as follows: Having the ball palmed in the right hand, the performer takes up a cup in the same hand, and with it covers the second cup, at the same moment introducing the ball beneath it in the ordinary manner, but with the addition of a little upward jerk, rather difficult to describe, but easily acquired with a little practice. The ball is thereby thrown to the top of the uppermost cup, and, in again falling, is received by the concave top of the lowermost cup.

4. Simulating the Action of Placing a Ball Under a Cup

This may be done in two ways.

The first is to raise the cup with the left hand, apparently placing the ball underneath it with the right, but really palming it. Care must be taken that the edge of the cup touches the table at the very moment that the fingers of the right hand are removed.

The second and more common method is to apparently transfer the ball to the left hand, palming it in the transit, and then bringing the closed left hand close to the cup on the table, raise the cup with the other hand, and immediately replace it with a sort of scraping movement across the fingers of the now opening left hand as if pulling the ball under the cup off the left palm and onto the table.

When the student has thoroughly mastered the various operations above described, there will be little to learn save the combination of the various passes, a matter of memory only. There are, however, one or two subordinate sleights with which one should make oneself acquainted before proceeding publicly to exhibit one's dexterity.

Balls from the Wand

The wand is supposed to be the reservoir from where the magician produces his store of balls, and into which they vanish when no longer needed.

The method of production is as follows: The performer, holding the wand in his left hand, and drawing attention to it by some remark as to its mysterious power of production and absorption, secretly takes with his right hand, from the *servante* or elsewhere, a ball, which he immediately palms. Lightly holding the wand at the end with the left hand in such a manner as to show that the hand is otherwise empty, he slides the thumb and fingers of the right hand (the back of which is naturally toward the audience) lightly to the opposite end, at the same moment rolling the ball with the thumb to the ends of the fingers. The ball thus comes in sight just as the hand leaves the wand, the effect to the eyes of the spectators being that the ball is, by some mysterious process, squeezed out of the wand.

To return a ball into the wand is the converse of the above process. Taking the wand in the left hand, as before, and the ball between the thumb and the second joint of the forefinger of the opposite hand, the performer lays the end of the wand across the tips of the fingers, and draws the hand gently downward along it, at the same time palming the ball by the first method.

One Cup Penetrates Another

This is an effective sleight, by no means difficult to acquire.

Taking one of the cups, mouth upward, in the left hand, and holding another in a similar position in the right hand, about a foot above it, the performer drops the right-hand cup smartly into that in the left hand (which latter should be held very lightly). If this is neatly done, the lower cup will be knocked out of the hand by the concussion, while the upper one will be caught and held in its place; the effect to the eye being as if the upper cup had passed through the other. The lower cup either may be allowed to fall on the table, or may be caught by the right hand in its fall.

Introducing the Cups and Balls

The successive appearances and disappearances of the balls underneath the cups are known by the name *passes*, the particular combination of such passes being governed by the taste and invention of the performer. The series most generally in use is derived from a work dating from the 1700s, the *Rècrèations Mathèmatiques et Physiques* of Guyot; and Guyot, we believe, borrowed it from a German source. The series given below, which will be found very effective, is derived mainly from that of Guyot, as improved by J. N. Ponsin, a later and very ingenious writer on the art of prestidigitation.

The cups and balls require, even more than conjuring generally, a running accompaniment of *talk*. Each pass should have it's own "patter," carefully prepared and frequently rehearsed. It would be impossible to give, within any reasonable limits, appropriate patter for each of the passes. This each performer must arrange for himself, so as to suit the style and character in which he performs. We shall, however, give a specimen or two in the course of the various passes. The introduction next following is a paraphrase of a similar address quoted by Robert-Houdin:

"Ladies and gentlemen: In an age so enlightened as our own, it is really surprising to see how many popular fallacies spring up from day to day, and are accepted by the public as unchangeable laws of nature.

"Among these fallacies there is one that I will at once point out to you, and that I believe I can very easily dispose of. Many people have asserted, including the celebrated Erasmus, that a material object can only be in one place at one time. I maintain, on the contrary, that any object may be in several places at the same moment, and that it is equally possible that it may be nowhere at all.

"I ask you to watch closely. In the first place I have nothing in my hands—except my fingers; and that between my fingers there is nothing save a few atoms of the mysterious fluid that we call the atmosphere.

"I have before me, as you will have noticed, three little cups. The metal of which these are composed is an amalgam of costly minerals, unknown even to the smartest scientists. This mysterious composition, which resembles silver in its solidity, color, and clearness of ring, has over silver this great advantage: that it will at pleasure become impalpable as air, so that solid bodies pass through these cups as easily as they would through empty space. I will give you a curious illustration of this by making one cup pass through another. [This the performer does in the manner already described, and after a moment's pause, continues, taking up the wand in the left hand, and secretly palming a ball in the right.] This little wand, you are possibly aware, goes by the name of Jacob's Rod. Why it is so called I really don't know; I only know that this simple-looking wand has the faculty of producing various articles at pleasure. For instance, I require for the purpose of my experiment a little ball. My wand at once supplies me." [A ball is produced from the wand and is laid on the table.]

With this or some similar introduction, the performer proceeds to exhibit.

1 Right hand tips ball on top of cup into left hand while secretly introducing extra ball under cup.

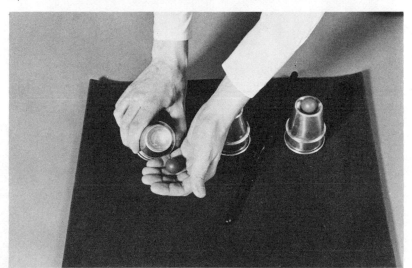

2 Ball held in third method—clipped by little finger—is easily introduced by right hand as rear edge of cup is lifted to tilt ball on top of cup into left hand.

3 Ball rolled from left hand into right hand, then apparently rolled back into left hand, is actually retained and concealed in right hand.

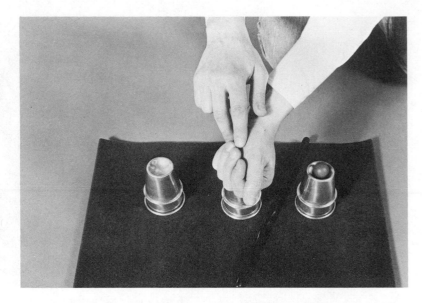

1 Left hand closes as if it contains ball, actually ball is held in right hand.

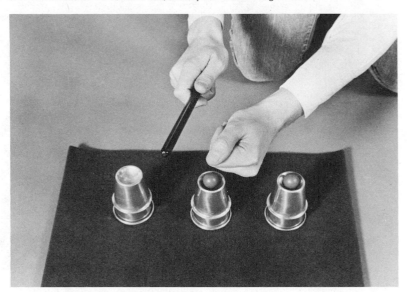

2 Pick-up wand with right hand.

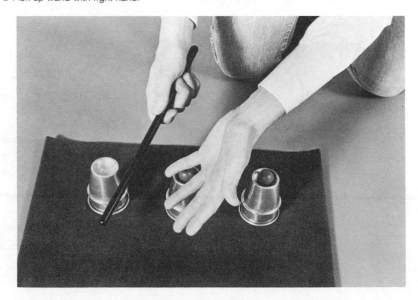

3 Wave wand over left hand, then open left hand to show ball has vanished.

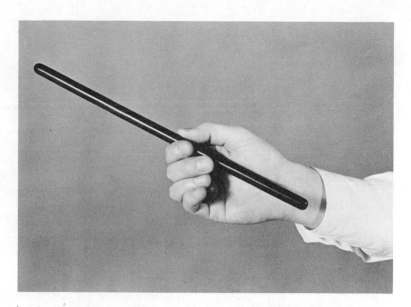

4 Ball remains concealed in right hand while hand holds the wand.

5 Ball is introduced into cup from clipped position in right hand. During performance, the front lip of cup is on the table.

6 Large balls are palmed and dropped into cups.

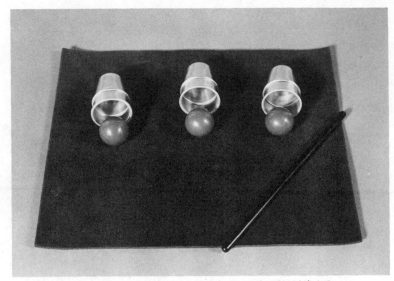

7 Finale: small balls disappear and a large ball is discovered under each cup.

Pass I

Having produced a ball from the wand, and having laid it on the table, the operator continues: "Allow me to show you once more that all the cups are empty" (they are raised one by one, and replaced), "and that I have nothing in either of my hands. I take this little ball" (picked up with the right hand, and apparently transferred it to the left, but really palmed in the right), "and place it under one of the cups." Here the cup is raised with the right hand, and the action of placing the ball under it with the left is simulated.

"I draw another ball from my wand" (really the same ball, which remained palmed in the right hand), "and place it in like manner under the second cup." He goes through the motion of transferring it to the left hand and then to the cup, as before, but this time actually does what on the former occasion he only pretended to do, and leaves the ball under the middle cup.

"I will produce another ball" (he half draws the wand through his fingers, but checks himself half-way). "I think I heard someone assert that I have a ball already in my hand. Please satisfy yourselves" (showing the palms of his hands, the fingers carelessly apart) "that such is not the case. A lady suggested just now, by the way—it was only said in a whisper, but I heard it—that I didn't really put the balls under the cup. It was rather sharp on the part of the lady, but you see she was wrong. Here are the balls."*

So saying, the performer lifts up the middle cup with his left hand, and picking up the ball with his right, holds it up that all may see, immediately replacing it under the same cup. The last movement is simulated only, the ball being in reality palmed in the supposed act of placing it under the cup.

"We have now a ball under each of these two cups. We only want one more, and (apparently producing a third ball but really the same again from the wand), "here it is. We will place it under this last cup." This is actually done.

---

*The reader will understand that nobody has in fact made any such observation, but the overhearing of an imaginary objection is often of great use, as enabling the performer to do some necessary act, which he could not well have done without such pretext. Thus, in this instance, the performer wants a plausible excuse—first, for altering his apparent intention of immediately producing a second ball from the wand; and second, for lifting the middle cup, and so regaining possession of the ball. A conjurer thus addressing an imaginary objector is said in French "parler à la cantonade," but the phrase has no precise equivalent among English performers.

"Now, ladies and gentlemen, we have three cups and three balls, one under each cup. So far, I admit that I have not shown you anything very surprising, but now comes the puzzle, to take the balls from under the cups. Perhaps some of you will say there isn't much difficulty in that. Lift the cup, and pick up the ball!" He suits the action to the word, lifting up the third cup with the left hand, and picking up the ball with the right. "A very good solution, but it doesn't happen to be the right one. The problem is to draw out the balls without lifting the cups."

Here he replaces the cup, apparently placing the ball beneath it, but really palming it, as already described in the case of the middle cup, and then returns to the first or farthest cup; touching the top of the cup, he lets the palmed ball drop to his fingertips, and immediately exhibits it, saying, "This is the way *I* take the balls out of the cups.

"The ball being no longer needed, I return it into the wand." This is done as above described, immediately afterward, if desired, handing the wand for examination. "In like manner I draw out the second ball" (the same process is repeated with the middle cup), "and pass that also into my wand. I need not even handle the cups. See, I merely touch this third cup with my wand, and the ball instantly appears on the top." The company cannot see any ball on the end of the wand, but a ball is nevertheless taken from there by the process already described, of letting the palmed ball drop to the tips of the fingers, as they come in contact with the wand. "I pass this also into my wand. Wait, though; on second thought, I'm going to want a ball for my next experiment, so I'll leave it here on the table."

We have given a somewhat elaborate description of this first pass, in order to give the reader some idea of the various feints and artifices employed in relation to the cups and balls. It would be impossible, from consideration of space, to do this for each of the passes, and the reader must therefore remember that the descriptions following give merely the essential outlines, which must be worked up to dramatic effectiveness by the ingenuity of the individual performer. Where practical, we will allow the few words put into the mouth of the performer to indicate the actions accompanying them, only giving special "stage directions" in cases where the performer does *not* suit the action to the words.

For the sake of distinctness, we will indicate the cups from the performer's view. So cup A is at the performer's left hand, cup B is directly before the performer, and cup C is at the performer's right hand.

Pass II

"Now, ladies and gentlemen, if you watch very closely, you will be able to see the ball travel from one cup to another.

"I take the ball" (apparently transfers it to left hand) "and place it under this cup (C). You all see that there is nothing under this one (B)." In raising B with the right hand the palmed ball is introduced under it.

"I will now command the ball that I just placed under the first cup (C) to travel under this one (B). Watch! You will see it pass." A motion of the wand is made from the one cup to the other. "There it goes! This cup (C), as you see, is empty, and under this one (B) is the ball. I will replace it under this same cup (B)." You in reality palm it. "There is nothing under this cup (A)." You secretly introduce the ball under A. "Now observe again. Pass! Did you see it? No? Well, I don't much wonder, for I can't always see it myself. Here it is, however" (lifts A), "and this cup (B) is empty."

You replace the cups on the table, and lay the ball beside them.

Pass III

Before commencing this pass, the performer, while placing the cups in line or otherwise engaging the attention of the audience with his left hand, takes a second ball from the *servante* with his right, and palms it.

He continues: "For my next experiment, I will need two balls. I could, of course, instantly supply myself from the tip of my wand; but there is a curious faculty about the balls themselves; they have a constant tendency to increase and multiply.

"For instance, without using the wand, I can instantly make this one ball into two" (he takes up the ball on the table in his left hand, taking care to hold it so that all may see there is nothing else in that hand), "and the most curious part of the matter is, that though mathematicians insist the whole is always greater than its parts, in this case each of the parts will be found precisely equal to the whole."

As he speaks he takes the ball from the left hand with the fingers of the right, at the same time dropping the palmed ball into the left hand, and now taking care to so hold his *right* hand as to show that it contains the one ball only. He then again replaces this ball in the palm of the left hand, where it lies side by side with the second ball. Rubbing the left palm with the second and third fingers of the right, with a circular motion, he gradually lifts the fingers, and shows the single ball apparently transformed into two, both of which he places on the table.

"You see there's nothing under this cup (C). I'll place this ball under it" (it is actually palmed); "neither is there anything under either of these two cups (B and A)." The cups are lifted one with each hand, and the palmed ball is secretly introduced under B.

"I take this second ball, and place it under this cup (A)." He really palms it. "We now have a ball under each of these two cups (A and C). I draw the ball out of this one (C)." He touches the top of the cup, and produces the ball last palmed at his fingertips. "I order it to pass under this middle cup (B)." He apparently transfers it to the left hand, but really palms it, and then makes a motion with the left hand, as if passing it into B. "It has passed, you see!" He raises B with his right hand, exposing the ball under it, and in replacing it secretly introduces the second palmed ball.

"Now I order the ball in this cup (A) to pass in like manner." He waves his wand from A to B, and then lifts B. "Here it is, and these two outer cups" (turning them over with the wand) "are perfectly empty."

Pass IV

"You have just seen these two balls pass under the middle cup; now, by way of variety, I will make them pass out of it.

"I will take the two balls, and place them under the middle cup." He really so places one only, palming the other.

"You see that there is nothing either under this (A), or under this (C)." Here the palmed ball is secretly introduced beneath C.

"Now I order one of the balls under the middle cup to pass under one of the outer cups. Let's see if it has left." He takes up and shows it with his right hand; then makes a gesture of replacing it, but really palms it.

"Let us see where it has gone to" (he lefts A with his right hand, and in replacing it secretly introduces the palmed ball under it). "It is not under this one. Then it must be under this." He lifts C. "Yes, here it is. Now I command the other ball in like manner to leave the middle cup, and pass under the other (A). Pass! Here it is, you see, and this one (B) is entirely empty."

Pass V

"So far what I have shown you has been child's play." He drops the right hand carelessly to the *servante* and takes up two more balls, one of which he holds between the fingers, the other in the palm.

"The real difficulty only begins when we begin to work with three balls. Now which of these two balls," (taking up the two balls from the table) "is the largest? This one, I think, so I'll pinch a little piece off it to make a third ball." He goes through the motion of pinching the ball with the fingers of both hands, at the same moment letting fall the ball in the palm to the tips of the fingers of the right hand.

"Yes, this will do. It isn't quite round, but that's easily rectified." He rolls it between the fingers. "That is better."

"Now watch me closely." He places the balls upon the table, with the exception of the fourth, which remains concealed between the fingers. "You see that there is nothing under any of the cups." He raises all three and introduces the fourth ball under the middle one (B). He then picks up one of the balls on the table and apparently transfers it to his left hand, but really palms it.

"I command this ball to pass into the middle cup. It has passed, you see" (raising the cup with the right hand, and in replacing it, introducing the ball now palmed). The operation is repeated in like manner, until three balls have been shown under the cup, the fourth finally remaining palmed in the right hand.

Pass VI

At the conclusion of the last pass the performer has brought three balls under the center cup B, a fourth remaining concealed in his hand.

In lifting B to exhibit the three balls, and in replacing it beside them, he takes the opportunity of introducing beneath it this fourth ball. He next takes one of the three balls thus exposed and places it on the top of this same cup (B), covering it with a second cup (A). Making any appropriate gesture he pleases, he commands the ball to fall through the lower cup onto the table. He then overturns (without separating) the two cups, their mouths being toward the spectators, when the ball which he had secretly introduced will be discovered, and will appear to be that which the spectators have just seen placed on the top of the cup (and which really still remains between the two cups); the two cups are then picked up together, mouth upward, with the left hand, while the right hand takes out that which is now uppermost (B). Both the cups are turned down upon the table, A being placed over the ball just shown. If this is neatly done, the other ball, which has remained in A, will not be discovered, but will as it falls be covered by A, which will now have beneath it two balls.

The performer now places one of the remaining balls on the top of A, covering it with either of the other cups, and again goes through the same process till he has shown first two, and then three balls under the cup, the fourth remaining, at the close of the pass, between the two cups last used.

Pass VII

The last pass was concluded by lifting two cups together to show three balls beneath the undermost. Now, holding the two cups in the left hand, turn them over, mouth upward. Taking with the right hand that which is now uppermost, place it on the table in the ordinary position, still retaining the other, in which, unknown to the spectators, a fourth ball still remains.

"Ladies and gentlemen, you may possibly imagine that there is some trick or sleight-of-hand in what I have shown you, but I am now about to perform an experiment in which that solution is clearly inadmissible. I propose to pass these three balls, one after the other, through the solid table into this empty cup. Please, watch me carefully. I take away one of the balls" (you take in the right hand one of the three on the table), "and hold it beneath the table" (which you do). "My left hand, as you see, is perfectly empty. I have only to say, 'Pass!' " (You palm the ball in the right hand, at the same time giving a gentle tap with one finger against the under surface of the table, and immediately bring up your hand, taking care, of course, to keep its outer side toward the spectators; then gently shaking the cup that you hold in your left hand, you tilt over the cup and the ball rolls out upon the table.) "Here it is, you see.

"Now I will put it back in the cup" (you pick up the ball with your right hand, and drop it into the cup, secretly letting fall with it the palmed ball), "and take another ball." You repeat the process, and show two balls in the cup; then again (each time dropping in the palmed ball), and show three, retaining the fourth ball, still palmed, in your right hand.

Pass VIII

Again place the three cups in a row on the table, secretly introducing under the right-hand cup (C) the ball that remained in the right hand at the close of the last pass, and then openly place the three other balls on the tops of the three cups. Then proceed, "I will take this ball" (that which is on B), "and place it under this same cup (B)." You really palm it.

"I take this other ball" (that which is upon A), "and place it under this cup (A)." You secretly introduce with it the ball you have just palmed.

"I take this last," (that upon C), "and place it under this cup (A); or, wait, I will pass it invisibly to this one (C)"—really palming it. "It has passed, you see." You lift C, and show the ball which is already there; and in again covering the ball with the cup, you secretly introduce that which you last palmed.

You now have in reality two balls under each of the end cups, and none under the center one; but the spectators are persuaded that there is one ball under each cup.

"We now have one ball under each cup. Now I shall command the ball that is under the center cup to pass into either of the end ones at your pleasure. Which shall it be?" Whichever is chosen, suppose C, you raise the cup and show the two balls under it. Then obstensibly replace the two balls under C, but really replace the one only, palming the other. Then raise the middle cup (B), to show that it is empty and in replacing it, introduce the ball you have just palmed under it. "Now I shall next order one of the two balls you have just seen under this cup (C) to go and join the one which is already under this other (A). Pass! Here it is, you see." You raise A to show that there are two balls under it. You also raise C to show that now only one ball is under it, and then leave all three balls exposed on the table.

Pass IX

At the conclusion of the last pass, three balls were left in view, while a fourth, unknown to the audience, was hidden under the middle cup.

Now pick up a ball with the right hand. "I take this ball, and place it under this cup (C)"; (in reality palm it). "I now order it to pass under the middle cup. Presto! Here it is." The middle cup is raised to show that the ball has obeyed the command, and, in again covering the ball, you secretly introduce into it the ball that has just been palmed.

"I take this one" (you pick up another), "and place it under this cup (A)"—here it's palmed as before—"and order it also to pass under the middle cup." You raise the middle cup, and show that there are now two balls under it, and, in again covering them, introduce the ball that has last been palmed.

"I take this last ball, and place it under this cup (C)"—it's palmed—"whence I shall command it to again depart, and join its companions under the middle cup. This time it shall make the journey visibly." Take your wand in the left hand, and with it touch cup C. "Here it is, you see, on the end of my wand. You don't see it? Why, it's visible enough. Look." You pretend to produce the palmed ball from the wand, and exhibit it to the company. "You can all see it *now*." You lay down the wand, and go through the motion of transferring the ball to the left hand, while really palming it in its passage.

"Now then, please watch me closely, and you will see it pass under the cup. One, two, three!" You make the gesture of throwing it through the middle cup, and open the hand to show it empty, immediately turning over the cups to show that there are three balls under the middle and none under the outer ones.

Pass X

For the purpose of this pass, a hat, small straw basket, bowl, or some other container is necessary. It is held in the left hand.

You then place the three balls in a row upon the table, and cover each with one of the cups. It will be remembered that a fourth ball remains palmed in your right hand. Now lifting up the right-hand cup (C), and placing it on the table close beside the ball it lately covered, you at the same time secretly introduce beneath it the palmed ball.

With the right hand you pick up the uncovered ball and go through the motion of dropping it into the container, really palming it the moment at which the hand is concealed inside the container, and at the same moment simulating, by a gentle tap against the inside, the sound the ball would make if actually dropped into the container.

Next, B is lifted in like manner, and the ball just palmed is introduced beneath it; motions are gone through of placing the second ball, which is thereby left exposed, in the container. The same is done with the third cup, at which time you return to the first (which the spectators believe to be now empty, and from which they are astonished to see produced another ball), continuing till you have raised each cup in succession eight or ten times, and, on each occasion of lifting a cup to uncover a ball, introducing beneath it the ball which you had previously palmed. To the eyes of the spectators, who believe that the balls are really dropped into the hat, the effect will be exactly as if new balls, by some mysterious process of reproduction, came under the cups at each time of raising them. When it seems the audience is sufficiently astonished, you remark, "I think we have about enough now; the container is getting rather heavy. Will someone hold a handkerchief to receive the balls?" When the handkerchief is spread out, you carefully turn over the container, and the general astonishment will be intensified at discovering that it contains nothing.

There is, of course, a ball left under each cup, and a fourth palmed in the right hand. This latter will not again be wanted, and you should therefore, while attention is drawn to the container, drop it upon the servante, or in one of your pockets.

Pass XI

While the attention of the spectators is still occupied by the unexpected ending of the last pass, you can prepare for this one by secretly taking with your right hand from the *servante*, and palming (by either the second or third method, the first being only usuable with the small balls), one of the larger balls.

Then address the spectators to the following effect: "Ladies and gentlemen, you see that I have no difficulty in increasing the number of the balls to an unlimited extent. I will now repeat the experiment in another form, and show you that it is equally easy to make them increase in size. You will see that, notwithstanding the number of balls I have just produced from the cups, there are still plenty more to come."

Here you raise C, and show that there is a ball still under it. Replace it on the table at a few inches' distance, and as you do, secretly introduce under it the larger ball which you just palmed. Taking up the small ball in your right hand, say, "To make the experiment still more surprising, I will pass the ball upward through the table into the cup." So saying, place the right hand under the table, dropping as you do so the little ball which you hold on the *servante*, and taking in its place another of the larger balls.

"Pass!" you exclaim, while giving a gentle rap on the under-surface of the table. You bring the hand up again as if empty. Do not touch the first cup, but repeat the operation with the second, B, and again with A; on each occasion of passing the hand under the table, exchanging a small ball for a larger one, and immediately afterward introducing the latter under the cup next in order.

The last time, however, merely drop the small ball on the *servante*, without bringing up any other in exchange. You now have, unknown to the audience, one of the larger or medium-sized balls under each of the cups; and if you were about to end this pass, you would merely lift the cups and show the balls, thus apparently increased in size, underneath. We will assume, however, that you propose to exhibit the following pass (one of the most effective), in which case the necessary preparation must be made in the act of raising the cups; and we shall therefore proceed at once, while the balls still remain covered, to describe.

Pass XII

The last pass having reached the stage just described—a large ball under each cup, but not yet exhibited to the audience, you secretly take in your *left* hand from the *servante* one of the still larger balls. These balls should be soft and elastic, and of such a size that, if pressed lightly into the cup, they require a slight tap of the cup on the table to dislodge them.

Having taken the ball in the left hand, you should hold it at the ends of the fingers behind the table, as near the top as possible consistent with its being out of sight of the spectators. Then saying, "Now, I must ask for your very closest attention," raise C with the right hand, and with the same movement lower it for a moment behind the table and cover with it the ball in the left hand, which will remain in the cup of its own accord. All eyes will go instinctively to the ball on the table, whose increased size is a new phenomenon, and not one in a hundred will, in this first moment of surprise, think of watching the cup, which is naturally supposed to have, for the moment, concluded its share of the trick.

Now replace the cup on the table lightly, so as not to loosen the ball, meanwhile getting ready another ball in the left hand, and repeating the operation with B. With A, make a slight variation in your mode of procedure. Taking a third ball in your left hand, hold it as before, but, as if through carelessness or clumsiness, allow it to be seen for a moment above the edge of the table. When you raise the third cup, move it behind the table as before, and make a feint of introducing the ball the spectators have just seen, but really let it drop on the *servante*, and replace the cup empty.

A murmur from the audience will quickly apprise you that they have, as they imagine, found you out. Looking as innocent as you can, you inquire what the matter is, and are informed that you were seen introducing a ball into the cup. "I beg your pardon," you reply, lifting up, however, not A, which you have just replaced, but C, which is the farthest remote from it. There is really a ball in this cup, but having been pressed in, and fitting tightly, it does not fall. The audience, seeing you raise the wrong cup, are more and more confirmed in their suspicion. "Not that one, the other," they exclaim. So you next raise B, the ball in which also does not fall, for the same reason. "No, no," the audience shout, "the other cup, the end one."

"You are really very obstinate," you reply, "but please satisfy yourselves." Turning over A as you speak, and showing the inside, which is obviously empty, your critics rapidly subside. Meanwhile, drop the left hand to the *servante*, and secretly take from it *two* similar balls. Then, addressing the audience, say, "Surely you don't think that, if I wanted to place a ball under a cup, I would set about it after such a clumsy fashion as this!" As you say this, place your left hand in your left pocket, as if taking a ball from there (as it obviously would not do to give the audience cause to suspect the existence of a secret receptacle in or behind the table), and bring out again the two balls, allowing only one to be seen while keeping the other concealed in the palm.

Bringing the cup over the hand, squeeze in *both* balls as far as you can, when the innermost will remain, but the outermost, not having sufficient space, will drop out again on the table. The audience, not knowing that there are *two* balls, believe the cup, which you now replace on the table, to be empty.

Meanwhile you continue: "Now, when I pass a ball under a cup, you may be sure that I don't let anybody see me do so." As you speak, you take the ball on the table in your right hand and make the movement of transferring it to the left hand, really palming it by the second method, and holding the left hand closed and high, as if containing it, and keeping the eyes fixed thereon; carelessly drop the right hand until the fingertips rest on the table, when you'll be able to let fall the ball upon the *servante*.

"I will now pass this ball under either of the cups you name. Indeed, I will do more; I will cause this ball invisibly to multiply itself into three, one of which shall pass under each of the cups. First, however, let me show you that there is nothing under the cups at present." You raise each in turn: "Nothing here, nothing here, and nothing here!" The balls still adhere to the sides of the cups, which, therefore, appear to be empty, but you replace each with a slight rap on the table, which thereby loosens the ball within it. "Now, then!" you bring your two hands together and gently rub them over each cup in turn, finally parting them and showing that both are empty, and then, lifting the cups, show the three large balls underneath.

Some performers, in lifting each cup with the right hand, introduce a fresh ball, held in the left hand, as already explained. The effect is the same as the multiplying-balls pass already described, with this difference: that on each occasion of uncovering a ball, the ball remains on the table, which thus becomes gradually covered with an ever-increasing number of balls. Some performers conclude by apparently producing from the cups objects much larger than they could naturally contain—large apples, Spanish onions, lemons or limes, small potatoes, tangerines, even small glasses of wine. This is effected in the same manner as the introduction of the large balls just described, except that in this case the object, which cannot really go into the cup, is merely held against its mouth with the third finger of the right hand, and dropped with a slight shake, as if there was a difficulty in getting it out.

There are many other cup-and-ball passes in an infinite variety of combinations. Many performers demonstrate the cups and balls using their jacket pockets or their lap, if seated, in place of the *servante*. If any reader desires to follow the subject further, we would refer him to a number of pamphlets and books available from publishers of magic literature in which this branch of prestidigitation is treated at considerable length. (See page 165).

THE BALL AND VASE

The leading idea of the trick we are about to describe is the magical appearance or disappearance of a ball. It resembles the cups and balls, but with the difference that the main effect is produced here by mechanical means, any sleight-of-hand employed being rather an accessory than the leading feature.

The oldest and simplest of the mechanical appliances for this purpose is that known as the *ball-box*, or the *ball and vase*, consisting of a box two to six inches in height, of the shape shown in the illustration, and containing a ball that just fills it. The box consists of three portions: the lower portion, or box proper; the lid; and an intermediate portion, being a hollow hemisphere colored on top in imitation of the ball, and so fitted with reference to the box and lid that it may be either lifted off with the lid, leaving the box apparently empty, or may be left upon the box when the lid is removed, the effect to the eye being as if the ball had returned to the box.

The ball-box is generally made of plastic, and is scored with concentric circles, which serve to disguise its double opening.

Simply stated, its effect is as follows: The solid ball is first shown in the box, and then openly taken from it, and the box covered with the lid. The ball is then got rid of in one or other of the methods before described, and a pretense is made of passing it invisibly into the box. The lid is removed without the intermediate portion, and the ball appears to have returned to the box. Again the lid is replaced, and again removed; but this time the intermediate portion is removed with it, and the box again appears empty.

The trick in this form is to be found in every toy-shop, and is so well known as to produce scarcely any illusion, but its transparency may be considerably diminished by previously palming (in the right hand) the moveable shell, the convex side being inward, and then handing round the remaining portions and the solid ball for inspection.

When they are returned, you apparently place the ball in the box, but really make a secret exchange, and place the intermediate shell in the box instead. Once again removing the lid, and with it the shell, the ball has disappeared; and as the audience have, as they believe, inspected the whole apparatus, the method of its disappearance is not quite so obvious as in the first case.

STAGE
TRICKS

The Cake in the Hat

This is a trick of a comic character, and in the hands of a spirited performer is sure to be received with applause, particularly by the younger members of the audience. We shall describe the effect and a variation, The Welsh Rabbit, from which the reader can choose elements when performing the trick himself.

The performer brings forward a plate with a number of ingredients (eggs, water, flour, pepper, sugar, lighter fluid—whatever appeals to the humor of the performer) and proposes to bake a cake and to give the audience, without extra charge, a lesson in cooking.

Chopping and mixing the ingredients together in a burlesque fashion, and seasoning with pepper and salt to a degree which no palate short of a salamander's could possibly stand, the conjurer pours the mixture into a hat, sprinkles it with lighter fluid, and tosses in a match, whereupon flames jump out of the hat. When the flames have subsided, the performer reaches into the hat and takes out the result—a perfectly baked cake. The hat is otherwise empty.

As an alternate, once the mixture has been poured into the hat, the performer can hold the hat over a lit candle, moving it backward and forward at a short distance over the flame, and then produce the baked cake, which is then cut up and handed round to the company for their approval.

This is an old favorite trick whose necessary apparatus which may be had from most magic *depôts*, consists of two parts. First is required a round pan four inches in depth with slightly tapered sides. This pan is open at each end, but is divided into two parts by a horizontal partition at about two-thirds of its depth. Second is needed a larger container five and a half inches in depth and so shaped as to fit somewhat tightly over the smaller pan. In the larger end of the small pan is placed a cake, and in this condition it is placed on the *servante* of the table or behind some large object on the table top. The performer takes the hat, and in passing behind the table, tips the cake and pan together into it. The chances are that the pan will fall small end upward (the opposite end being the heaviest); but if not, the performer turns the pan, so as to bring it into that position. Placing the hat mouth upward upon the table, the conjurer announces his intention of making a cake in it. The ingredients are mixed in the larger container and poured from this into the hat, actually into the small pan. As it's being poured, the large container is brought lower and lower, till at last, as if draining the last drop of the mixture, the mouth of the container is lowered right into the hat, and brought down over the smaller pan. On being again raised, it brings away with it the smaller pan and its liquid contents, the cake being left in the hat.

The Welsh Rabbit

This trick is similar to the above as the performer proposes to cook a Welsh rabbit for the audience. Originally it was performed with a special pan and a hat, the mixture of ingredients being exchanged for the rabbit concealed in the false bottom of the pan. Today, the *dove pan* or *duck pan* is used and the cooking done in the pan rather than the hat. Once the ingredients have been mixed and set on fire, the lid of the pan is capped on it. Then, taking off the lid, the performer brings the pan forward to the company, and exhibits, not the expected Welsh rabbit, or "rarebit," but a genuine live rabbit, every vestige of the ingredients having disappeared.

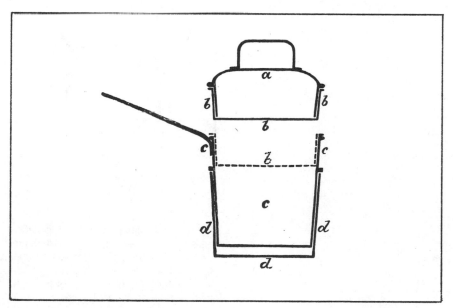

The secret of this trick lies in the construction of the pan, which consists of three parts: the pan itself; a lid with rather deep sides; and an inner pan which fits inside the lid and is inserted into the pan proper when the lid is put on the pan. It is inside this fake pan that the rabbit is concealed prior to production. These pans are available from magic *depôts* in several sizes allowing for the production of a dove, duck, rabbit, birthday cake, or whatever strikes the performer's fancy.

Some fun may be created by selecting beforehand an assistant from the juvenile portion of the audience, and dressing him up with an apron to act as assistant cook.

A guinea-pig or small kitten may be substituted for the rabbit, the performer accounting for the wrong animal being produced by supposing that he must have made some mistake in mixing the ingredients.

The Cut and Restored Rope

This is a trick of such venerable antiquity that we should not have ventured to allude to it were it not that the mode of working we are about to describe, though old in principle, is new in detail, and much superior in neatness to the generally known methods.

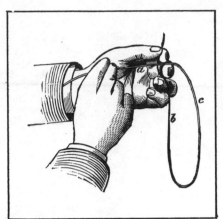 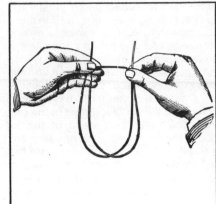

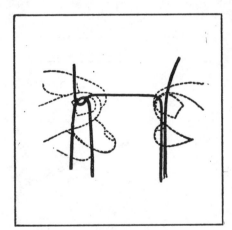 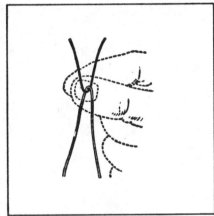

A four-foot length of string or rope and a pair of sissors are needed. The soft, thick rope sold by magic *depôts* is ideal for this effect. After having offered the rope for examination, the performer takes the ends (pointing upward) between the first and second finger and thumb of the left hand, and the first finger and thumb of the right hand, letting the remainder of the rope hang down in a loop between them. Now bringing the right hand close to the left, he draws that portion of the rope which is held in the right hand toward himself between the first and second fingers of the left hand (thus crossing at right angles that end of the rope which is held in the left hand), and continues to pull until half the length of the rope has passed the left hand, at the same time slipping the third finger of the left hand between the two parts of the string, which will be seen in the illustration. The first finger and thumb of the right hand, still retaining the end they already hold, seize the rope at a point just below the left hand, the third finger of the left hand at the same time drawing back the portion of the rope between the left fingers and right hand toward the palm of the left hand. The rope will thus be brought into the position shown in the illustrations, the part now held horizontally between the two hands, which appears to be the middle of the rope, really being only the immediate continuation of the end held in the left hand.

The whole operation of arranging the string in proper position, though tedious to describe, does not take half a second in practice.

The performer next requests some person to cut the string, thus arranged, in half, and this being (apparently) done, he transfers the string altogether to the right hand, keeping the point of junction of the crossed pieces hidden between the finger and thumb. He now gives either end to someone to hold, and, placing his open left hand near to the end thus held, winds the rope rapidly round it, sliding off as he does so the short piece, which, as soon as it is clear of the longer portion, he presses with his thumb between the second and third fingers of the same hand. On again unwinding the rope from the left hand, it is found to be whole as at first.

The principle of the trick being very generally known, you will frequently find someone in the audience who will tell you how it's done, saying that you have merely cut a short piece off the end of the rope.

"Pardon me," you reply, "But that method of performing the trick has long since been exploded. I will at once show you that I do not make use of any such shabby expedient. Of course, if a piece was, as you suggest, cut off the end, the string would be that much shorter after it was cut. Will someone be kind enough to measure it?"

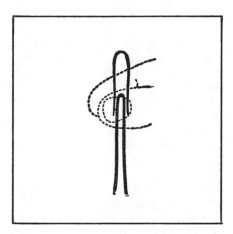

While this is being done, you secretly double-loop the little piece that was cut off on the former occasion, and which has still remained in your right hand. When the rope is returned to you, you double it in half, and allow it to hang down between the first finger and thumb of the right hand, drawing up immediately above it the little loop you have just formed. You now ask someone again to cut the rope, which is apparently done, but which in reality merely divides the little loop. You go through any magical gesticulations you please, and ultimately again conceal the cut ends between the fingers, and produce the rope once more restored. On being measured, it is found to have lost nothing of its length.

The trick in this second form being performed by wholly different means, the repetition will puzzle even those who knew, or believed they knew, the modus operandi in the first case.

My Grandmother's Necklace

The trick that bears this title is also a very old one, but is little known in the improved form we are about to describe.

In its older form it is performed with three wooden balls or beads, each with a hole drilled through it, threaded on a couple of ribbons, whose ends are held securely by two of the spectators. The problem is to detach the beads without breaking the ribbons.

This is effected as follows: The ribbons, which should be from four to six feet in length, are beforehand doubled in the middle, and slightly joined at the bend of each with fine thread of the same color. The ribbons are thus really middle to middle, though to a casual observer they appear to be merely laid side by side.

You come forward with the ribbons, thus prepared, thrown over the left arm (taking care that the point of junction shall be on the side toward your body, and therefore concealed), and with the beads in your hands. These latter, which are merely wooden balls from one to two inches in diameter, drilled through with holes so the ribbons can be threaded through them, you hand for examination. When they are returned, you thread them one after another upon the ribbons, holding the latter in a loop, so that the balls may sink down to the middle, and so cover the point of junction.

You next request two of the company to come forward to hold the ribbons, and hand two ends to the one and two to the other. Each person believes that he holds one end of each ribbon, though, in reality, each has both ends of the same ribbon. You take from each person one of the ends that he holds, and crossing the tapes in a tie, give to each the end that the other previously held.

Holding your hands, a hat, or a basket below the balls, you request each person to pull smartly at the word *three*. The words of command are given; "One, two, *three!*" and the thread breaking, the balls fall into the hands, though the ends of the ribbons still remain in the hands of the holders.

The improvement to which we have alluded consists in the use of *six* balls, three red and three black. The red balls having been first threaded on the ribbons, and the two ends having been crossed and returned to the holders in the manner already described, the black balls are in turn threaded on the ribbons at either end, and you, holding your hands beneath, and addressing one of the persons who hold the ribbons, say, "Which will you have, the red balls or the black?"

Whichever the answer, the result is the same, for the red balls only can come off the ribbons, the black remaining still upon them; but in either case the performer is able to satisfy the choice that has been made. If the red balls have been chosen, you say on their falling, "You chose the red, I think. You see that your commands are obeyed at once." If, on the other hand, the black are chosen, the performer says, "You prefer the black? Then *I* will take the red," which you do accordingly. The audience, having heard the choice freely offered, and not being aware of the subterfuge by which the implied undertaking is fulfilled, naturally believe that you were able to take off or leave on the ribbon whichever group of balls you pleased.

The Bonus Genus

While upon the subject of old-fashioned tricks, we may briefly examine one known by the name of the Bonus Genus, which has puzzled many generations of our forefathers, and, though now rarely exhibited by professional performers, is still a great favorite with juvenile audiences.

The Bonus Genus is a little wooden figure of a man, four to six inches in height, and more or less grotesque in color and design. A little cloak, made small above and full below, like the skirt of a doll's dress, and with no opening except at the bottom and at the top where the head of the figure passes through, completes the apparatus.

There are, however, two points about the doll and his cloak that are unknown to the spectators. First, the head of the doll is movable, a wooden peg forming the neck, and fitting somewhat tightly into a corresponding hole in the body; secondly, there is stitched on the inside of the cloak, just below the opening for the neck, a little patch pocket of such a size as to contain the head easily.

The performer, holding up the figure, and introducing it to the company as his flying messenger, warranted to outstrip the telephone, covers it with the cloak, so that nothing but the head is seen. Grasping the figure under the cloak with the right hand, the performer holds a burlesque conversation with him, finally entrusting him with a message to be immediately delivered to the President of the United States or any other individual at a distance.

The figure does not move. "Well, are you going?" asks the performer. The figure shakes his head from side to side, an effect easily produced by turning the body to and fro under the cloak,. "You won't. Why not? Oh! I see what you mean. I haven't given you your traveling expenses." As these last words are said, the performer grasps the figure and the cloak from the outside round the neck with the left hand, and draws away the right from beneath the cloak, secretly carrying with it the body, and putting his hand in his pocket as though in search of money. Leaving the body of the figure in the pocket, he brings the hand out empty, but as if holding a coin between the finger and thumb. "There," he says, "there is a quarter for you," making the gesture of giving it. "You don't see the coin? Well, I have to give you invisible money, for the weight of an ordinary coin would interfere with the rapidity of your flight. Now, get going, you have nothing to wait for now."

The performer has, meanwhile, again put the right hand under the cloak, and with two fingers holds the little pocket open for the reception of the head. Saying the last words, he gives the head a sharp downward rap with the fingers of the left hand, and lets it fall into the little pocket, the effect being as if the figure had suddenly vanished.

The performer shakes the cloak, and turns it inside out to show that it is empty, taking care always to grasp it by that part which contains the head, while all other portions of the cloak may be shown freely. As the audience are not aware that the figure is divisible, and supposing it to be indivisible and clearly much too large to be concealed in the closed hand, there is nothing to lead them to guess the secret.

If it is desired to make the doll reappear, the head is pushed up again through the opening of the cloak, the hand beneath supporting it by the peg that forms the neck, and it may thus be made to vanish and return any number of times.

With tolerable skill in palming, the little pocket may be dispensed with, the head being simply held in the hand. This mode of working is, in our own opinion, to be preferred, as the cloak may then be handed for examination without giving even the infinitesimal clue that the pocket might suggest.

Some performers, to still further hoodwink the spectators, make use of two figures, the first of which is handed round for inspection, being solid, and being afterward secretly changed for its counterpart with the movable head. Others again use only one figure, which is solid throughout, but provide themselves with a separate head (whose existence is, of course, not suspected by the spectators), and having handed round the solid figure for examination, conceal this, and work with the head only.

The Imp Bottle

This bit of apparatus is more suitable for close-up performances than for stage conjuring. Obtainable at nearly all magic shops, it consists of a little bottle about two inches in height, with a rounded bottom, and so weighted that it will only rest in an upright position. The bottom of the bottle is made of a half bullet, spherical-side downward, so that the center of gravity is at the bottom of the bottle, which compels it to stand upright no matter what position it is placed in.

For you, the conjurer, however, there is a charm by which it is possible to conquer the bottle's obstinate uprightness. For you, and for you only, it will consent to be laid down, and even to stand at an angle of forty-five degrees, though the bottle will again rebel if any other person attempts to make it do the same.

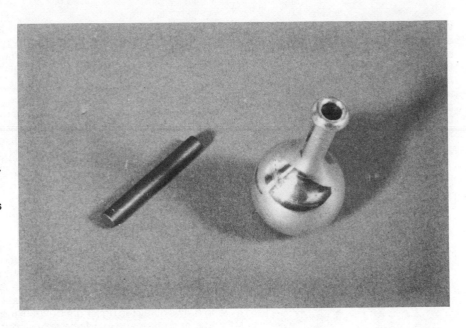

As the center of gravity is at the bottom of the bottle, it will bob back upright no matter how it is placed. You, however, have a little piece of iron, about the size of a cigarette lighter flint, which is easily slipped into the bottle. If this bit of metal is held concealed between the finger and thumb, it is a very easy matter in picking up the bottle to slip it in, and this slight additional weight, neutralizing the effect of the half-bullet base, causes the bottle to lie still in any position.

Having shown that the bottle is obedient to the word of command, you again pick it up with the neck between the first and second fingers and thumb, carelessly turning it bottom upward and thus allowing the bit of metal to slip out again into the palm of your hand, when you are able to again offer the bottle for experiment. Partaking of the nature of a puzzle as well as a conjuring trick, this little toy has amused thousands, and if neatly manipulated may be repeatedly exhibited, even for the same spectators, with little fear of detection.

The Vanishing Gloves

This is a capital trick with which to commence an entertainment; when coming, as it should do, unannounced, and before the performance proper has begun, it has an air of improvisation which greatly enhances its effect, and at once awakens the attention of the audience.

The performer comes forward in evening dress. While saying a few words by way of introduction to his entertainment, he begins to take off his gloves, starting with that on his right hand. As soon as it is fairly off, he takes it in the right hand, waves the hand with a careless gesture, and the glove is gone. He begins to take off the other, walking as he does so behind his table, whereon his wand is laid. The left-hand glove, being removed, is rolled up into a ball, and transferred from the right hand to the left, which is immediately closed. The right hand picks up the wand, and with it touches the left, which being slowly opened, the second glove is found to have also disappeared.

The disappearance of the first glove is effected by means of a length of elastic cord, attached to the back of the jacket or the back middle loop of the trousers, and then passing down the sleeve. This should be of such a length as to allow the glove to be drawn down and put on the hand, you yet to pull it smartly up the sleeve and out of sight when released. It is desirable to have a hem round the wrist of the glove, and to pass the elastic through this like the drawstrings on a bag, as it thereby draws the wrist portion of the glove together, and causes it to offer less hindrance to its passage up the sleeve. Upon taking off the glove, the performer retains it in his hand, and lets it go when he pleases. He must, however, take care to straighten his arm before letting it slip, as otherwise the elastic will remain comparatively slack, and the glove will, instead of disappearing with a flash, dangle ignominiously from the coat-cuff.

The left-hand glove is got rid of by palming. The performer, standing behind his table as already mentioned, rolling the glove between his hands, and quickly twisting the fingers inside, so as to bring it into more manageable form, pretends to place it in his left hand, but really palms it in his right. He now lowers the right hand to pick up his wand, and as the hand reaches the table, drops the glove on the *servante* or in the well. He touches the left hand with the wand, opening the hand and showing that the glove has departed.

Some performers vanish both gloves by means of elastic, one up the right sleeve, the other up the left, but in doing so they offend one of the cardinal precepts of the art, viz., never to perform the same trick twice in succession by the same means. The audience, having seen the manner of the first disappearance, are all on the alert, and are not unlikely on the second occasion to guess the means employed. If, on the other hand, the performer adopts the plan indicated above, the two modes of producing the effect being different, each renders it more difficult to observe the secret of the other.

The Egg-Bag

This is a very old fashioned trick, but, if performed with address, is by no means ineffective. It was exhibited in a modified form by the Japanese jugglers who visited London in the 1870s. I shall first describe it in the simple form adopted by them, and shall then proceed to explain the older and more elaborate version.

The Japanese egg-bag is about eight inches in depth and six in breadth, and made of some opaque material. Its only peculiarity is that one of its sides is double, the material being folded down inward from the mouth of the bag to about two-thirds of its depth, and stitched at the sides, but left open at its lower edge. The effect of this arrangement is to make a sort of pocket, mouth downward, inside the bag. If any small article, such as an egg, be placed within the bag, and the bag is turned upside down, the article will not fall out, but will fall into the pocket, which, in the reversed position of the bag, will be mouth upward. This enables you to conceal the presence of any article in the bag, as you may turn it upside down, and even inside out, without any fear of the article falling; and so long as you take care to keep the "pocket" side of the bag toward yourself, the spectators have not the least reason to suspect that the bag is other than empty.

The uses to which this little bag can be put are various. Among others, it is available either to produce or cause the disappearance of an egg, and may thus, in combination with other apparatus, be made useful for many tricks. I shall describe one of the modes of using it.

The performer comes forward, having in hand the bag, in which is beforehand placed a small egg. The bag is turned upside down and inside out, thus proving, to all appearance, that it is perfectly empty. Taking the bag in the left hand, the conjurer dips his right hand into it, and produces an egg (or rather, *the* egg). This is placed in his jacket pocket or into a container on the table. He again dips his hand in the bag, and produces a second egg, of which is disposed of in the same way, repeating the operation until a dozen or more have been apparently produced. With the reader's present knowledge, it is hardly necessary to suggest to him that the egg, though fairly put in the pocket or container, is palmed out again, rendering it a very simple matter to produce (apparently) another egg from the bag. Although so absurdly simple, the trick is effective, and if neatly performed, produces a complete illusion.

A bag that is the older form of the "egg-bag" is a much larger affair, measuring eighteen to twenty inches in width, and fourteen or fifteen in depth. In its most approved form, one side of the bag is made double, the double side being stitched all around, save for about four inches at one corner of the bottom of the bag. The little opening thus left affords the sole access to the space between the double sides. Between these double sides, and immediately below their upper edge, is stitched a broad band, with a row of a dozen or more little pockets, each capable of holding an egg, end upward. Each pocket covers about two-thirds of the egg, which is prevented from falling out spontaneously by a little piece of elastic around the edge of the pocket, though it will slip out and fall into the space between the double sides on the slightest pressure being applied to it.

The bag is prepared for use by placing an egg in each of the little pockets. The eggs used are either blown shells or imitation eggs of wood or plastic, with one real one for the performer to break as a specimen, and so lead the audience to believe that all are equally genuine.

The bag being brought forward is turned upside down—of course nothing falling from it. The performer then, thrusting arms down to the bottom, and seizing the bag by the corners inside, turns it inside out, taking care, however, to keep the double side toward himself. Having thus conclusively proved its emptiness, he again brings back the bag to its normal condition, and in the act of doing so squeezes with his finger and thumb (through the stuff) the genuine egg out of its pocket. It falls into the space between the double sides, and by gently sloping the bag downward in the direction of the opening at the corner, the conjurer brings the egg into the outer bag, dips one hand into the bag, produces the egg, and breaks it to show its genuineness. Again the bag is turned inside out, shaken and twisted, and again an egg is produced from it as before, the operation being repeated until the supply of eggs is exhausted. Sometimes the proceedings are varied by trampling or jumping on the bag, which is laid for that purpose on the floor, with its lower edge toward the audience. The eggs are thus on the side remote from the spectators, and in trampling on the bag it is very easy for the performer to avoid the particular line in which he knows them to be.

It was formerly the fashion, after bringing out a number of eggs as above described, to finish by producing the hen that was supposed to have laid them. This was done by an adroit exchange of the bag just used for another containing a hen, hung in readiness behind a chair, or some other convenient cover. This latter bag, having no double side or other preparation, might safely be abandoned to the inspection of the most curious spectator. Where it is not intended to produce the bird, it will still be well to have the second bag, so as to be able to make an exchange, and to hand the bag for inspection.

It is a great improvement to the egg-bag to have the lower portion, say the last three inches of its depth, made of net, so that the spectators can at once see each egg as it falls to the bottom of the bag. It is hardly necessary to observe that in this case the inner lining of the double side must terminate where the net begins.

The Drawer Box

This is a very useful piece of apparatus. In appearance it is an ordinary drawer, with an outer box or case of wood painted or simply stained. It is made in various sizes, according to the size of the articles with which it is intended to be used, and which may range from a pack of cards to a live rabbit. Its use is to produce or to cause the disappearance of a given article; the drawer having the faculty of appearing full or empty at pleasure.

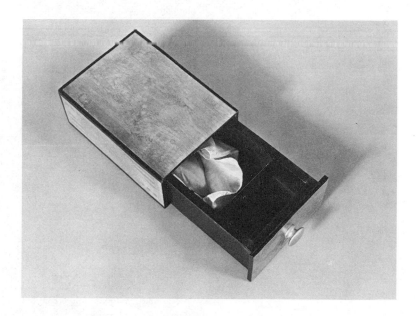

The drawer is in reality double, consisting of two parts, the latter sliding backward and forward freely within the former, which is, in fact, a mere case or shell, open at one end. If any object, suppose an orange, is placed in the inner drawer and both drawers are drawn out together (the inner drawer fitting snugly into the inside of the outer shell drawer) the orange will be visible. But if the inner drawer is held back (through a hole in the bottom of the box large enough to admit a finger) and the outer drawer drawn out, the box will be apparently empty.

Fire and Water from Thin Air

The performer comes forward with a shawl in hand, which is spread out and exhibited on both sides, to show (as is really the fact) that there is no preparation about it. Then the conjurer swings the shawl about, finally throwing it over the left shoulder and arm, the arm being held square before him. The arm now gradually sinks down, and the form of some solid object is seen defined beneath the shawl, which, being removed, reveals a glass bowl brimming with water, and with goldfish swimming about in it. This is repeated a second time.

The bowls used are saucer shaped, measuring eight to twelve inches in diamter, and one and a half to two inches in depth. These bowls are available from some magic suppliers and vary in the way they are kept sealed—a larger rubber cover can be used or the bowl can have the water sealed in it; the goldfish are plastic and also to be had from magic *depôts*. The bowls are concealed before production on the person of the performer. The precise mode of concealment varies. Where three bowls are to be produced, one is generally carried beneath the coat-tails, in a sort of bag open at the sides, suspended from the waist, and the other two in pockets, opening perpendicularly inside the breast of the coat, one on each side.

Sometimes, by way of variation, bowls of fire are produced. These bowls are metal, and have no covers. An inflammable material (a wick moistened with lighter fluid) is attached to the bottom of the bowl and is ignited by a mechanical or electronic spark device that can be triggered with one hand. The bowl is lit under cover of the shawl and the shawl immediately pulled away. Some bowls have a mechanical arrangement for instantly changing, by means of a spring flap, the fire to spring flowers. These "fire bowls" are available from certain magic shops.

The Mysterious Funnel

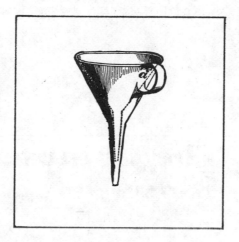

This is a funnel, made double throughout, with a space of one-half inch or so between its inner and outer sides. It is, in fact, a funnel within a funnel, joined at the upper edges. It has an air-hole, generally on the side of the handle. When required for use, the hidden space is filled with water, milk, juice, or some other liquid. The simplest way of doing this is to stop the spout of the funnel with the finger, and then fill it with liquid, which, seeking its own level, will gradually rise to the same height in the outer space as it stands at inside the funnel. This must be done with the air-hole open. When the space between the inside and outside walls of the funnel is filled, the air-hole is stopped with a piece of soft wax or tape, and the liquid remaining inside the funnel allowed to run out. The funnel will now appear perfectly empty, and may be used as a funnel in the ordinary way. Such funnels in metal or plastic are standard props at conjurer's shops.

A young woman is invited to have a glass of water. After she drinks it, the performer asks a young man if he would also like a glass. The reply is pretty sure to be in the affirmative, but the performer pretends to find that there is no more water, and begins to apologize for the supposed disappointment—but as if suddenly thinking of something, says, "However, you won't be disappointed. If I can't supply you in the natural way, I must do so in a supernatural way. Suppose we take back the water this young woman has just drunk. Let me see, where is my magic funnel? Oh, here it is. Let us make sure first it is quite clean." Water is poured through it, after which it's held up to the light in such a manner that the audience can see right through, thus proving to them that it's empty.

"Now, Miss" (addressing the young woman who drank the water), "I am going to take back that glass of water. Be kind enough to bend your elbow. First we must pierce your elbow." So saying, the performer brings forth an awl. This magic awl is another conjurer's prop, looking like an ordinary awl, but with a blade so arranged as to recede into the handle on the slightest pressure, again reappearing (being, in fact, forced forward by a spiral spring in the handle) as soon as the pressure is removed. The performer proceeds therewith to bore a hole in the helper's elbow.

"There, now will you please hold your elbow directly over the top of the funnel," the performer asks, putting aside the awl and holding the funnel under the elbow. "And you" (addressing the second assistant), "perhaps will be kind enough to take this woman's other arm, and work it gently up and down. In fact, we are going to transform her into a pump. Start pumping." The performer holds the glass under the funnel, and as soon as the pretended pumping starts, opens the air-hole with the scratch of his fingernail, at which point water will run into the glass.

129

The Butterfly Trick

This is a trick of Japanese origin. In effect it is as follows: The performer brings forward an ordinary fan, and a couple of bits of tissue-paper, each torn into a fanciful likeness of a butterfly. These, taken in hand, are gently fanned, the motion of the air causing them to rise above his head. Still gently fanning them, the conjurer causes them to hover, now high, now low, now fluttering along the wall, now descending to the table, fluttering here and there at his pleasure.

The point that most strikes an attentive observer is the fact that, whether they fly high or low, the butterflies always keep *together*. Sometimes they may be a couple of feet apart, sometimes only a few inches, but they never exceed the above limit; and the spectator naturally concludes that an extraordinary degree of dexterity must be necessary to enable the performer to keep them from diverging more widely. Here, however, lies the secret of the trick, which is that the so-called butterflies are connected by a piece of very fine silk thread a couple of feet in length, which, when the butterflies are in motion, is absolutely invisible to the spectators. The remainder of the trick is a matter of practice, though it is less difficult than would be imagined by anyone who had never tried it.

Some performers have the thread attached to one of the buttons of the coat. This arrangement will be found greatly to facilitate the working of the trick. Other performers attach the end of the thread to the fan.

The paper for the butterflies is better torn than cut, and should be about two inches square in the shape shown in the illustration.

The Chinese Linking Rings

A number of rings are given for examination, and found to be solid and separate; but at the will of the performer they are linked together in chains of two, three, or more, becoming connected and disconnected in a moment, and being continually offered for examination. Finally, after the rings have become linked in one long chain, a slight shake suffices to disentangle them, and to cause them to fall singly upon the stage.

These rings of brass or steel, 3 to 10 inches in diameter and varying from ¼ to ⅜ inch in thickness, are available at magic *depôts*, and range in quality (the larger-size sets of rings made for professional conjurers have a clear, bell-like ring to them when they hit together).

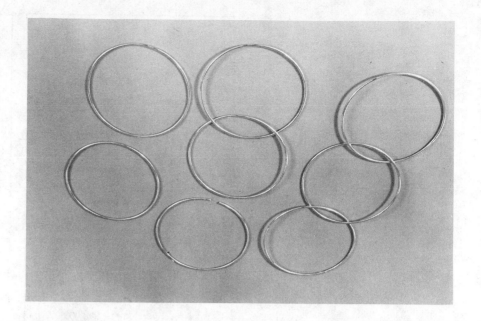

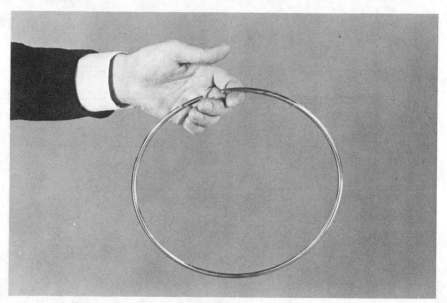

The sets sold at magic shops are usually eight rings in number, and consist of one "key" ring, two single rings, a set of two linked together, and a set of three linked together. The key ring, in which lies the secret of the trick, is simply a ring with a cut or opening in it. For use upon a stage, where the performer is at a considerable distance from his audience, there may be a gap of half an inch to one inch between the ends, but for close-up use, they should just touch each other.

We shall describe the trick as performed with the set of eight rings. We must point out, however, that the manipulation of the rings admits to almost infinite variation, and that the practice of performers differs greatly as to the mode of working them.

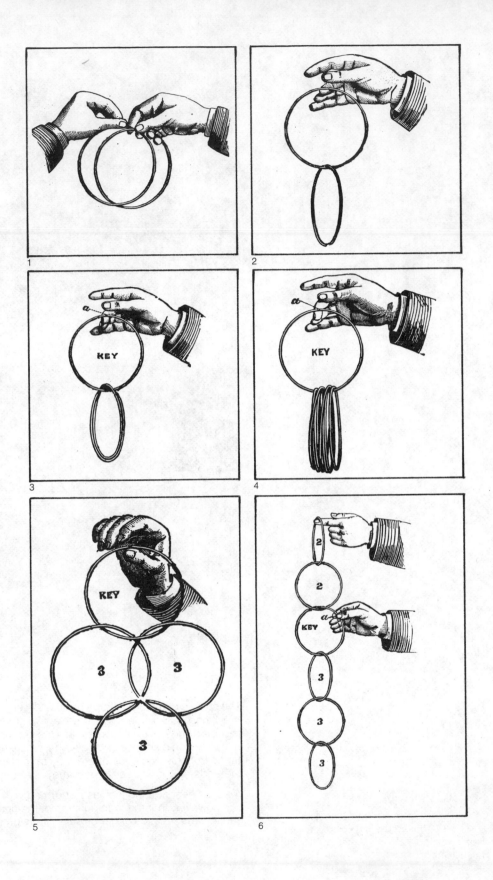

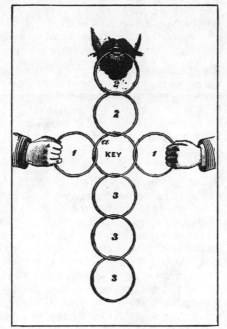

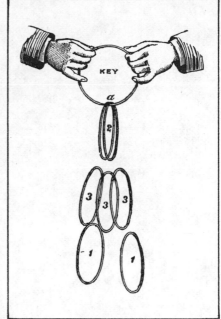

1

2

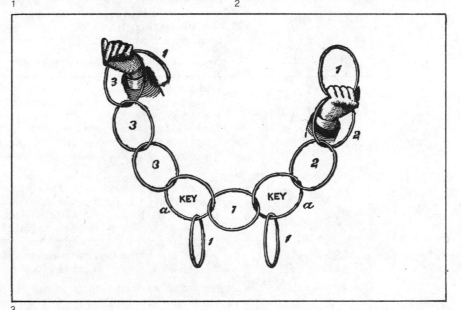

3

The performer comes forward holding the eight rings in the left hand, arranged as follows. First (i.e., innermost) comes the set of three; then the key ring (the opening uppermost in the hand), then the set of two, and lastly the two single rings.

The first of these single rings is handed to a spectator for examination, and then passed when returned to another person; the second ring is carelessly handed to be examined in like manner. This should be done without any appearance of haste, and with an air of being perfectly indifferent as to how many of the rings are examined. The two "singles" having been inspected, the performer requests one of the spectators to take both of them in his right hand, at the same time taking in his own right hand the next two rings, which, it will be remembered, are the set of two, though the audience naturally believe them to be, like the first, separate.

"Now, sir," the professor says, "will you be good enough to link one of the rings you hold into the other." The person addressed looks more or less foolish, and finally gives up.

"You can't?" asks the performer in pretended surprise. "Why, nothing is easier. You only have to do as I do. Look!'' Laying down the rest of the rings, he holds the two as in the illustration, and makes a gentle rubbing motion with the thumb upon the rings, and then lets one of them fall, which naturally drops to the position shown in the illustration. He now hands these two rings for examination.

The spectators seek for some joint or opening, but none is found; and meanwhile the performer transfers the next ring (the key) to the right hand, keeping the opening concealed therein. Now, taking back with the left hand the two single rings, the conjurer immediately transfers one of them to the right hand, pressing it through the opening in the key ring, into which it falls, with exactly the same effect as the apparent joining of the two linked rings a moment before. Again they are separated and again the two rings are joined. The second single ring is now linked onto the key ring in like manner so that the two single rings hang from the key ring.

The performer remarks, ''We now have three joined together. Here are three more, as you can see (shaking those in the left hand) all solid and separate, and yet at my will they will join like the others.'' While making a rubbing motion with the hand as before, two of the three are dropped, one by one, from the hand, when they will appear as a chain of three. These are handed for examination, while the set of two is taken back, and linked one after the other onto the key ring, to which four rings are now attached. Again taking back the set of three, the professor links these also one by one into the key ring, which thus has seven rings hanging from it. Using both hands, but always keeping the opening of the key ring concealed behind the fingers, he now takes off these seven rings, commencing with the single ones, and again offers them for examination; then takes off the set of two. Last of all, the set of three is unlinked, and then, held at length in the performer's left hand, the upper one is joined to the key ring, thus making a set of four, of which the key ring is uppermost. Next the lowermost of the four is taken, and linked into the key ring, bringing the four rings into a diamond shape, as shown in the illustration.

Again unlinking the lower ring, the performer takes up the set of two, and connects them with the key ring, holding them above it, and thus making a chain of six, the key ring being third from the top. (See illustration). Putting the upper ring over his head (if the diameter of the ring permits) or clipping it between his chin and chest, he links the two single rings into the key ring on either side, making the figure of a cross. As the hands are now occupied in holding the single rings forming the arms of the cross he can no longer keep the opening of the key ring concealed by his hand, but it is extremely unlikely that among so many rings, so slight a mark in one of them will attract notice.

Regaining possession of the key ring, the professor links all one by one onto it, so as to again bring them to the condition where all seven rings hang from the key ring. Then, holding the key ring with both hands, and with the opening doward, about a couple of feet from the floor, he shakes the rings violently, at the same time gently straining open the key ring, when the seven rings will all in succession drop through the slit, and scatter themselves about the floor, the general impression being that they all fall separate, though the grouped sets, of course, remain still united.

It is not an uncommon thing to see a a performer commit the mistake of handing all the rings, except the key ring, to be examined in the first instance—the key ring being hidden under the coat, and being added to the set in returning to the table. The spectators are thus needlessly made acquainted with the fact that certain of the rings are already linked together, and this once admitted, the trick loses nine-tenths of its effect.

In manipulating the rings the performer should study neatness and lightness rather than speed. The effect should be as though the rings *melted* into and out of one another, and the smallest appearance of force or exertion should be avoided. It is a very good effect, in disengaging the rings one from another, to hold them together for a moment or two after they are actually disconnected, and then holding them parallel to each other, to draw them very slowly apart. The precise moment of their separation is thus left uncertain, the illusion being thereby materially heightened. A single ring may in this way be drawn along a chain of three or four, the effect being as if the disengaged ring passed *through* the whole length of the chain.

The Passe-Passe Bottle and Glass

The performer brings forward a bottle and a small tumbler, which are placed side by side upon the table. A couple of metal covers, or a size to just go over the bottle, are produced, one being placed over the bottle, and the other over the glass. Now the two articles are commanded to change places, and when the covers are removed, the glass and bottle are found to be transposed. Again they are covered, and again they change places; this is repeated as often as the conjurer pleases, who occasionally pours out wine or other liquid, to show that the bottle is a genuine one, and not a mere make-believe.

The reader will already have anticipated that there are in reality two bottles and two glasses. The bottles are of metal, but with the bottom only about a couple of inches below the neck, leaving an open space beneath for the reception of the glass. Each bottle has near the bottom, on the side kept away from the audience, an oval opening or finger-hole, measuring about an inch and a half by one inch. When it is desired to lift the glass with the bottle, the middle finger is made to press on the glass through this opening, thereby lifting both together with perfect safety. The outer cover just fits easily over the bottles, and if lifted lightly leaves the bottle on the table, but if grasped at the top, with the finger inserted into the top and into the neck of the bottle, allows the bottle to be carried away.

The method of working the trick will now be readily understood. The bottle that is brought forward has a second glass concealed within, which is kept in position while the bottle is brought in by the pressure of the finger. The cover that is placed over this bottle is empty. The other cover, which is placed over the glass, contains the second bottle, which, being hollow below, enables the performer to rattle the wand within it, and thus (apparently) prove the cover empty. Having covered the glass and bottle, the performer raises the cover of the first, leaving the glass concealed by the second bottle, but lifts the other carrying the bottle with it, revealing the glass which has hitherto been concealed within it. By reversing the process, the bottle and glass are again made to appear, each under its original cover. Where it is desired to pour wine from either bottle, the performer takes care, in lifting it, to press the glass through the finger-hole, and thus lifts both together. For obvious reasons the glass into which the wine is poured should be a third glass, and not either of the two which play the principal part in the trick.

Top Hat Tricks

The tall silk hat has been the object of much well-merited abuse. It is ugly, inconvenient, and expensive. As a set-off to so many vices, it has one virtue. No other head-gear that could be devised would offer such facilities to the conjurer, who should devoutly pray that it may never go out of fashion. Even in the hands of a very moderate performer, the familiar "chimney-pot" becomes a storehouse of surprises.

To appreciate its full capacity was to have witnessed the performance of Hartz, in whose hands the old and hackneyed trick of the Inexhaustible Hat became something approaching a miracle. Standing on an all but naked stage, Hartz continued for more than twenty minutes to produce from a borrowed hat, in rapid succession, an endless variety of articles. These included not only an avalanche of playing cards and a quantity of soft goods such as silk handkerchiefs and ribbons, but lighted lanterns of metal and glass, cigar-boxes, and soda-water tumblers of various colors, silver goblets, champagne bottles, a large bird-cage with a living bird, and last but not least, a human skull—the latter object rising spontaneously from the hat, placed on a small glass table at a distance from the performer.

I do not propose to give instructions for imitating Hartz's performance, for it would be practically impossible to do so. I could give the dry bones of the trick, but unless by some mystic spell I could put Hartz himself inside the reader, he would be as far as ever from being able to work it.

The general principles of the trick are familiar to the merest tyro in conjuring. These are supplemented in some small degree by ingenious mechanical contrivances, but the main secret lies in the artistic way in which each word and gesture of the performer has been studied and combined, so that the production of each successive article or group of articles facilitates and covers the introduction of the next.

Hartz possessed in an extraordinary degree the faculty which has been said to be tantamount to genuis, namely, "an unlimited capacity for taking pains." His "hat trick" was the culmination of years of gradual experimentation. Within my own remembrance I saw it further and further developed, and I knew its author devoted days and weeks of labor (carried often into the small hours of the morning) to work out some new idea or hypothetical improvement casually suggested in conversation. It is of such material that the true artist is made, and the devotion of Hartz to his life-work was repaid by the attainment of a degree of finish perhaps never exceeded. There are many conjurers who have a more brilliant stage manner, and from that fact enjoy greater popularity with the groundlings, but for combined ingenuity of contrivance and neatness of manipulation, Hartz, so far as my observation extends, was unrivaled.

Eggs from Handkerchief

The conjurer displays a handkerchief, folds it in half, and reaches inside to produce one egg after another, each egg being put in a container after it is produced, and the handkerchief shown empty between each production.

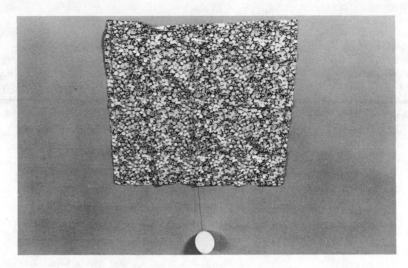

A large square handkerchief is best for this trick. In the center of one side (which we shall call A) a piece of fine black silk thread is attached. The length of the thread is just one-half that of the side, and fixed to its free end is a blown or plastic egg. The length of the thread and the resultant position of the egg is that if the handkerchief is held taut by the two corners of A, the egg will hang down just below its center or it may at pleasure be concealed in the hand that holds the one or the other corner. Things are in this latter condition when the handerkchief is first shown to the audience. The egg is palmed in the right hand, which holds one corner of A, while the left hand holds the other. One side of the handkerchief having been shown, the hands are crossed so as to show the opposite side. This done, and the hands brought back to their original position, the egg is released from the palm, when it naturally falls behind the handkerchief. A slight "drop" of the hands at the same moment will prevent its swinging too far, and showing itself beyond the opposite edge.

Having shown the handkerchief thus apparently empty, tell the audience that you are going to try to get a few eggs from it, and that you will pour them direct from the handkerchief into a hat or other container that stands on the table.

Transferring the corner held by the right hand to your mouth, and holding it with your teeth, slide the right hand along the handkerchief to the center of A, and fold the handkerchief vertically down the center. The suspended egg, of course, hangs in the fold. Then transfer the right hand to the joined corners of A, and the left hand to the opposite joined corners, and tilt the sort of bag thus made into a horizontal position above the container. Sloping it a little farther so that the corners in the left hand are highest, the egg rolls out of the fold on the side A, and falls into the container, the length of the thread allowing it ample fall.

Now comes a movement not very easy to explain, but which it is essential that the reader should understand, as it is in truth the backbone of the trick.

The left hand releases the corners it holds and travels toward the corners of A. It seizes the outermost of the corners and the two hands once more draw A taut. The effect of this movement is to spread the handkerchief with its broad side to the spectators, and at the same time to lift the suspended egg from the container (which is for the moment screened by the handkerchief), to its old position in the rear. Again the handkerchief is folded and again the egg produced; and this may be repeated as often as the performer pleases, attention being specially called to the fact that the hands remain all the while empty, and that they approach nothing from which the eggs could possibly be obtained.

When all is over, the thread may be broken, and the handkerchief carelessly handed for inspection.

The Bewitched Fan

A fan is produced. You open and fan yourself with it. It appears to be a perfectly ordinary fan. You close it, and hand it to a lady, inviting her to make use of it. She opens it accordingly, but a strange thing happens. It falls apart in her hands, and assumes a dislocated appearance, each section of the fan falling loose from the others. You take it from her, breathe upon it, and lo! it is whole again.

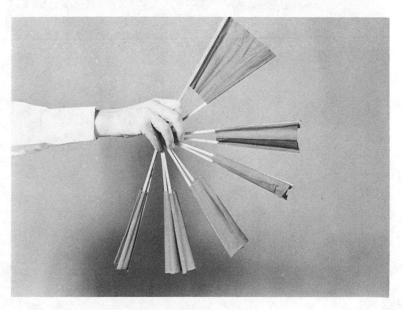

The secret lies in the construction of the fan, which is so made that by a peculiarity of construction (readily intelligible on inspection but practically impossible to explain in writing), the fan when opened from *left to right* in the ordinary manner assumes the customary appearance of a respectable fan, but when opened from *right to left* parts in the way that has been described.

By giving the fan a turn-over in the hand, before opening it, the needful "change" is spontaneously effected, and the opening may always be in the same direction. These fans are available at any conjuring shop.

A Shower of Flowers

One of the prettiest illusions of the eminent magician Buatier de Kolta consists in the production from a large sheet of paper, freely shown on both sides and then rolled into a cone, of a quantity of paper flowers of all sizes and colors. Each flower is widely expanded, and of considerable size, and enough are produced from the empty sheet of paper to fill a large basket.

The main secret of the trick lies in the construction of the flowers, which is extremely ingenious.

They are made as follows: The first step is to cut out a number of pieces of green tissue paper (not too thin) of the shape shown in *a* in the illustration. The extreme length of each may be 4½ inches, and its greatest width 1¾ inches. Next should be cut out double the number of mixed colors—red, yellow, blue, pink, mauve, and white. These should be of the shape shown at *b* in the same illustration. They may be of the same width as the green leaves, but are only 1¾ inches in length.

The next step is to provide the necessary "springs" to make the flowers expand. These are made by cutting a sheet of hardened brass or sheet steel the thickness of brown paper into strips 2 inches long and a little less than ¼ inch wide; each strip must then again be cut down its center to within ⅜ inch of the opposite end, as *c*, and the two portions then bent apart as *d* in the same illustration—when it will be found that however often they may be closed, they will when released revert to the expanded position. Taking one of the green papers, fold it across the middle, and placing one of the steel springs between, secure it with strong paste to the center of the leaf, pasting a strip of the same paper, ⅜-inch wide, over it to conceal the spring. Lay these aside to dry, and meanwhile taking pairs of the smallest pieces of paper (each pair being of the same color), paste two of their edges together, and let them dry in like manner. This done, take one of these and, inserting it in the opening of one of the green papers, paste the free edges to the corresponding edges of this latter. The effect will now be, as shown in the illustration of the completed flowers, a sort of compromise between a sweet-pea and a butterfly. By pressing the sides together, the flower may be made perfectly flat, though it will instantly expand again as soon as the pressure is removed.

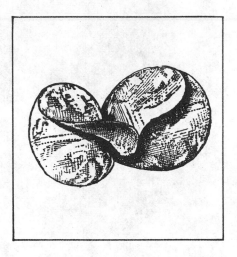

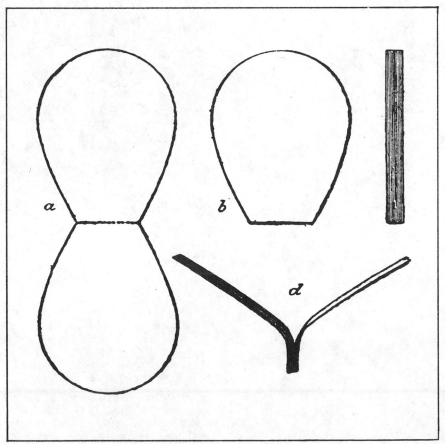

I have explained the mode of construction of the flowers for the better elucidation of the trick, but I should strongly recommend the reader *not* to attempt to make them for himself, but to procure them from one of the recognized conjuring *depôts,* some of which have improved considerably on the original pattern. The trick, well done, has such a pretty effect that it is worthy of the slight extra expense needed to produce a really finished article.

Having provided yourself with the flowers, of which a couple of hundred will be required, you should divide this quantity into (say) three "loads." Taking the flowers one by one between finger and thumb, press each flat on its predecessor, and when you have thus dealt with a sufficient quantity, secure them with an elastic band, or better still, between two slips of stiffish cardboard, 3 by 2 inches, with an elastic band passed round these in the direction of their greater length. If the ends of the cardboard are pressed they naturally separate in the middle, and at once free the flowers. The getting off of a couple of elastic bands from the flowers themselves takes longer, and even seconds are of importance to the effect of a conjuring trick.

Having thus prepared your "loads" (which will comprise about seventy flowers in each), and disposed them about your person so as to be instantly get-at-able when needed, you are ready to show the trick. Your only further requirements will be a full-sized sheet of stiffish paper and a pin, which you may stick into your lapel until needed.

Advancing to the company, and showing both sides of the sheet of paper (and incidentally that your hands are otherwise empty), you twist the sheet into a conical container, and fasten it with the pin. Next comes the introduction of the load. Some performers do this in the act of making the cone, getting the load into the hand (say, from the jacket pocket, or from under the edge of the jacket, or the waistband) a moment earlier, and forming the cone round the hand that contains it—then dropping it to the bottom. Another plan is to introduce the load under the pretext of showing that you have nothing that you can possibly introduce. To this end you smile a self-satisfied sort of smile into the cone just formed, and begin to shake it a little, as though to simulate the production of the expected mystery, meanwhile the unoccupied hand, which we will suppose to be the left, gets possession of and palms the load. Suddenly you pause, and look about you. "Pardon me, I think I heard someone say that I have something already in the paper. Please satisfy yourselves that I have nothing of the kind." (You show the interior of the cone.) "Neither have I anything in my hands." In order to show the right hand free you transfer the cone to the left, grasping it with the fingers inside, and thereby introducing the load. Having shown the right hand empty, you again take the cone in the right hand, grasping it by its smaller end, and show the left hand in like manner. The load meanwhile gently slides down to the bottom, and the trick is practically done.

The right hand grasps the cone outside the load, and prevents its too-rapid development. The left hand dips into the cone, and under pretense of taking out the first one or two flowers, frees the remainder, and arranges them for subsequent production. As you diminish the pressure of the encircling hand, the flowers naturally expand, and seem to well up spontaneously to the mouth of the cone, whence they are shaken into any convenient receptacle. The production should not be too rapid, as the effect of quantity is enhanced by a discreet amount of deliberation.

The production of a second load is a very easy matter, for the general attraction being drawn to the gush of flowers from the mouth of the cone enables the performer to have ample opportunity to palm and introduce a further supply.

For the third load, however, the method of production should be somewhat varied. Getting the load into the palm of your left hand, and shaking out the last remaining flowers from the cone, you should remove the pin and open out the paper. Then spreading the paper over your right hand, bring the left hand violently down on its center, as if merely crushing the paper, and forthwith twist it into a crumpled ball, the load just introduced being of course in the center. Crush and knock about the ball of paper thus produced, as though merely to carry still greater conviction to the minds of the audience that it contains nothing. When you have maltreated it sufficiently, again unfold the paper with due precaution, and again a gush of flowers will come welling from it—this last effect being, to most spectators, the most surprising of any.

ILLUSIONS

The present chapter will be devoted to such tricks as by reason of the cumbrousness or costliness of the apparatus required for them are, as a rule, exhibited only upon the public stage. The stage performer may, if he pleases, avail himself of the aid of mechanical apparatus, electrical appliances, etc., which enable him to execute a class of tricks beyond the scope of an ordinary amateur performance.

The Sphinx

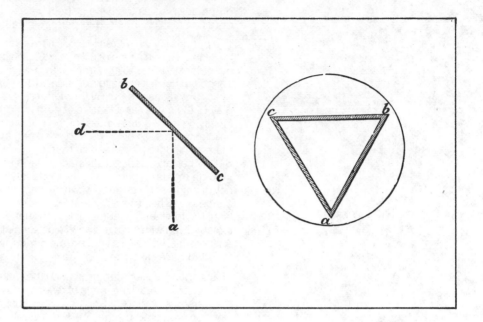

Few tricks have caused so great a sensation as this now well known illusion, which was first introduced to the London public by the late Colonel Stodare in 1865. We cannot better preface the explanation of the trick than by quoting a portion of the *Times* notice on the subject, of October 19, 1865:

> . . . Most intricate is the problem proposed by Colonel Stodare, when, in addition to his admirable feats of ventriloquism and legerdemain, he presents to his patrons a novel illusion called the "Sphinx." Placing upon an uncovered table a chest similar in size to the cases commonly occupied by stuffed dogs or foxes, he removes the side facing the spectators, and reveals a head attired after the fashion of an Egyptian Sphinx. To avoid the suspicion of ventriloquism, he retires to a distance from the figure supposed to be too great for the practice of that art, taking his position on the borderline of the stalls and the area, while the chest is on the stage. Thus stationed, he calls upon the Sphinx to open its eyes, which it does—to smile, which it does also, though the habitual expression of its countenance is most melancholy, and to make a speech, which it does also, this being the miraculous part of the exhibition. Not only with perspicuity, but with something like eloquence, does it utter some twenty lines of verse; and while its countenance is animated and expressive, the movement of the lips, in which there is nothing mechanical, exactly corresponds to the sounds articulated.
>
> This is certainly one of the most extraordinary illusions ever presented to the public. That the speech is spoken by a human voice there is no doubt—but how is the head to be contrived which, being detached from anything like a body, confined in a case, which it completely fills, and placed on a bare-legged table, will accompany a speech, that apparently proceeds from its lips, with a strictly appropriate movement of the mouth, and a play of the countenance that is the reverse of mechanical? Eels, as we all know, can wriggle about after they have been chopped into half-a-dozen pieces; but a head that, like that of the Physician Douban, in the Arabian tales, pursues its eloquence after it has been severed from its body, scarcely comes within the reach of possibilities; unless, indeed, the old-fashioned assertion that "King Charles walked and talked half-an-hour after his head was cut off," is to be received, not as an illustration of defective punctuation, but as a positive historical statement. . . ."

For the benefit of those who have never seen this illusion presented upon the stage, we will describe its effect a little more minutely. The Sphinx is always made a separate portion of the entertainment, as it is necessary to lower the curtain for a few moments before and after its appearance, in order to arrange and remove the necessary preparations. The curtain rises, and reveals a round or oval table, supported upon three slender legs, and utterly devoid of drapery. This stands in a curtained recess ten or twelve feet square, open on the side toward the audience. The performer comes forward bearing a cloth-covered box, fifteen to twenty inches square, and places it upon the table. The box is then unlocked, and the front of it drops down so as to give a perfect view of the interior, in which is seen a head of Egyptian fashion, colored in perfect imitation of life.

The performer now retires to a position in the very midst of the audience and, raising the wand, says in a tone of command, "Sphinx, awake!" The Sphinx slowly opens its eyes, looking first to the front with a strong gaze; then, as if gradually gaining consciousness, it looks to one side and the other, the head moving slightly with the eyes. Questions are put by the performer to the head, and are answered by it, the play of the mouth and features being in perfect harmony with the sounds uttered. Finally, in answer to a query of the operator, the Sphinx declaims a neatly turned oracle in verse. Should the audience call for an encore, the performer addresses them to the following or similar effect: "Ladies and gentlemen, I am glad that the Sphinx has afforded you satisfaction, and I should be only too pleased to be able to indulge the desire which you kindly testify of seeing it again. Unfortunately, this is not possible. The charm by which I am able, as you have seen, to revivify for a space the ashes of an ancient Egyptian who lived and died some centuries ago, lasts but for fifteen minutes. That time has now expired, and the head that has astonished you with its mysterious eloquence has again returned to its original dust." As those last words are spoken, the performer again opens the box, and the head is found to have disappeared, leaving in its place a handful of ashes.

This singular illusion depends upon the well-known principle, common to optics as to mechanics, that "the angle of reflection is equal to the angle of incidence." To wit: If a person standing at point a in the illustration looks into a mirror placed in the position indicated by the line b c, he will see reflected not himself but whatever object may be placed at the point d. By an ingenious application of this principle a mirror may be used to conceal a given object behind it, while at the same time an image reflected in the glass may be made to represent what would presumably be seen if no glass were there, and thus prevent the presence of the mirror from being suspected. This is the secret of the Sphinx. The table, as already mentioned, has three legs, one in front and one at each side. Between these legs the spectator sees apparently the curtains at the back of the recess, but really a reflection of the curtains at the sides. The space between the middle leg and that on either side is occupied by mirrors (see the illustration which represents a ground plan of the arrangement), extending from a to b to c. The glass extends quite down to the floor, which is covered with cloth of the same material and color as the surrounding curtains. The spectators, therefore, looking toward the table, see above it the curtains at the back, and below it the reflection of the curtains at the sides; which, however, if the relative angles are properly arranged, appears to be simply the continuation or lower portion of the curtains at the back. The illusion is perfect, and the spectators, from the position assigned to them, cannot possibly discover, by the evidence of their senses, that they are looking at any other than an ordinary bare-legged table, with the background visible in the usual way.

The rest is a very simple matter. The person who is to represent the Sphinx is beforehand placed, duly attired, underneath the table. There is a trap in the table through which the head can be passed at the proper moment. This trap is a round piece of wood, covered to match the surface of the table, and working on a hinge on the side nearest to the audience. It has no spring, but is kept closed by means of a hook on the opposite side, and when released hangs down perpendicularly. It must be long enough to allow passage of the somewhat elaborate headpiece of the Sphinx, and would therefore leave an open space visible round the neck. This difficulty is met by the expedient of having a wooden collar, whose upper surface is a facsimile in size and pattern of the trap, fastened round the neck of the representative of the Sphinx. When the head is lifted up through the trap, this collar exactly fills the opening, and thus shows no break in the surface of the table. The box is bottomless, and when brought forward by the performer is empty. A little caution has to be observed in placing it upon the table, for, if the performer were to approach the table *from the side*, his legs would be reflected in the glass, and would thereby betray the secret. He must therefore make his appearance from some quarter *outside* of the curtained recess, and advance to a position well in front of and at some little distance from the table, when, by moving in a straight line from the audience toward the middle leg a, he prevents this inconvenient reflection. The acts of placing the box upon the table and unlocking it allow time for the representative of the Sphinx to get his head into position within it. This done, the box is opened, and the rest depends on the dramatic talents of performer and assistant. The performance being concluded, the box is again locked, and the head withdrawn, a handful of ashes being introduced in its stead.

The angle at which the two mirrors should be set cannot be determined absolutely, but will vary according to the distance and position of the surrounding drapery.

Some performers use a shawl or a screen of cardboard in place of the box, but we doubt whether any method is more effective than that above described.

The ghastly illusion of the so-called Decapitated Head, which drew crowds to the Polytechnic some few years since, was merely the Sphinx in a less pleasant form.

The Cabinet of Proteus

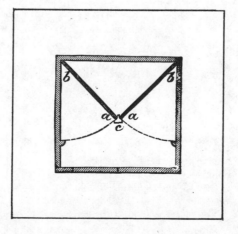

This is another adaptation of the principle on which the Sphinx illusion is founded. It is the joint invention of Messrs. Pepper and Tobin, by whom it was patented in 1865. The first steps toward a patent for the Sphinx were also taken in the same year, but the latter invention never proceeded beyond provisional protection.

The Cabinet of Proteus is a wooden closet, seven to eight feet in height by four or five feet square, supported on short legs, so as to exclude the idea of any communication with the floor. It has folding doors, and an upright pillar extends from top to bottom of the interior, at about the center of the cabinet. At the top of this pillar, in front, is fixed a lamp, so that the whole of the interior is brightly illuminated.

The cabinet may be used in various ways. One of the most striking is as follows: The folding doors are opened, disclosing the interior perfectly empty. The exhibitor directs the assistant to walk into the cabinet. This is done, and the doors are closed. Meanwhile, a couple of spectators, selected by the audience, are invited to stand behind or beside the cabinet, and see that no one gets in or out by any secret openings. Nowithstanding these precautions, when the doors are again opened, the assistant is found to have vanished, and another person, different in dress, stature, and complexion is found in the original's place. This person steps forth, makes a bow, and retires. Again the cabinet, now empty, is closed, and after an interval of a few moments, again opened. This time a human skeleton is found to occupy the vacant space. This ghastly object having been removed, and the door having been once more closed and opened, another person, say a lady, appears. This woman having retired, the doors are again closed; and when they are again opened, the person who first entered is once more found within. A committee from the audience is now invited to examine the cabinet within and without, but all their scrutiny cannot detect any hidden space sufficient to conceal even a mouse.

An examination of the illustration representing a ground plan of the cabinet will make plain the seeming mystery. A moveable flap *a b*, working on hinges at *b*, extends from top to bottom of each side, resting when thrown open against the post *c* in the middle, and thus enclosing a triangular space at the back of the cabinet. The outer surfaces of these flaps (i.e., the surfaces exposed when they are folded back against the sides of the cabinet) are, like the rest of the interior, covered with wall paper, of a crimson or other dark color. The opposite sides of the flaps are mirrors, and when the flaps are folded back against the posts, they reflect the surfaces against which they previously rested, and which are covered with paper of the same pattern as the rest.

The effect to the eye of the spectator is that of a perfectly empty chamber, though, as we have seen, there is in reality an enclosed triangular space behind the post. This is capable of containing two or three persons, and here it is that the persons and things intended to appear in succession are concealed. The assistant, entering in sight of the audience, changes places, as soon as the door is closed, with one of the other persons. This second person having retired, and the door being again closed, those who are still within place the skeleton in position in front of the post, and again retire to their hiding-place. When all the rest have appeared, the person who first entered presses the flaps against the sides of the cabinet, against which they are retained by a spring lock on each side, and the public may then safely be admitted, as their closest inspection cannot possibly discover the secret.

The Aërial Suspension

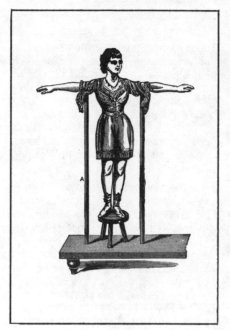 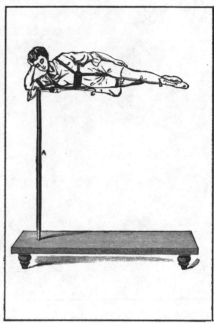

This is a very old trick, performed originally by the Indian jugglers, who kept the modus operandi a profound secret. The ingenuity, however, of Robert-Houdin penetrated the mystery, and in 1849 he made it a special feature of his *séances fantastiques*. At that time the public mind was much interested in the anaesthetic qualities of ether, which had then recently been discovered. Robert-Houdin manipulated this fact into a valuable advertisement. He gave out that he had discovered in that popular anaesthetic a still more marvelous property, viz., that when inhaled under certain conditions, it neutralized the attraction of gravitation in the person inhaling it, who became, for the time being, light as air. In proof of this, he brought forward his youngest son, then a child of ten or thereabouts, and after having made him smell at a small phial, really empty, but supposed to contain ether, caused him to recline in mid-air, with no other support than that afforded by, to all appearance, an ordinary walking-stick, placed in a vertical position under his right elbow. (It is characteristic of Robert-Houdin's minute attention to the *mise en scène* of a trick that while his son sniffed at the empty bottle, his assistant, behind the scenes, poured genuine ether upon a hot shovel, so that the fumes, reaching the nostrils of the audience, might prove, indirectly but convincingly, that ether was really employed.)

After the retirement of Robert-Houdin from the stage, the trick fell comparatively out of notice, till it was revived in a new form by the Fakir of Oolu (Professor Sylvester) in England, and contemporaneously by De Vere on the Continent. A full-grown young woman was in this case the subject of the illusion, and was made, while still suspended in air, to assume various costumes and characters. The illusion, in this new form, took the fancy of the public, and brought forth a host of imitators; but few have presented it with the same completeness as the two performers named. For a time it produced quite a marked sensation, equal crowds thronging to see Sylvester in London, and De Vere in Paris, St. Petersburg, Brussels, Pesth, Dresden, Strasbourg, and other Continental cities. Recent mechanical improvements, to which the last-named Professor has materially contributed, have greatly heightened the effect of the trick—the lady being made to rise spontaneously from the perpendicular to the horizontal position, and to continue to float in the air after her last ostensible support has been removed.

Apart from these special mysteries, which we are not at liberty to reveal, the trick is as follows: The performer brings forward the girl or boy who is to be the subject of the illusion, and who is dressed in some fancy costume. A low bench or table, say five feet in length by two in width, and on legs about six inches in height, is brought forward, and shown to be wholly disconnected from the floor or stage. On this is placed a small stool, which the subject of the experiment (whom, in the present instance, we will suppose to be a young woman) mounts. She extends her arms, and under each is placed a stout rod or pole of appropriate length (broomsticks and, in the twentieth century, microphone stands, are also employed as the upright).

The performer makes pretended mesmeric passes over her, and in a minute or two her head is seen to droop, and after a few more passes her eyes close, and she is, to all external appearance, in a mesmeric sleep. The operator now takes the stool from under her feet, when she hangs suspended between two rods. Again a few more passes, and the operator removes the rod that supports the left arm, and gently mesmerizes the arm down to the side. Still the woman hangs motionless, with no other support than the single upright rod on which her right arm rests. The operator now bends her right arm so as to support her head and lifts her gently to an angle of forty-five degrees to the upright rod and finally raises her to a horizontal position.

An inspection of the diagrms will already have furnished the clue to the mystery. Of the two upright rods, one (that placed under the left arm) is wholly without preparation, and may be freely handed for examination. The other is either of iron throughout (this was the case with the pretended walking-stick used by Robert-Houdin) or of well-seasoned wood with a metal core, and capable of bearing a very heavy weight. The lower end of this sinks into a socket in the low board or platform already mentioned, and thus becomes, for the time being, a fixture. In the upper end is hollowed out a small space, about an inch in depth. The subject of the experiment wears, underneath her costume, a sort of metal corset, or framework. At the point in the framework under the woman's arm is an iron plug which just fits into the cavity in the top of the rod. There is an opening in the underpart of the sleeve to give passage to this plug, which, when inserted in the cavity, makes a fixture. The remainder of the metal framework (and with it the woman) remains movable, to the extent that it can be made to describe and arc of ninety degrees to the upright rod.

The mode of operation will now be clear. When the young woman mounts on the stool and extends her arms, the performer, in placing the upright beneath them, takes care that the lower end sinks properly in the socket on the platform and that the plug under the woman's arm fits into the cavity at the top of that same rod. The apparatus is now in the position shown in the first illustration, and when the stool is removed the woman is left apparently resting only on the one upright, but in reality comfortably seated in her metal cage, the different parts of which are all carefully padded, so as to occasion her no discomfort. As the support terminates above the right knee, the legs are kept extended by muscular power. This attitude is therefore very fatiguing, and for that reason cannot be continued more than a few moments. Eventually the woman is replaced in the upright position. The stool is again placed under her feet, and the second upright under her left arm, before the operator begins to demesmerize her, which he does after the orthodox fashion with reverse passes, the lady simulating as best she may the bewildered and half-scared expression of one newly awakened from a mesmeric trance.

The Vanishing Lady

The capital trick that goes by this name is the invention of the ingenious Buatier de Kolta. Its very success has been its ruin. There is unfortunately no copyright in magical illusion, and the one in question has been pirated all over the country, in many instances so clumsily as to let out the best half of the secret. Most people have by this time a sufficient notion of "how it's done" as to make it at present scarcely worth the doing; but in competent hands, and notably in those of the inventor, it is one of the most brilliant of stage illusions.

It will be convenient first to describe the effect of the feat, as it appears to the eye of the spectator.

The performer comes forward with an eight-page newspaper, and spreads it upon the floor of the stage. Upon the center of the paper he places an ordinary-looking chair, with cane back and seat. He then introduces a young lady, clothed in a soft silk dress, rather clinging, and with no superabundance of drapery. She seats herself on the chair. The operator begins to make mesmeric passes before her face. Her eyes close and she appears to sleep. The operator then throws a long veil of thin black silk over her, covering her from head to foot. This he secures with a pin behind her head.

The operator again resumes the mesmeric passes, meanwhile appearing very solicitous that the drapery shall fall right and completely cover the figure, and smoothing it down in various directions to that end. Suddenly, he grasps the veil by its center, and jerks it off. The chair is vacant; the newspaper beneath it is undisturbed, but the lady has vanished, presently to reappear with a calm smile at the wing, and relieve the natural anxiety of the spectators as to her fate.

The trick, as performed by Buatier and the more ambitious of his imitators, had an additional effect in the vanishing of the veil itself at the moment when it was removed to show the disappearance of the lady.

Explanation: The first requirement is a trap in the stage, about fourteen inches from back to front, and fifteen to sixteen in width. This trap is hinged at the back, opening downward by its own weight, but kept closed, when not in use, by a strong iron bar crossing its underside. The stage is carpeted, the top of the trap exactly matching the rest of the carpet.

The newspaper used has one of its sides (the one that in its folded condition is *not* exhibited to the audience) fortified with cardboard, and in this is cut a trap corresponding with that in the stage, save that it is a quarter of an inch smaller each way, and closed by a double flap, meeting in the center. The performer holds it expanded at arms' length, but folded in half along the upper edge. The trap portion is in the half held toward himself, and he lays it on the floor with this portion downward and with the fold away from the audience. He then draws the upper surface, which is the unprepared half, over toward himself, thereby exposing the trap surface. Certain marks on the carpet show him where to lay the paper, so as to bring the trap in the paper exactly over that in the stage.

The next proceeding is the placing of the chair, which has a point in each leg. These are so placed as to correspond with the punctures made in the paper by previous use, thereby ensuring the chair being exactly in the right position.

The woman now takes her seat, and the performer throws the veil over her. As he does so, she drops her hands to the sides of the seat, immediately above the two front legs, and pushes out two thin strips of steel which, when protruded, curve inward round each of her knees, though without pressure. The performer now steps behind the woman, and spreading the veil for a moment by its two upper corners, draws its upper edge over her head, and secures it in that position with a shawl-pin. This gives him an opportunity to effect another necessary arrangement.

Behind the back of the chair (whose pretended open canework is only a delusion, the interstices being in reality backed with some dark and opaque material), hinged vertically behind the top-rail, is a metal rod, carrying at its free extremity a little wire "cap." The length of the rod is so adjusted that when this end is upward, the cap in question shall just cover the top of the woman's head. From the rod projects, on either side, a wire arm, carrying at its extremity a sort of epaulette which, when the rod is lifted, rests on the lady's shoulder. A subsidiary mechanical arrangement provides that these epaulettes shall, when the center rod is despressed, be close against it, sliding to the extremities of their respective "arms" only when the rod is uplifted. There is a coiled spring in connection with the hinge, which forces the rod normally to point downward, in which condition, being entirely behind the back of the chair, it is of course out of sight. But on pulling a cord terminating in a ring just under the seat of the chair, within easy reach of the left hand, the free end of the rod describes a semicircle, and rises into an erect position about ten inches or a foot above the back of the chair, in which position it is held by a spring-catch.

This is the operation to which we have referred. At the moment when the performer, standing a little behind the woman, spreads the veil preparatory to securing it behind her head, she slips her thumb into the ring, and pulls the cord. The rod rises, the wire cap adapts itself to the woman's head and the two epaulettes to her shoulders. The performer then pins the veil behind her head as already described, though the pressure really falls on the cap, and not on the head of the woman. (It is hardly necessary to remark that with this elaborate mechanical arrangement behind, the chair cannot be turned round with its back to the spectators. There is no particular reason that it should, and the omission can hardly be regarded as a serious defect, but Buatier de Kolta, with that minute attention to "finish" which makes his performance so perfect, has set himself to cure it, and now brings on his chair with the back to the audience; the necessary "head-and-shoulders fake," of specially light and portable construction, being supplied from his own person under cover of the veil.)

It may be well at this stage to mention a further peculiarity of the chair, which is a most elaborate and carefully constructed piece of apparatus. The seat of the chair, with the exception of a frame a couple of inches wide on either side and at the back, is movable, being hinged to the back. It is supported in position by a double-action bolt, securing it on both sides simultaneously, but withdrawable by a pull upon a hook beneath the seat.

Now come the mesmeric passes, and the performer's pretended anxiety that the veil shall be properly and elegantly draped, to which end he smoothes it down every now and then, standing of necessity with his back to the spectators, and so interposing his own body between the company and the lady. This, again, is for a purpose. An attendant under the stage, taking his cue from the patter of the performer, has unfastened the trap, which noiselessly opens; the corresponding trap in the newspaper opening in like manner.

Meanwhile, the woman herself has not been idle. Under cover of the pretended passes, she draws her feet back under the chair, grasping the seat on either side, so as to take her weight off it. She then draws the bolt, and releases the movable portion of the seat (which falls accordingly); still supporting herself by grasping the sides, she again puts forward her feet so as to rest on the front edge of the opening. This is done with all possible precaution against unnecessary movement. So soon as she feels that the way is clear, she drops her feet through the opening, where they fall on the top step of a step-ladder; and gently lowers herself down. To do this neatly demands a considerable amount of practice, and the gesticulations of the performer are designed to cover any possible disturbance of the veil during the operation. If the trick is skillfully performed, the uninitiated spectator has not the least notion that the woman has already departed. The cap and epaulettes take the place of the head and shoulders of the woman, and the wire springs mentioned keep the lower part of the veil distended, apparently by her knees.

The trick is now (as far as the disappearance of the woman is concerned) practically done. The attendant beneath the stage pushes up the seat of the chair into its normal position (sometimes placing the woman's handkerchief on it in addition) and closes the trap. The performer unpins the veil from behind the supposed head, jerks it in the air, and the woman is gone.

We have still to account for the disappearance of the veil. In the case of so large an object, the favorite explanation "up his sleeve" appears to be out of the question, but this is precisely how it's done.

The operation is effected as follows: The veil is oblong, about six feet by four, and of very thin soft silk, so as to be capable of being folded or crumpled into very small dimensions. Firmly sewn to its center is a little hook. In an earlier chapter we have described the Buatier pull, an ingenious contrivance by which any small object is drawn up the sleeve of the performer. The ordinary length of the pull, however, is in this case under two feet, and the veil, even when held by the center, is nearly three feet, six inches. The length of the pull has therefore to be increased accordingly. One end of the cord terminates in a loop which passes over the thumb of the right hand. Thence it is carried up the right sleeve, across the chest beneath the shirt, and down the left sleeve to the left wrist. Attached to the left wrist, by means of a broad leather wristband, is what is known to mechanics as a "lazy" pulley, i.e., a pulley attached to a jointed swivel, which permits it to take any angle at pleasure. (When there is no pull upon it, it lies flat, hence its peculiar name.) Passing over this pulley, the cord returns up the sleeve, across the chest and down the right arm again, terminating in a second loop. The length is so adjusted, however, that this second loop only reaches the right hand when the arms are flexed, and held close to the body. The moment they are extended it is drawn quite up the sleeve, and rests on the chest. And here it of necessity remains during the greater part of the trick. To enable the performer to get at it when necessary, a piece of very thin cord is threaded through the loop and brought down to the right hand.

Under cover of final manipulations with the veil (before showing that the lady has departed), the performer draws down the loop. This done, he takes out the pin which secured the veil behind to the cap. Standing sideways (with his right side to the audience) to the chair, he slips loop No. 2 over the hook in the center of the veil, and at the same time, with his left foot, presses a brass stud (the head of a spring-bolt) immediately behind the leg of the chair on the side on which he stands. This pulls a wire, and thereby withdraws the locking catch of the "head-and-shoulders fake," which thereupon flies back to its original position behind the chair. Almost at the same moment, he extends his arms and makes a half-turn of the body, under cover of which the veil disappears, with a "flash," up his sleeve.

SECRETS
OF THE
MASTER
CONJURERS

Robert-Houdin's Cards in Flight

This trick was a special favorite of Robert-Houdin, and we shall proceed to describe it as nearly as possible in the form in which it was presented by him.

The performer brings forward a pack of cards, still in the official envelope. These he hands to a spectator, with a request that they be opened and counted. This is done, and the volunteer finds that there is a full complement (in Houdin's day cards came in packs of 32 and 52, depending on their use). The next request is to cut the pack into two portions, pretty nearly equal, and to choose one of the packets. Having made a selection, the spectator is further asked to count the cards in the packet chosen. The general attention being, meanwhile, drawn away from the performer, there is ample opportunity to get ready in his right hand, duly palmed, three cards of another pack, but of similar pattern to those of the pack in use. (These may previously be placed either on the *servante* or in the performer's right-hand pocket; or he may, if he prefers it, have them ready palmed in his right hand when he comes upon the stage to commence the trick.)

The spectator, having counted the chosen pack, declares it to consist, say, of twenty-five cards. "A fine number for the trick," remarks the performer. "Now, will you be kind enough to take these seventeen cards in your own hands" they are pushed carelessly toward the volunteer, the three palmed cards joined in with them), "and hold them well up above your head, that everyone may see them Thank you. Now, as your packet contains twenty-five cards, this other should contain twenty-seven. Let us see whether you have counted right." The performer himself audibly counts the remaining packet, card by card, on the table; immediately afterward he takes the heap in his left hand and, squaring the cards together, thus obtains the opportunity to separate and palm in his right hand the three top cards.

He continues: "Twenty-seven cards here and—how many did you say, sir?—yes, twenty-five, which the gentleman holds, make fifty-two. Quite right. Now will someone else oblige me by taking charge of these twenty-seven cards?" He hands the cards with the left hand, and at the same moment drops the three palmed cards into the *profonde* or *servante*, immediately bringing up the hand, that it may be seen empty.

"Now, ladies and gentlemen, I will show you a very curious phenomenon, all the more astonishing because you will bear me witness that, from the time the cards were counted, they have not been even one moment in my possession, but have remained in independent custody. Will you, sir" (addressing the person who holds the second packet), "hold up the cards in such a manner that I can touch them with my wand? I have but to strike the cards with my wand once, twice, thrice, and at each touch a card will fly from the packet which you are now holding, and go to join the twenty-five cards in the other packet. As this trick is performed by sheer force of will, without the aid of apparatus or dexterity, I shall be glad if you will all assist me by adding the force of your will to mine, which will greatly lighten my labor. At each touch of the wand, then, please, all present, mentally command a card to pass in the manner I have mentioned. Are you all ready! Then we will make the experiment. One, two, three! Did you see the cards pass? I saw them distinctly, but possibly my eyes are quicker than yours. Will each of the gentlemen who hold the cards be good enough to count his packet?"

This is done, and it is found that one holds twenty-eight cards, the other twenty-four only.

It is obvious that the two packets now collectively contain duplicates of three cards, while three others are missing; but it is extremely unlikely that anyone will suspect this, or seek to verify the constitution of the pack.

Comte's Ladies' Looking-Glass

This capital trick was a great favorite of Comte, who christened it, for reasons best known to himself, by the poetical name of The Ladies' Looking-Glass.

The cards having been freely shuffled, you invite a person to draw two cards, allowing him free choice. Opening the pack in the middle, you ask him to place his cards together in the opening. You bring them to the top by the pass, make the first of the false shuffles, and conclude by leaving them on the top.

Offer the cards to a second person to draw a couple, but in opening the cards for him to return them, make the pass, so that they may be placed upon the pair already drawn, which are thereby brought to the middle of the pack. Again make the pass, so as to bring all four on the top, and offer the cards to a third and fourth person, each time repeating the process. Make another false shuffle for the last time, so as to leave all the drawn cards in a body on the top of the pack, with one indifferent card above them.

The audience believe that they are thoroughly dispersed, and your first care must be to strengthen that impression. If you are expert in card-palming, you may palm the nine cards, and give the pack to be shuffled by one of the spectators; but this is not absolutely necessary, and there is some risk of the company noticing the absence of part of the pack. You remark, "You have all seen the drawn cards placed in different parts of the pack, and the whole have been since thoroughly shuffled. The drawn cards are therefore at this moment scattered in different parts of the pack. I can assure you that I do not myself know what the cards are" (this is the only item of *fact* in the whole sentence); "but yet, by a very slight, simple movement, I shall make them appear, in couples as they were drawn, at top and bottom of the pack.

Then, showing the bottom card, you ask, "Is this anybody's card?" The reply is in the negative. You next show the top card, and make the same inquiry. While you do so, you slip the little finger under the next card, and as you replace the card you have just shown, make the pass, thus bringing both cards to the bottom of the pack. Meanwhile, you ask the *last* person who drew what his cards were. When he names them, you "ruffle" the cards, and show him first the bottom and then the top card, which will be the two he drew. While exhibiting the top card, take the opportunity to slip the little finger of the left hand immediately under the card next below it, and as you replace the top one make the pass at that point. You now have the third couple placed top and bottom. Make the drawer name them, ruffle the cards, and show them as before, again making the pass to bring the card just shown at top, with the next following, to the bottom of the pack, which will enable you to exhibit the second couple in like manner. These directions sound a little complicated, but if followed with the cards will be found simple enough.

You may, by way of variation, pretend to forget that a fourth person drew two cards, and, after making the pass as before, appear to be about to proceed to another trick. You will naturally be reminded that so-and-so drew two cards. Apologizing for the oversight, you beg him to say what his cards were. When he does so, you say, "To tell you the truth I have quite lost sight of them; but it is of no consequence. I can easily find them again."

Then nipping the upper end of the cards between the thumb and second finger of the right hand, which should be slightly moistened, you make the pack swing, pendulum fashion, a few inches backward and forward, when the whole of the intermediate cards will fall out, leaving the top and bottom cards alone in your hand. These you hand to the drawer, who is compelled to acknowledge them as the cards he drew.

De Kolta's Flying Handkerchief

A favorite feat of Buatier de Kolta is that of making a silk handkerchief "pass" from a decanter held in the hand of the performer into another standing on a table at a considerable distance.

The decanters to be used are first exhibited. They are of "pint" size or thereabouts, and of the round-bellied kind generally used as water-carafes. They have tolerably wide necks, and no stoppers.

Having submitted them to inspection, the performer borrows a handkerchief, and taking one of the decanters by the neck, asks a spectator to tie the handkerchief over it. The bottle being held upside down, the handkerchief is thrown over it, and tied round the neck. This done, it is placed upon a table, where it remains till the conclusion of the trick.

The performer then takes a small silk handkerchief, and with the aid of his wand, thrusts it down into the second decanter, wherein it remains visible, the bottle not being covered in any way. Taking this by the neck, and standing sideways to the audience, with face turned toward the covered decanter on the table, he says, "One, two, three!" at the same time waving his arm up and down pump-handle fashion. At the word *three*, the handkerchief, which has remained visible up to that moment, vanishes from the decanter that he holds; and on the second decanter being uncovered, the missing article is found to have transferred itself therein.

So much for the effect of the trick. Now for the solution, which, as usual, is simple enough when you know "how it's done."

Under cover of the wrapping-up of the first decanter, the performer loads into the neck a duplicate silk handkerchief, which he holds palmed in readiness for that purpose. After showing round the second decanter and handkerchief, he secretly attaches the latter by its center to a little hook, which in turn is attached to a silk cord, coming down his right sleeve. The cord in question passes across the body and out through the left armhole of the vest, terminating in a loop which hangs down beside the performer's waist, at his left side. The attachment duly made, he proceeds to thrust the handkerchief into the visible decanter, pushing it down with his wand as above described; then he grasps the bottle by the neck and begins the up-and-down movement. All eyes being fixed on the bottle, it becomes an easy matter to slip the left thumb into the loop of the cord. At the word *three* he gives a smart downward pull, which draws the handkerchief out of the decanter and up the sleeve. The decanter is now free, and may be handed for examination; and on uncovering the second decanter, the duplicate is found therein.

The movement of the handkerchief, when withdrawn from the decanter, is so rapid that the eye cannot follow it, and though an acute person may suspect, he cannot claim to have actually seen the manner of its disappearance.

Stodare's Flying Glass of Water

This capital trick was, I believe, first introduced to the public by Colonel Stodare, to whom the profession is indebted for many first-class illusions.

The necessary apparatus consists of a couple of ordinary glass tumblers, exactly alike, with a rubber cover (available at conjurer's shops) just fitting the mouth of one of them, and a colored silk or cotton handkerchief made double (i.e., consisting of two similar handkerchiefs sewn together at the edges), with a wire ring (of the size of the rim of one of the tumblers, or a fraction larger) stitched loosely between them, in such a manner that when the handkerchief is spread out the ring is in the middle.

Beforehand, you nearly fill one of the tumblers with milk or water, and then put on the rubber cover, which, fitting tightly all round the edge, effectually prevents the water escaping. The glass, thus prepared, you place in your right-hand pocket.

You then bring forward the other glass, a pitcher of water or milk, and the prepared handkerchief, and in full view of the audience fill the glass with liquid up to the same height as you have already filled the one in your pocket, and hand round the glass for inspection. When returned, place the glass upon the table, a few inches from its back edge, and standing behind it, cover it with the handkerchief, first spreading out and showing both sides of the latter, proving, to all appearance, that there is no preparation about it. In placing the handkerchief over the glass, draw it across in such a manner as to bring the hidden ring as exactly as possible over the top of the glass. Then placing your left hand over the handkerchief and taking the wire ring in your fingers as if it were the rim of the glass through the handkerchief, raise the handkerchief, apparently with the glass, but really the empty handkerchief only, which is kept distended by the ring. At the same time, under cover of the handkerchief, gently lower the glass of water with the other hand onto the *servante* (it may also be lowered into a well in the table, but more care must be taken). This is by no means difficult, as your pretended carefulness not to spill the liquid allows you to make the upward movement of the left hand as deliberate as you please.

All that is really necessary is to take care *to follow with your eyes the movement of the left hand*, which will infallibly draw the eyes of the audience in the same direction.

Having raised the supposed tumbler to a height of about two feet from the table, you bring it forward to the audience, and request that someone with a steady hand give you his assistance. The volunteer, having given satisfactory replies as to the steadiness of his nerves and the strength of his constitution generally, is requested to place his hand under the handkerchief and take the glass. As he proceeds to do this, you let go of the handkerchief with your left hand, still retaining one corner with the right, and let the right arm with the handkerchief drop to your side. Pretending to believe that the gentleman has taken the glass, and not to notice its disappearance, you turn carelessly aside, and bring forward a small table or chair, saying, "Put it here, please." Looking, generally, somewhat foolish, the victim replies that he has not got it.

If you are a good actor, you may here make some fun by pretending to believe that the victim has concealed the glass, and asking him to return it. At last you say, "Well, if you won't give it to me, I must find it for myself," and you proceed to tap with your wand the sleeves and pockets of the unfortunate individual, without success, until, on touching him between the shoulders, you pretend to tell by the sound that the glass is there.

"Yes, here it is," you remark. "I am sorry to have to ask you to turn your back to the company, but to show them that there is no deception on my part, I must ask you to do so. Will you please turn round for one minute?"

On his doing so, you again shake out the handkerchief, showing both sides of it to prove it empty, and spread it over the back of the victim. Again you tap with your wand, which, striking the ring through the handkerchief, causes an unmistakable hard sound to be heard; and then grasping the ring as before through the handkerchief, you deliberately raise it up in a horizontal position, the effect being as if the glass had again returned to the handkerchief.

You then say, "I don't think I will trouble this gentleman again; he is too much of a conjurer himself," and turning rapidly to the audience, say, "Catch!" and flick the handkerchief quickly toward the spectators, who duck their heads in expectation of a shower.

"Pardon me, I'm afraid I alarmed you; but you need not have worried, I never miss my aim. That gentleman" (you designate anyone you please), "has the glass. May I ask you to step forward for one moment?" On that person doing so, you place him facing the audience, and under cover of his body take the second glass out of your pocket and throw the handkerchief over it, saying, "Yes, here it is, in this gentleman's back pocket." Then taking hold of the glass with your left hand beneath the handkerchief, clip with your first finger and thumb, through the handkerchief, the edge of the rubber cover, and thus drawing off the cover inside the handkerchief, hand round the glass and liquid for inspection.

Two improvements have recently been made in this trick, which, though trifles in themselves, greatly heighten the effect.

Upon a performance of the trick as already described, it is not uncommon to find some person, more acute than average, guess that there is a ring in the handkerchief. The first of the improvements is designed to make the ring no longer a fixture, and yet to insure bringing it into the right position when needed. This is done by stitching the two handkerchiefs together, not only round the edge but also in a V shape from one corner to the middle back to the other corner on the same end. This confines the ring to a triangular enclosure within which, however, it is allowed to move freely, not being attached to the handkerchief in any way. If the handkerchief is held by the two corners (which should be distinguished by a mark of colored silk or a small button sewn at the corner between the two layers), the ring will take its proper place in the middle. If, on the other hand, the handkerchief is held by only one corner, the ring is free to move about, and the handkerchief, if grasped and shaken until the ring has moved to one of the corners open to it, then held just below that corner, may be twisted or pulled, proving with apparent conclusiveness that there is no ring or shape concealed in it.

The second improvement is to have ready on the *servante* a small piece of sponge, dipped in water. This is picked up by the right hand of the performer as the genuine glass is placed on the *servante*. When the conjurer has moved away from the table, at the moment of requesting the volunteer to take the glass, he places the right hand for a moment under cover of the handkerchief, and squeezes the sponge, the water that immediately pours from it being, apparently, accidentally spilt, and so convincing the spectators that the glass is really in the handkerchief. With these two additions the trick is one of the most effective that can possibly be performed, whether at close-up or on the stage.

Dr. Lynn's Second Sight Trick

This is the trick with which Dr. Lynn made a great success at the Egyptian Hall in the late 1800s.

A number of small slips of paper were handed to members of the audience, each of whom was invited to write on the slip the name of some person *deceased*. Much stress was laid on this qualification by Lynn, the idea being, no doubt, that a genuine dead person would be more in the way of the "spirits" who were supposed to prompt the performer. The slips of paper, thus inscribed, were folded up, and placed in a hat. Lynn, taking one of them, handed it to a spectator, with a request that it be opened and examined; he, himself, meanwhile, in order not to be suspected of peeping, turned his back on the company, and walked up the stage. Presently he turned round, and after a due amount of hesitation, deciphering first the initial, and then the other letters piecemeal, read out the complete name.

A second slip was taken from the hat, handed to another spectator, and deciphered in like manner; this continued until some four or five slips had been duly read. When this point had been reached, Lynn, putting his hand in the hat, took out a handful of the folded papers and invited a spectator to choose any one of them. The chosen paper, still folded, was laid on Lynn's arm, outside his coat-sleeve, and the spectator was invited to breathe softly upon it. The paper was then unfolded, and the name upon it—say, Charles Dickens—publicly stated. The performer bared his arm, and on the spot where the paper had rested appeared, in blood-red letters, the same name.

Few tricks have produced, in their time, a greater sensation. Victor Hugo, witnessing it, was persuaded that it was the outcome of some new and mysterious principle in nature, and gave the ingenious exhibitor a capital advertisement by declaring that Lynn's performance "demanded the attention of science."

And yet the explanation of the supposed mystery is almost absurdly simple. Dr. Lynn had in his pocket or *pochette* (say) four folded papers, each bearing the name Charles Dickens, and the same name was written in red ink upon his arm. A fifth paper, bearing the name of some other deceased celebrity, say, Lord Beaconsfield, was concealed in his palm. Some ten or twelve blank papers were handed out to the audience, and, when each had been duly written on, a spectator was asked to collect them in a borrowed hat.

So far nothing could be fairer; but when Lynn presently dipped his hand into the hat and took one, handing it (apparently) to a spectator for safekeeping, he in reality retained the paper he had taken, and gave instead his own paper—which, as we have seen, bore the name Lord Beaconsfield. While this paper was being opened, he discreetly turned his back and moved a few steps away, meanwhile quietly opening the paper he had abstracted (which bore, we will suppose, the name of Napoleon Bonaparte), noting the contents, and refolding it. He then proceeded to read out, simulating more or less difficulty, the name on the paper held by the spectator: "Lord Beaconsfield." This being found correct, he again dipped his hand in the hat, taking out another paper, and handing not that paper but the one bearing the name Napoleon Bonaparte to a second spectator. This he repeated as often as he thought fit, "reading" each time the paper he had just examined, and meanwhile taking a quiet peep at a new one.

When he considered that the company had had enough of this phase of the trick, he would remark that he would now show them a still more striking method of ascertaining the concealed name. During his last journey up the stage, which he made empty-handed, he would have got into his hand, and palmed, the four papers with the name Charles Dickens. Dipping his hand once more into the hat, he would bring out these four papers (which the audience naturally took to be some of those inscribed by themselves), and throw out those remaining upon the floor or table.

Placing the four he had retained upon the crown of the hat (this use of the hat giving the necessary pretext for throwing out the other papers), he'd ask someone to choose one of them, and throw the rest carelessly aside; then, placing the paper on his arm as above described, would show that the name thereon had by some occult means been reproduced upon his arm.

THE ART OF MAGIC

The art of magic, as it is now understood, is no longer a secret and mystic profession; it is a written art, and may be easily acquired by the clever mechanician, or any person having dexterous hands and a large amount of self-possession and impudence. I say "impudence," because most of the best tricks are really so extremely simple that many persons of a timid or self-conscious disposition would feel ashamed to venture to perform them, in case of what they think must be inevitable detection and exposure. But so blind is poor human nature that the clever conjurer can always select his man for "forcing a card upon him," even though he makes his dupe believe he has selected one at his own will and choice.

My object in the foregoing chapters was to show the reader, first, that the art of magic is merely the art of a very clever illusionist, who, by swiftness of execution and a thorough knowledge of the laws of mechanics and optics, can make his audience *deceive themselves*; second, to afford some entertainment to my readers; and, third, to set the ingenious at work to solve the mysteries of the art upon the basis I have given in these chapters. I venture to think, from the observations I have heard, that all these objects have been attained.

It now only remains to give the neophyte a few parting hints of general application. In getting up any trick, even the simplest, your first task should be to carefully read and consider the instructions given, and to make quite certain that you perfectly comprehend their meaning. This being ascertained, the next point will be to see whether the trick involves any principle of sleight-of-hand in which you are not thoroughly proficient; and if it does, to set to work and practice diligently, till the difficulty is conquered. Having thus mastered the elements of the trick, you should next attack it as a whole, and in like manner practice, practice, practice, till from beginning to end you can work each successive step of the process with ease and finish.

Having achieved this much, you may perhaps consider that your task is at an end.

By no means.

Being perfect in the mechanical portion of the illusion, you must now devote yourself to its dramatic element, which, as regards the effect upon the spectator, is by far the more important portion.

As a performer, you should always bear in mind that you fill the character of a person possessing supernatural powers, and should endeavor, in every word and gesture, to enter into the spirit of your part. As the true actor, playing Hamlet, will endeavor actually to *be* Hamlet for the time, so you as the self-styled magician must, in the first place, learn to believe in yourself. When you step upon the stage you should, for the time being, persuade yourself that your fictitious power is a reality, and that the wand you hold is not only the emblem, but the actual implement of your power. Every time you pronounce the mystic "Pass!" or touch an object with your wand to effect some pretended transformation, you should force yourself to forget the commonplace expedients by which the result is really attained, and to believe that the effect is produced by a genuine magical process.

When you go through the motion of passing a coin from the right hand to the left, you should have imagination enough to persuade yourself, for the moment, that the coin has really been transferred as it appears to be. If, as a performer, you have sufficient imaginative faculty to do this—if you can so enter into the spirit of your part, yourself believing in the marvels you profess, you will achieve an almost unlimited mastery over the imaginations of your audience.

As we have already intimated, each individual illusion should have its appropriate words and gestures—in technical language, its "patter"—carefully arranged and rehearsed, so as to produce the maximum of effect. These are, in truth, the very life of the trick. How much depends on *mise en scene* is forcibly illustrated by one of the simplest of card tricks as performed by Robert-Houdin.

The trick has already been described, but we will recapitulate its effect in a few words: The performer offers the pack to a spectator, and requests him to draw a card. (This card may or may not be forced.) The card having been drawn and replaced in the pack, the performer makes the pass to bring it to the top, and palms it, handing the pack to be shuffled. If the card was forced, he already knows it; if not, he takes the opportunity to glance at it while the cards are being shuffled. The pack being returned, the drawn card is placed on the top, and the pack placed in the pocket of a second spectator. The performer now announces that he not only already knows the card, but that he is able to pick it out without seeing it from the remainder of the pack, which he does accordingly.

Presented in this barren form, the trick would attract only the most passing notice. We will now proceed to describe it, quoting from Robert-Houdin, as it should actually be presented:

"Ladies and gentlemen, I shall commence my performance with an experiment that is wholly independent of dexterity. I propose simply to show you the extreme degree of sensibility which may be acquired by the sense of touch. We possess, as you all know, five senses—sight, hearing, smell, touch, and taste. In the ordinary way, each of these senses enjoys one faculty only; but when the mysterious influences of magic are brought to bear, the case is altered. All five of the senses may be exercised through the instrumentality of one—touch, for example; so that we can not only touch, but hear, see, smell, and taste with the tips of the fingers. You smile, but I assure you that I am serious; and I venture to think that in a few minutes you will be fully convinced of the reality of the singular fact which I have mentioned.

"Here is a pack of cards. Madam, will you be kind enough to take whichever card you please; hold it for a moment between your hands, so as to impregnate it with the mesmeric influence of your touch, and then replace it in the middle of the pack.

"In order to exclude all possibility of sleight-of-hand, we will now thoroughly shuffle the cards; after which, for still greater certainty, I will show you that the card is neither at top nor bottom from which you may be persuaded that it is placed just where chance has chosen to put it.

"Will some gentleman now have the kindness to empty his breastpocket, and allow me to place the pack in it?" (This is done.) "Now that the cards are placed in perfect darkness, I will try, by virtue of that five-fold sensibility of touch which I have just mentioned, to discover, by the aid of my fingers only, the card that this lady drew. To make my task still more difficult, I will try to draw the card at such number as you yourselves may choose. What number shall it be?" (We will suppose the reply is "seventh.") "Seventh, all right. Then six times in succession I must avoid taking the drawn card, and produce it on the seventh occasion only. One, two, three, four, five, six. (He shows six cards one by one, taking them from the bottom of the pack.) "Now to find the lady's card. Yes, I think I have it. Before taking it out, I will read it with my little finger, which is the cleverest of the five. Yes! It is not a small card; it is not a club, nor a spade, nor yet a diamond. It is the king of————." (He draws out the card, and places it face downward.) "Will you please, madam, finish naming the card before I turn it over, and we shall see whether my little finger has been correct in its assertions." (The woman names the king of hearts, which the performer turns up.) "My little finger was right, you see. Will you be good enough, sir, to take the remainder of the cards out of your pocket, and examine them to see that the experiment has really been performed exactly as I have stated."

The above example will show how, by the exercise of a little tact and ingenuity, a simple piece of parlor magic may be elevated to the dignity of a stage trick. The great secret is the directing of the minds of the audience into such a channel, that the effect of the trick for the moment seems to be a natural result of the causes artfully suggested by the performer.

This may, to a considerable extent, be effected, as in the example given above, by the language and gesture of the performer in the individual trick; but still more may be done by the artistic grouping of one trick with another, a comparatively simple feat being employed to prepare the minds of the spectators for the greater marvel to follow. Thus, in the recent performances of the Fakir of Oolu, the aërial suspension, which formed the staple of his programme, was preceded by the exhibition of a wooden rod or wand which (by means of certain projecting wire points, so minute as to be imperceptible at a very short distance), was made to defy the laws of gravity by clinging to his fingertips in various positions without visible support. This minor illusion, being somewhat similar in effect (though wholly different as to the means employed), prepared the minds of the audience to receive the greater marvel of a living woman made to recline in mid-air.

In arranging an entertainment, the performer should continually bear the principle in mind of the possibility of the artistic combination of two or three different tricks in such manner as to enhance the effect of the whole. The programme should consist not of a number of absolutely unconnected tricks, but of a series of ten or a dozen *groups* of tricks. As compared with each other, these groups should have as much diversity as possible; but, individually, each should consist of the same or similar effect repeated in a more and more striking form (though produced by different means), or else a string of tricks united by some natural sequence, as in the case of the production, vanish, and reproduction of a rabbit.

Having arranged your programme, and the appropriate patter for each group of tricks, you should conclude your practice by having a series of three or four "dress rehearsals," with an intelligent friend to play the part of audience, who should be invited to criticize with the utmost freedom. At these rehearsals there should be no "make believe," but each trick should be worked throughout with the same completeness in every particular with which it is afterward to be exhibited in public. In the course of these final rehearsals you should tax your invention to see what amount of "incidents," or by-play, you can introduce in the course of the different tricks. If, for instance, you have occasion for an egg or lemon in the course of a trick, it will greatly enhance the effect if, instead of having the necessary article brought forward by your assistant, you can produce it youself from behind a spectator's ear. These little matters, though small in themselves, tend to keep alive the attention of the audience, and to create a sort of magical atmosphere, which will aid materially in disposing the spectators to receive with due respect the occult pretensions of the performer.

With respect to stage arrangements, you will quickly learn by experience how best to arrange your apparatus for the purpose of your entertainment. One suggestion is that a working programme should be kept for the use of the performer and any assistants, with a note of the articles required for the purpose of each trick. This will enable them to have everything ready at the right moment, without delay or confusion.

When you have made your bow to the audience, there are still one or two little points that you will do well to bear in mind. They may be summarized as follows:

1. *Don't be nervous*. The reader may possibly consider that this is a matter in which there is no choice; but nothing could be a greater mistake. A slight lack of confidence is excusable on the first presentation of a new programme, but never afterward.

2. *Take your time*. Deliver your patter like an actor playing his part, and not like a

schoolboy repeating his lesson. Further, give your audience time to see and appreciate your movements. Young performers are very apt to exhibit the second phase of a transformation without having sufficiently indicated the first to the spectators. The change of, say, an orange to an apple falls decidedly flat if nobody noticed that the article was an orange in the first instance.

3. *Don't make any parade of dexterity, and don't affect any unusual quickness in your movements*. If you are about to vanish a coin, don't toss it endlessly from hand to hand as a preliminary; but make the necessary pass as quietly and deliberately as you possibly can. Don't talk about "the quickness of the hand deceiving the eye," and still less do anything to support such an idea. The perfection of conjuring lies in sending away the spectators persuaded that sleight-of-hand has not been employed at all, and unable to suggest *any* solution of the wonders they have seen.

4. *Don't force yourself to be funny*. If you are naturally humorous, so much the better; but in any case perform in your natural character.

5. *Never plead guilty to a failure*. Keep your wits about you, and if anything goes wrong, try to save your credit by bringing the trick to some sort of a conclusion, even though it be a weak one. If you are so unfortunate as to experience a complete and unmistakable break-down, smile cheerfully, and ascribe the fiasco to the moon being in the wrong quarter, to a little misunderstanding between two of your "controlling spirits," or any other burlesque reason, so long as it be sufficiently remote from the true one.

Bearing in mind these parting counsels, and thus armed against failure as well as prepared for success, you may safely ring up the curtain, and begin to bewitch the world with the marvels and mysteries of
MODERN MAGIC.

Robinson's Guide to Magic Sources

1. **Books:** Since the publication of *Modern Magic* in 1876, there have been many excellent texts on the art of conjuring. Unfortunately the great majority of them are out of print, but search your public library for these classics:

Our Magic by Nevil Maskelyne and David Devant, New York, 1911.

The Art of Magic by Thomas Nelson Downs, Buffalo, 1909.

Magic Without Apparatus by Camille Gaultier, Berkeley Heights, New Jersey, 1945.

Illustrated Magic by Ottokar Fischer, New York, 1931.

Modern Magic Manual by Jean Hugard, New York, 1939.

Greater Magic by John Northern Hilliard, Minneapolis, 1938.

In addition, Walter Gibson wrote a number of introductions to magic under his own name as well as several for Houdini, Thurston, and Blackstone. All of Gibson's introductions are similar, so any one of them will suffice. Several have been published recently in remainder editions and can be purchased at discount book chains.

One magic book that is easily found is *The Amateur Magician's Handbook* by Henry Hay published by Signet in a $1.95 paperback edition.

Most magic books are available only from magic dealers. There are catalogs devoted solely to books on magic—two notable examples are published by Magic Inc. in Chicago and Supreme Magic in Devon, England (*See Mail Order Magic*). There are manuscripts, pamphlets, and bound books that will tell you how to locate a chosen card or float a person in mid-air. Among the many volumes for serious magicians, I especially recommend:

The New Modern Coin Magic by J. B. Bobo, Chicago, 1966.

Rices Encyclopedia of Silk Magic, Volumes 1, 2, and 3 by Harold R. Rice, Wynewood, PA, 1948, 1953, 1962.

2. **Instruction:** Personal instruction from a professional magician is probably the best way to learn the art of magic. Many professionals do give lessons, others present lectures before magic societies. Consult the yellow pages of the telephone directory under *Magic, Magic Shops,* or *Magicians.* Local magic shops and magic clubs are the best place to inquire about professional lessons.

There are two mail-order magic courses written to give the basics of magic through home-study techniques. The most famous of these was written by Harlan Tarbell in the late 1920's. *The Tarbell Course In Magic* is presently available in seven bound volumes from magic dealer and publisher Louis Tannen (*See Mail Order Magic*). The other course is sold by Mark Wilson, a well-known professional. *The Mark Wilson Course In Magic* (P. O. Box 440, North Hollywood, California, 91603) costs about $40 and comes with necessary apparatus.

3. **Magic Shops:** Those lucky enough to have a magic shop in their city or town realize how wonderful it is to escape into the world of magic by spending an afternoon at a magic shop. Consult your phone directory. Since the rebirth of magic as a hobby (mostly because of Doug Henning's *The Magic Show* on Broadway), magic shops have sprung up across the country, not only in large and medium-sized cities, but also in suburban shopping malls.

There are a few magic shops that are particularly worthwhile to visit:

Abbott's Magic Mfg. Co., Colon, Michigan 49040.

Flosso-Hornmann Magic Co., 304 West 34th St., New York, New York 10001.

Magic, Inc., 5082 North Lincoln Avenue, Chicago, Illinois 60625.

Hollywood Magic, Inc., 6614 Hollywood Blvd., Hollywood, California 90028.

Louis Tannen, Inc., 1540 Broadway, New York, New York 10036.

Yogi Magic Mart, 310 North Charles Street, Baltimore, Maryland 21214.

Ken Brooke, 145 Wardour St., London W.1., England.

L. Davenport & Co., 51 Great Russell St., London W.C.1., England.

International Magic Studio, 89 Clerkenwell Rd., Holborn, London, E.C.1., England.

Supreme Magic Co., 64 High Street, Bideford, Devon, England.

M. Hatte-Mayette Magic, 8 rue des Carmes, Paris 11, France.

Al's Magic Shop, 1205 Pennsylvania Ave., N.W., Washington, D.C. 20004.

4. **Mail Order Magic:** Many magicians order equipment by mail from catalogs published by one of the large magic dealers. The following dealers issue catalogs worthy of your attention (the catalogs cost about $2 or $3.):

Abbott's Magic Mfg. Co., Colon, Michigan, 49040.

Abracadabra Magic, Highway 27, Colonia Shopping Plaza, Colonia, New Jersey, 07067.

Creative Magic Products, 786 Merrick Rd., Baldwin, New York 11510.

Eagle Magic Store, 708 Portland Avenue, Minneapolis, Minn. 55415.

Fabulous Magic Co., 3319 East Charleston Blvd., Las Vegas, Nevada 89104.

Flosso-Hornmann Magic Co., 304 West 34th St., New York, New York 10001.

Miami Magic, 9734 Bird Rd., Miami, Florida 33165.

Magic, Inc., 5082 North Lincoln Ave., Chicago, Illinois 60625.

Magic Methods, P. O. Box 4105, Greenville, South Carolina 29608.

Haines House of Cards, 2044 Ross Avenue, Norwood, Ohio 45212.

Mak-Magic, P. O. Box 2843, Columbus, Ohio 43204.

James Swoger, 2037 Plainview Ave., Pittsburgh, Pennsylvania 15226.

Silk King Studios, 640 North Evening Star Lane, Cincinnati, Ohio 45220.

Louis Tannen, Inc., 1540 Broadway, New York, New York 10036.

Ken Brooke, 145 Wardour St., London W.1., England.

Hughes House Of Magic, The Grange, Willow Park, King's Lynn, Norfolk PL30 1EJ, England.

Supreme Magic Co., 64 High St., Bideford, Devon, England.

Hank Lee's Magic Factory, 24 Lincoln Street, Boston, Mass. 02111.

Chu's Magic Studio, 401 Chatham Road, Kowoon, Hongkong, T.S.T. P. O. Box 5221.

Abbott's, Tannen, Supreme, Magic, Inc., and Mak-Magic (U.F. Grant) all offer a particularly large selection of conjuring apparatus.

5. **Magazines:** There are a number of excellent monthly magic magazines. Most carry dealer ads, new tricks, magic news, and historical articles. Write for subscription prices.

Genii, The International Conjurors' Magazine, Box 36068, Los Angeles, California, 90036.

The Magigram, Supreme Magic Co., 64 High Street, Bideford, Devon, England.

The Magic Magazine, P. O. Box One, Marion, Ohio 43302.

The New Tops, Abbott's Magic Co., Colon, Michigan 49040.

6. **Societies:** There are a dozen or so magic societies, some dating back to the turn of the century. In the U.S., the oldest is the Society of American Magicians; in England, the most prestigious is The Magic Circle. These societies have branches in many major cities around the world, with local monthly meetings among magicians of the area. Most of the societies publish a monthly club magazine. Information about these magic societies can be found at magic dealers and through advertisements in magic magazines.

7. **Conventions:** There are seven or eight major magic conventions each year. Three or four of them are held in various cities in the U.S. under the auspicies of the major magic societies. In addition, both Louis Tannen and Abbott's Magic Company hold their own four day wing-dings. Conventions are advertised in magazines like *Genii* and *The New Tops,* and anyone with the price of registration is welcome. The conventions are hectic affairs with professional shows each evening, famous magicians lecturing during the day, talent contests, dealers' rooms and many other attractions to keep you up day and night for the duration of the event.

8. **Magic shows:** There are several full evening magic shows working in America. Harry Blackstone, Jr. and Doug Henning have two of the best evening shows and both travel extensively each year. Live magic can be seen in resort areas like Las Vegas as well as in cabaret reviews in major cities around the world, such as The Magic Castle, 7001 Franklin Avenue, Hollywood, California 90028. Call for information.

9. **Magic on television:** Magicians are frequently seen on television these days, particuarly on talk shows. Amateur magicians will find it valuable to use Sony's Betamax or other system to videotape these performances for later viewing and reviewing.

10. **Professional apparatus.** Major illusions such as those used by Doug Henning are manufactured by skilled craftsmen who specialize in the construction of apparatus for professional magicians. One such firm is Owen Magic Supreme, 1240 South Chapel Avenue, Alhambra, California 91801.

INDEX